The High Aces

MAJOR RAOUL LUFBERY
Greatest of American flyers, who was killed May 19, 1918 with an official score of 18.

The High Aces
French, American, British, Italian & Belgian pilots of the First World War 1914-18

Laurence La Tourette Driggs

The High Aces
French, American, British, Italian & Belgian
pilots of the First World War 1914-18
by Laurence la Tourette Driggs

First published under the title
Heroes of Aviation

Leonaur is an imprint
of Oakpast Ltd

Copyright in this form © 2009 Oakpast Ltd

ISBN: 978-1-84677-956-5 (hardcover)
ISBN: 978-1-84677-955-8 (softcover)

http://www.leonaur.com

Publisher's Notes

In the interests of authenticity, the spellings, grammar and place names used have been retained from the original editions.

The opinions of the authors represent a view of events in which he was a participant related from his own perspective, as such the text is relevant as an historical document.

The views expressed in this book are not necessarily those of the publisher.

Contents

Preface	9
Introduction	11
The *Escadrille Lafayette*	21
Early French Heroes	46
Roland Garros, the First Air Fighter	61
The Cigognes	76
Georges Guynemer the Miraculous	88
Raoul Lufbery	104
The British Aces	121
René Fonck	158
Other French Aces the Spectacular Career of Armand Pinsard	175
Balloon Observers	206
The Bombers	214
Extraordinary Exploits in Air	223
The Belgian and Italian Aces	233
The American Aces	248
Appendix Aces of all Nations	268

To Our Heroes of Aviation
This Book
is Gratefully Dedicated

Preface

The author is deeply indebted to M. Jacques Mortane and *La Guerre Aerienne* of Paris for portions of the material used herein relating to the French Air Fighters. M. Mortane, himself an airman and the devoted friend of all fliers, has done more for the cause of Aviation in France than any other living man. His researches in war-aviation will for the years to come form a most valuable history of the birth and growth of the Fourth Arm in Warfare.

I desire to here express my further obligations to the London periodicals, *Flight, Flying, Aeroplane and Aeronautics*, for many of the incidents relating to the British pilots.

The inborn reluctance of the British youth to speak of his own heroic deeds prevents the world from estimating the marvellous part he has played in sweeping Germany from the skies. The Hun pilots flood the world with the information of their victories. It was not until I visited England as the guest of the British Government in the fall of 1918 that I discovered that twenty British airmen have exceeded by over one hundred the number of victories claimed by the best twenty Aces of the Huns. And the great majority of these British airmen are still silently carrying on, while but five of the twenty Huns survive!

Laurence La Tourette Driggs

September 24, 1918.

Introduction
THE FOURTH ARM IN WARFARE

Those venerable old campaigners, infantry, cavalry, and artillery, have held for centuries the highest pinnacles of achievement in warfare. The three arms have stood united, exclusive, unchallenged, and unafraid. Today enters a fourth arm whose coming prostrates these old soldiers and whose future dazzles the imagination of the world.

So valuable are the "eyes of the army" that supremacy of the air is now a first requisite to successful offense or defence. This vital discovery was made by the Allies in the first week of the war, when their aeroplane scouts brought in the information that not thousands but millions of German troops were pouring through Luxemburg into France. Had this intelligence been wanting, it is likely that the decisive battle of this war would have been fought then, and the overwhelming German forces would have occupied France and advanced upon England within the month.

From that hour began the tremendous struggle for mastery of the air. Germany had the advantage. Before the war began she had produced an aeroplane engine that had won world records in duration and altitude flights. With customary foresightedness, she had on hand more machines and had trained more pilots than other nations. She had established aerial routes across the land, had experimented with night landing-grounds, with aeroplane guns, bombs, and bomb carriers.

The writer witnessed the daily sortie over Paris of the celebrated German pilot Lieutenant Immelman early in the month of September, 1914. German troops were then but twenty-five miles from Paris. French aeroplanes were all in service at the front, and the city was left undefended from air attack.

Regularly at five o'clock in the afternoon Lieutenant Immelman appeared circling over Paris. It was a daily program that afforded excitement, if not amusement, to the citizens below. So inadequate were the defences of Paris at that time that the fearless scout scorned to fly above rifle range. The whir of his propeller could be plainly heard, and the aeroplane could be discerned several miles away.

Terror-stricken people ran for the nearest doorways and cellars, and reappeared only after the noise of exploded bombs announced that he had passed. Then, with furious gestures, they would gaze up into the sky from the centre of the streets after their disappearing enemy.

In certain open parks, on certain bridges, and at other vantage points great crowds gathered every afternoon to witness the approach of the daring raider. Interest, and not alarm, actuated such persons. Oblivious of the fact that what goes up must come down, that thousands of guns were shooting up at the flying enemy, and that a score of bombs would doubtless be dropped into Paris, these crowds stood with "nose in full air", rapt in wonder, and, I believe, with much sneaking respect for the pluck and audacity of the airman.

One could hear the heavy booming of the big guns from the outlying fortifications. A rattle of promiscuous rule firing grew in intensity as the aeroplane approached over the centre of the city. Several regiments stationed along the river quays aimed upwards and fired in volleys; the machine guns on the Eiffel Tower, a short distance up the Seine, could be heard—pop—pop—popping fiercely. Taxicab drivers and their fares produced revolvers and blazed away. Literally millions of bullets were speeding up after this one solitary human being in the sky. The awful odds he was taking in this storm of lead produced some feelings of pity, if not admiration for his sportsmanship.

Among his daily shower of small bombs there invariably appeared a laconic note, dropped within a bag of sand, addressed to the people of Paris, which was regularly published in the papers the following morning, couched in this style:

> People of Paris! Surrender! The Germans are at your gates! Tomorrow you will be ours!
> Lieutenant Immelman,
> Air Scout.

While but slight damage resulted from the light bombs he tossed over the side, it has always remained a mystery to me why many injuries did not result from the bullets falling upon the streets of Paris. Not one casualty was ever reported from this cause.

Paris Today is efficiently protected from raids by either aeroplanes or Zeppelins. Besides the anti-aircraft land defences, including field guns, observation towers, listening towers, and searchlights encircling the city, the aeroplane patrol above Paris is continued day and night, not by one but by three aeroplanes at three different altitudes, approximately at one thousand feet, six thousand feet, and ten thousand feet elevation.

Air raids, or "stunts", as they are called in Europe, and the home defence against such attacks are of secondary importance from the military point of view. Today at the front the smallest movements of the enemy are watched by the air scouts; lines of communication far in the rear are photographed, hidden artillery discovered, mobilization of cavalry bombed and stampeded, and threatened attacks of infantry foreseen.

Each morning before daylight the air squadrons are assembled and given their instructions. Most vital of all is the return of the trained observers to the commanding officer with their reports. Consequently all preparations are made to this end. First there is despatched a fast-climbing patrol. He attains a height of eighteen or twenty thousand feet before the others leave the ground. He surveys the front and watches for anti-aircraft movements.

Soon he observes his command rising up with spiral climbs in squadron formation. There are twelve or fourteen tractors, each armed with a machine gun fastened to the left-hand side of the fuselage, weighing less than eighteen pounds and capable of firing five hundred shots per minute. A synchronizing device is attached to the trigger of the gun and connected with the propeller shaft, which permits firing only when the blades of the propeller are out of the way of the stream of bullets. As these propellers are making at least nine hundred revolutions per minute, the four blades are passing the muzzle of the gun at the rate of thirty-six hundred per minute!

Three of the aeroplanes carry pilot and observer. The others are "single-seaters", and, being lighter, are faster and quicker to manoeuvre. Their duty is to advance and receive the attack of enemy aeroplanes, to cover the retreat of their own observers, and, if opportunity arises, to prevent the crossing of their front by enemy scouts. A minute study of the enemy front must be made. The squadron has to inspect an area of fifty miles front and twenty-five miles deep.

Five thousand feet above ground was considered a safe level in the early days of the war. Practice, better field guns, and newly devised range-finders drove the aeroplanes to the higher levels of at first eight thousand, then ten thousand, and now twelve thousand feet over enemy lines. Even at this altitude an occasional lucky "Archibald" bursts in the vicinity of the plane and a piece of shrapnel finds its mark. An altitude of eight thousand feet defies the rifle bullet and small-bore machine gun.

The airmen of the various fighting forces are chosen for their youth and cleverness. From eighteen to twenty-three years is the age that combines the proper proportions of daring and caution required for a successful flier. After a certain number of months' strain and a certain quantity of narrow escapes the average pilot gets "used up" and is retired at his own suggestion. He then becomes a staff officer, a trainer in the flying schools, or an observer, according to the necessity of circumstances.

To return to our early morning expedition, which we left

climbing up to the required altitude in squadron formation. The three two-seaters, being more heavily loaded, reach eight thousand feet at about the same time the lighter machines have attained ten or eleven thousand feet. Here they separate, each directing his course to the allotted segment of the front—one to the left, one to the right, and one takes the centre. The three observers sit in the front ends of the machines, a speaking tube under the helmet connecting each with his pilot in the seat immediately behind him. A map of yesterday's front is spread smoothly on a board above his knees. Any alteration of the landscape is immediately noted and corrected on the map.

Scrutiny is first centred on the narrow strip of ground separating the trenches. Twenty yards in some places, it widens out to several hundred yards in others. Trees have been shot into splinters in this "No Man's Land." Occasional stumps remain which have been spared by both sides because they are not worth wasting shells upon.

One of these stumps seems to have something new about it. The aeroplane circles around it several times. Field-glasses disclose an aperture in the rear. Ah! There are two wires running from the stump back to the enemy's trench!

The Germans have crept over one of these nights, silently dug up the old landmark, and have substituted a hollow telephone booth exactly similar to the familiar old stump. Probably information was telephoned back all day yesterday by the watchful spy within. The aeroplane observer jots down note No. 1.

Farther on a new trench is discovered and traced. Here a group of trees have been cut down during the night. Over there appears freshly-dug earth on a hillside, denoting a machine-gun emplacement. To the right on the top of the hill is a suspiciously green covered area not explained on the map. The observer directs the pilot's attention to this spot, and in a moment they are volplaning down directly toward it. A nearer view discloses an unusual thickness of green branches standing in an unnatural position, and a dim wagon rut leads directly to this spot from the rear. The observer presses a button on the dashboard twice, and takes two photographs of the hill from the camera attached to the bottom of the fuselage. A signal to bank off to the left and ascend is given by a gesture of his left arm, and while the shells of the enemy are bursting on all sides the officer tranquilly jots down the site of the newly discovered concealed battery of artillery.

As the pair ascend to a higher level they search the ground for aerodromes and scan the horizon for enemy aircraft. Many aeroplanes are about them, and some are distinguished by their colours, painted on wings and tail. Others are too distant to identify, but from their actions they are assumed to be Allies.

Far to the left along the river can be seen extraordinary activity. That must be thirty miles in the enemy's rear. It deserves watching, but our observer feels that he has valuable information to deliver to his commanding officer and is undecided as to the wisdom of undertaking further risks. His attention is awakened by a sudden swerve of the machine. Above the roar of the engine exhaust and the rush of wind in his face he can detect a curious hum. It is another aeroplane directly upon them. Before he can turn his head he is conscious of a rush under him, and a series of little shocks tells him that a stream of bullets is being poured into his machine.

From far up in the clouds an enemy scout has been trailing him. Carefully manoeuvring for position, the Fokker suddenly shoots down with tremendous velocity. When within fifty yards of his prey, he opens fire, pouring in a stream of lead until he passes underneath and spirals away to the rear.

Already our defenders are upon him, however, and the observer drops down over his own lines within the danger zone. Above his own aerodrome he sees a flock of his comrades taking the air—six, eight, twelve, in all. Behind him and above him are the enemy—in a superior position. He descends to within a thousand feet and skims along blithely to rejoin his squadron.

And now comes a battle royal. The observers leave the field and speed homeward with their reports. The combatants count their forces and those of the enemy. Both sides are jockeying for the upper berth in the air. For the upper berth gives many advantages. They can shoot down upon their adversaries, while they themselves are out of range of their opponents' guns; they have a wider view; they are safely above field-gun danger; and, most important of all, they can use their additional height to accumulate added speed when a sudden dive is essential.

Such are the tactics and strategy of the air. By its use small forces often overcome double their numbers. Darting, firing, banking, circling, climbing, and darting again and again, the battle in the air continues until many of the combatants are shot down or crippled and limp away to safety.

Many are the qualifications required for such fighters, and well do they exemplify the old adage, *Tackle a little job as though it were a big one, and a big job as though it were a little one.* Numerous conflicts have ended with the deliberate ramming of one aeroplane against the enemy, both men falling together—down, down, down, to a spectacular death.

The foregoing describes but one of the functions of this new arm of military science. Equally valuable, perhaps, is the aeroplane patrol of the seas, for from its vantage height the pilot can discover the lurking submarine at any depth, and he can explode the small submerged bombs strewn in the ships' path.

The submarine menace is probably the most perplexing fear of this war. The merchant ship is suddenly brought to by a round shot. If she runs, she finds herself easily overhauled and soon riddled with shells. She is permitted but one small 4.7 gun mounted on the stern for defence. Further arming will constitute her a war vessel, and she may be sunk without warning. Yet the stern gun is of no use for defence when the submarine appears off the bow. Any attempt to turn away will bring destruction.

Of England's total loss of merchant boats to date probably less than ten per cent, have been torpedoed. Ninety per cent, are shelled to death by submarines which lie off, two or three miles away, their decks flush with the surface, their guns and crews alone visible above the waves, tiny targets at best. Before rising to the surface the submarines have leisurely ascertained the exact range through their periscopes.

The almost invisible submarine scorns shrapnel, shot, or shell. The gun and crew on deck may suffer damage by a rare chance, but to sink the submarine herself by such missiles is next to impossible at such a distance. Experiments have shown that the walls of the submarine may be split open by the concussion of a high explosive. Seventy-five pounds of "T. N. T." timed to explode thirty feet underwater within a radius of fifty yards will crack her open like a watermelon dropped to the ground.

Hence the double peril of the aeroplane to the under-seas craft. Not only can the air scout locate the submarine by her dark mass under water and by the longitudinal ripple following her wake on the surface but he can drop down to any level over the victim, cut loose one of his high explosive bombs, and her career is ended. No dreadnought of the first line can accomplish such a feat.

Ship channels can be adequately and inexpensively defended against the submarine only by the aeroplane scouts. The military advantage of transport ships and supply ships saved from destruction by this means adds another value to the aeroplane arm. His wide horizon enables the lofty air observer to scan the sea for forty or fifty miles on every side for floating craft. His wireless equipment gives immediate information to his officer of the location of the enemy.

As an artillery fire "spotter" the aeroplane service has produced wonderful efficiency. Circling over the enemy, the observer signals back the errors of marksmanship, and almost perfect bull's-eye hits are scored. No stalemate can result in this war if one side gains the courted mastery of the air!

Zeppelin raids over England have not been a success from any viewpoint. England has minimized her losses and has censored all facts, but, estimating the loss to Germany of the many expensive airships destroyed and the additional military loss of her highly trained Zeppelin crews, it is extremely doubtful if the score stands in Germany's favour. Probably the greatest advantage to Germany lies in the fact that her Zeppelin raids have kept the shores of England an armed aeroplane camp for defence, thus greatly reducing England's air force in France.

But without this aeroplane defence England would be at the mercy of the Zeppelin. Field guns are not credited with the bringing down of any of the nine airships lost to Germany. The listening-tower equipment acquaints England with the coming of the monsters, and their searchlights never fail to pick them out of the night sky, but it is the aeroplane equipped with the Lewis machine gun that has brought to earth these midnight marauders.

Incasing the huge bulk of the Zeppelin is a belt of non-inflammable gas which not only is unaffected by the flaming bullet, but actually extinguishes it. The exploding bullet, therefore, is employed, although its use where it may cause "unnecessary human suffering" is forbidden by the Hague treaties.

If it is difficult to hit a Zeppelin from the ground, what possibility is there of "getting" an aeroplane! The Zeppelin at twelve thousand feet moves at sixty miles per hour and is a target of five hundred feet by forty feet. The aeroplane moves at one hundred and twenty miles an hour and presents a vulnerable target of approximately only four feet square, consisting of the pilot's person and his fuel tank. All other parts of his machine may be considered invulnerable, for a hit would only make a hole through his plane, or possibly break a strut, his rudder or his propeller, permitting him to alight in safety several miles away.

Flying at only one hundred miles an hour, this four-foot target moves about one hundred and fifty feet each second. It is impossible to get the range with any accuracy, and his constant evolutions would render marksmanship guesswork at best. From the time the shell leaves the ground until it reaches the twelve-thousand-foot level at which he is flying requires about ten seconds. In these ten seconds the aeroplane has travelled away some five hundred yards! Further speculation is unnecessary. The only adequate defence against aeroplane is aeroplane.

Aeroplane bombs are no longer carried in a basket and tossed over the sides by the pilot. Scientifically designed "squints" are adjusted to the altitude level, indicated by the barograph, and remarkably accurate bomb dropping is accomplished. The bombs are carried attached to a rack underneath the fuselage. An electric wire touches each fuse and is controlled by a switch on the dashboard. The fuse will not function until the switch is thrown on, so that the unused explosives can be brought down to earth in perfect safety.

The bomb-dropper goes aloft with ten bombs suspended under him. Some weigh ten pounds, some fifty pounds, some one hundred and fifty pounds, or one may weigh a ton. When he arrives near his target, he pushes the switch around, arming all the fuses. Alongside his right knee are ten push buttons. He ascertains his altitude, estimates the wind and his speed, adjusts his "squint sight", and flies on a level line towards his objective. When his "squint" points at the enemy target ahead and below, he presses one of the buttons, releasing the ten-pound bomb, or the one-hundred-and-fifty-pound bomb, as desired.

The bomb—long, slender, and "feathered"—is kept to its line of trajectory by its rudder. Upon impact the bomb explodes, flinging shrapnel, shot, pieces of shell, or inflammable material as prearranged.

A device is sometimes attached to precede the falling bomb by twenty or thirty feet. This touches the ground first, causing the bomb to explode twenty or thirty feet in the air with great destructiveness. Fancy a regiment of cavalry attacked by several of these destroyers!

It is apparent that both combatants in this world's war are stretching every muscle to obtain or retain the supremacy and mastery of the air. Thousands upon thousands of war planes are now ready. Delicate mechanisms and sensitively trained youths are being polished up to decide the issue in one dizzy, deadly combat "somewhere in France" over the upturned faces of the three hopeful beneficiaries below—the three dependent arms—infantry, cavalry, artillery.

CHAPTER 1

The *Escadrille Lafayette*

From time immemorial a nation's call to arms has brought leaping forward her gallant sons—her pride. The proudest are the first. With no thought of the risks and the costs, with no expressed scorn for those who remain behind, this eager spirit of the heroic volunteer has ever inspired the approbation and applause of the world.

The sad sacrifice of this glorious class of our youth to remorseless war is a spectacle so familiar to civilization that it is accepted as a matter of course. Its tragedy is smothered beneath the songs of the poets and the spontaneous praise of the populace.

On the college rolls in England I have seen the broad black band of mourning inclose three fourths, four fifths, nine tenths of the graduates' class rolls within the dread yet noble roll of honour. The best blood of the nation is lost; the higher the breeding, the gentler the training—the quicker comes the impulse to go.

With the advent of aviation in warfare a new call was sounded to attract the adventurous and strong. The very love of sport itself seemed to spiritualize the aviators' service at the front. With its natural appeal to those instincts of sportsmanship with which every youth is endowed, the Flying Service at once became the Mecca of every young hero's desire.

Rivalling the romance and glory of the tales in Greek mythology these free lances of the air went daily forth to dazzling adventure and awakened anew the chivalrous pride of old-time combat. The whir of their aeroplanes in the limitless skies never failed to attract the interest and admiration of the world below—be that world friend or foe.

Into this glamour of war went, early in the year 1915, a group of young Americans who were actuated by a common impulse to hurl their strength against the spoilers of Belgium long months before their tranquil fellow-countrymen at home awoke to the dreadful necessity of defending themselves against the same dire peril.

And with that heroic act of self-sacrifice whereby this small group united its little effort with these other defenders of French soil there was forged that first imperishable link in the mighty chain which now binds France and America together and which served to stem the furious tide of German soldiers in the spring of 1918.

Thus a double page must be provided in history on which to record the names and deeds of this immortal band of gallant Americans who were the first to volunteer their lives and all against the enemy of their country; who first encouraged the land of Lafayette with the hope of our support; who first organized a squadron of airmen which eventually stood third in all France in its number of victories over the enemy. For these young heroes did more than that. Most of them died in the conflict! And by their glorious deaths they awakened in the youth of America the quick consciousness that noble ideals are more precious than life!

William Thaw alone of the original seven who formed the first squadron of American aeroplane pilots remains to fight for France and home. Thaw shares with Norman Prince the distinctive honour of conceiving and organizing this group. In point of service Thaw's record begins first, for he was in France at the outbreak of war and immediately offered his services.

Thaw had learned to fly in America. Abroad on pleasure bent during the summer of 1914, he welcomed this opportunity of putting his training at the disposal of France. The keen insight of the aeroplane pilot within him was well assured of the im-

First Group of American Aviators in France

Left to right—Kiffen Yates Rockwell of Ashville, N.C., killed Sept. 23, 1916, after 3 victories to his credit: Commanding Officer Captain Thénault, French, 1 enemy shot down; Major William Thaw of Pittsburgh (behind), with 2 Germans brought down; Lieut. Norman Prince of Beverley Farms, Mass., killed October 15, 1916, after shooting down 4 enemy aeroplanes; Lieut. Elliot Cowden of New York City; Lieut. Bert Hall of Bowling Green, Ky.; Kenneth Marr of San Francisco; Sergt. James McConnell of Carthage, N.C., killed March 19, 1916; Sergt. Victor Chapman of New York, killed June 22, 1916, with 2 victories. Not homologated.

portance that aerial observation was to play in repelling the advancing hordes of Huns. It would afford Thaw the pleasure of flying and would give France the advantage of knowing the exact position and strength of the enemy—so what could be more natural than the immediate acceptance of his offer to fly for France?

But the laws of France permitted her to receive foreigners in but one organization of the military. This was the heterogeneous and miscellaneous collection known as the Foreign Legion. Into the Foreign Legion therefore Thaw speedily went. The first month of the war found him earning his penny a day and accumulating a military knowledge which doubtless served him abundantly when he later became the chief of his *escadrille*.

Another American hailing from Texas and Kentucky likewise found himself in Paris at the beginning of hostilities. This was Bert Hall. He too joined the Foreign Legion. Thaw and Hall quickly formed a friendship which soon included James Bach, the son of a millionaire and an especial chum of Hall who was in the same company. During the hard months which followed, as Thaw, Hall, and Bach stood knee-deep in the slush and filth of the trenches, gazing with envious eyes at the soaring aeroplanes overhead, Thaw beguiled the time by describing to his companions the luxury of an airman's life.

In December, 1914, Thaw, Hall, and Bach secured their transfer into aviation. The nucleus of the *Escadrille Lafayette* was forming.

Thaw, already a skilful pilot, was the first to be sent to the front. After a few weeks' training in the various machines then in use he was sent to Lunéville and attached to the bomb-dropping *escadrille*, Caudron 46. Hall and Bach, who were then training at Avord, later went to Pau, and here they were among the first of the pilots to fly the new single-seater Nieuport, the speediest and cleverest combat aeroplane then in existence.

In April, 1915, Norman Prince of Massachusetts and Elliot Cowdin of New York, both Harvard men and American-trained aeroplane pilots, arrived in Paris from the United States and entered the French Air Service. Prince was obsessed with the plan of organizing an all-American Flying Corps among the pilots and volunteers then in France. He knew several of them who were rich enough to buy their own machines and equip them, and thus provided he felt sure the French Government would find a way to use them.

Full of enthusiasm over his idea he at once set about putting his plan in operation. A committee of Americans was selected in Paris, of which William K. Vanderbilt was the head. Frederick Allen, the American representative of the Ambulance Division, and Doctor Edmund Gros were pressed into the plan. Robert Bacon and the American Minister himself were convinced that the American *Escadrille* could and should be organized. In the meantime, while official red tape was being cut by these efficient gentlemen, Prince and Cowdin left for the front where they were enrolled with the Voisin Bombardment 103 Escadrille.

Partly through the aid of Frederick Allen and partly through natural inclination several Americans then in the Ambulance Division secured their release about this time and enlisted in the French Aeroplane Service, in preparation for the approaching time when their own national group might be permitted to organize into one distinctive squadron. A few months' training now would put them in readiness to join the American *Escadrille* when the French Authorities could be persuaded to permit its separate establishment.

Among these was James McConnell of Carthage, North Carolina, a gifted writer and a man exceptionally popular among his comrades. He had already received the *Croix de Guerre* for distinguished service in performance of his ambulance duties. Lawrence Rumsay, a noted polo player of Buffalo, Clyde Balsley of El Paso, Texas, Dudley Hill of Peekskill, and Charles Chouteau Johnson of New York, were other ambulance drivers who, having experienced all the thrills that accompany collecting the wounded under shell fire, now burned with the desire for an occupation more exciting. All were sent to Pau.

Two of the most striking figures of the American squadron,

when some months later the infant organization was baptized in the inferno of Verdun, were at this period still occupying their places in the trenches with the Foreign Legion. These were Kiffin Rockwell of Asheville, North Carolina, a graduate of the University of Virginia, and Victor Chapman of New York who, like Prince, was an old boy of the Fay School and Harvard University. Both had intimate friends in Prince, Thaw, and Cowdin. In August, 1915, after a full year in the trenches, where both had received wounds in combat and citations from the French Army for distinguished conduct, Chapman and Rockwell were transferred to aviation and were sent to Avord for schooling.

During all this time Raoul Lufbery, quite independent of the other Americans who were aspiring to the Air Service of France, was engaged in Escadrille M. S. 23 as mechanic to Marc Pourpe with whom he had been associated in exhibition flying for the past four years. Pourpe was killed in December, 1914, and Lufbery applied for permission to fly to avenge the death of his friend and patron. It was granted. With little or no preparation at the training schools Lufbery entered the *escadrille* as a pilot of a bombardment machine and remained there until Thaw and Prince sought him out months later and drew him into the squadron of the Americans.

Lufbery's mother was French. His father married again and settled in Wallingford, Connecticut, but Raoul knew more about the other countries of the world than about his own, for he had spent most of his life wandering over the earth, seeking adventure.

Another resident of Connecticut who later entered the Lafayette Corps was Paul Pavelka. He, like Lufbery, had spent the bulk of his years in globetrotting and after some months in the Foreign Legion entered aviation to seek the excitement that made every other existence tame in comparison. Pavelka, after surviving three years of the great war, met his death in Monastir on November 10, 1917, by being thrown from a horse.

Didier Masson is another of this group who richly deserves to be mentioned. Masson was French in origin but subsequently became a naturalized American citizen. During the Mexican troubles he was in the service of the anti-Carranza revolutionists with his aeroplane and for some time he constituted the entire Air Service of Mexico. He hastened to France at the outbreak of the world's war and enlisted at once in the defence of his ancestral home. He still survives, claiming quite the longest career of actual uninterrupted flying, in war and out, that exists today.

So seven Americans were flying at the front before the end of 1915, Thaw, Lufbery, Prince, Cowdin, Hall, Bach, and Masson. Several other Americans were at that time in British aerodromes at the front, but did not sever their connection with these units to join the new American *Escadrille*.

Thanks to the persistence of Norman Prince and the assistance of his American friends in Paris the way was at last opened for the organization of the all-American aviation unit.

Prince called together as many of his aviator friends as could be collected in Paris on April 17, 1916, and gave a dinner at a famous restaurant to his guests who included Chapman, Balsley, McConnell, Thaw, Rockwell, Johnson, and Rumsay. He read them the official roster of the new *escadrille* which was dated March 14, 1916, and contained the following names:

William Thaw, Pittsburgh, Pennsylvania.
Norman Prince, Marblehead, Massachusetts.
Elliot Cowdin, New York.
Bert Hall, Bowling Green, Kentucky.
Kiffin Rockwell, Asheville, North Carolina.
James McConnell, Carthage, North Carolina.
Victor Chapman, New York.

Moreover, the seven American pilots were ordered to depart forthwith for their aerodrome quarters at Luxeuil in the Vosges Mountains near the eastern edge of France. The first American *Escadrille* was to be sent into the thickest of the fray—Verdun! And they were to fly Nieuports! After a joyous evening of celebration the boys separated to make a list of their requirements for the morrow, four of them, Prince, Chapman, Rockwell, and

McConnell, taking the train that same night for their new aerodrome.

Thaw, the most experienced pilot among them, was commissioned a lieutenant. Hall, Prince, and Cowdin were sergeants and the others corporals. The following day all were assembled at the flying field of Luxeuil and proceeded to make the acquaintance of their French comrades in aviation who were already stationed on the same grounds. The official number "Nieuport 124" was given them, and their French captain and lieutenant, Captain Thenault and Lieutenant de Laage de Meaux immediately began to teach the Americans the battle tactics and formation flying of the fighting squadron.

The German aeroplane squadrons entered the Battle of Verdun with an acknowledged superiority in the air. German observation and photographing machines circled over the French lines with impudence and impunity. Their swift Fokker single-seater fighting aeroplanes with synchronized machine guns firing through the propeller were the best duelling machines known to aviation until the improved Nieuports appeared at Verdun and gradually wrested from them the contested areas over the French positions.

On the fourth day of their stay at Luxeuil the American Escadrille scored its first victory. Kiffin Rockwell in his first duel shot down an enemy aeroplane in single combat back of Thann. The German observation machine fell in flames just back of the trenches, and Rockwell flew back to the aerodrome to find that the news of his great victory had preceded him. It had cost him just four bullets.

Whether this success convinced the French officers of the ability of the Americans to hold their own in combat or whether they considered a two weeks' training on the fringe of the big battle was sufficient, at all events the N. 124 was moved early in May to the Bar-le-Duc aerodrome adjoining the famous *escadrille* of the Cigognes, the N. 3 which contained a group of the finest fighting pilots in France. This was Captain Brocard's command, and among his pilots were Guynemer, Dorme, Heurteaux, Auger, Deullin and De la Tour. On the same field was Nungesser's Escadrille, N. 65. France was concentrating the cream of her air force against the Hun's attack upon Verdun. The American *Escadrille* found itself in fast company.

All of our American pilots now had their own Nieuports and had baptized them in shell fire and in the hailstorm of machine-gun bullets from enemy airmen. Lufbery here joined the group, and a day or two later Clyde Balsley and Charles Johnson were transferred from the air squadron guarding Paris to the *escadrille* of their fellow Americans below Verdun. In the course of a week or two Dudley Hill and Lawrence Rumsay finished their schooling and hastened to Bar-le-Duc. And finally came Didier Masson and Paul Pavelka from the French *escadrilles* where they had been attached and further swelled the membership of the all-American *Escadrille* to a total of fifteen.

James Bach had in the meantime been captured by the Germans and is still detained a prisoner. He had a narrow escape from a worse fate. He had engaged in what was called a "special mission" while in the bombing *escadrille* to which he was assigned with Hall, Cowdin, and Prince before the organization of the American *Escadrille*. This special mission consists in taking a spy in an aeroplane and depositing him well back in the enemy's territory and returning home. After a given number of hours the pilot returns to the rendezvous to collect his passenger. This is a feat which brings the successful pilot a citation and a decoration, but to the unsuccessful one comes the fate of an accomplice.

In Bach's case the spy was captured, and a trap was laid for the returning airman. Bach was ensnared and fell red-handed into the grasp of the enemy. Twice he was tried at a court martial by the Germans, but the fact that he was wearing his uniform when captured and that he had not himself carried the spy into the German lines saved him. At last accounts Bach was in a prison camp near Nuremberg where he was ruminating over the sad distinction of being the first captured American airman.

Dennis Dowd of Brooklyn, New York, was the first and only member of the early American *Escadrille* to meet death while training. Dowd too had served in the Foreign Legion, where he was wounded during the Champagne battles. As soon as he was able to be about he applied for a transfer into aviation. His request was granted, and he began training at the Buc school under the most auspicious circumstances.

Standing at the very head of his fellow pupils and just on the eve of leaving the flying school to join the *escadrille* at Bar-le-Duc, Dennis Dowd on August 11, 1916, fell from the trifling height of two hundred feet while making a landing on his aerodrome and was killed instantly. But another loss preceded his.

The American flyers at the front had thrust themselves into a terrible conflict above Verdun. Their Nieuports were at that time more agile but less sturdy than the enemy Fokkers, and they were less conveniently armed. The German pilots first perfected formation flying and thus scored heavily against their opponents who still flew singly and often deep within the enemy territory.

On May 24, just four days after the arrival of the Americans at Verdun, during which period they had busied themselves with putting their machines in order, their first great conflict occurred. Getting aloft before dawn the newcomers speedily found the game they were hunting. Scores of German aircraft were sweeping the skies above Verdun.

Thaw and Kiffin Rockwell got above the German lines and took on a Fokker and an Aviatic at the same moment. With the first dive at his enemy Thaw shot down the Fokker in flames, and it fell just inside the German lines. The Aviatic eluded Rockwell's attack and fled homeward in safety.

The two scouts returned to their field for petrol, soon filled up their tanks, and again set out for the foe. On this occasion both Thaw and Rockwell came to grief. Thaw engaged a group of Fokkers and while intent upon one of the circling aeroplanes another descended upon him from the side and riddled his machine with bullets. Thaw was struck in the arm and shoulder. Almost fainting with pain, he succeeded in directing his crippled aeroplane over the lines, where it fell heavily only a few feet behind the French trenches. The *poilus* dashed forward to his rescue and soon had him in safety. He was later removed to the Paris hospital, where he spent several weeks waiting for the shattered bones to mend.

Rockwell in the meantime had attacked another group of enemy machines, and he too received a facer. Almost before the combat began he received an explosive bullet in his small windshield which splintered it and sent the fragments flying violently into his face and neck. He landed normally on his field and was soon on his way to a Red Cross station for treatment.

He had no sooner arrived there than the great news overtook him that he had brought down the aeroplane with which he was engaged when he was wounded. It was seen to fall in flames, and he had received the official credit for its destruction.

Victor Chapman during this same period had established a reputation for aerial duelling that made him a hero among heroes. In his first attack upon three Aviatics, Chapman was slightly wounded by a slicing cut along his forearm. Ignoring the pain, he continued the combat until he shot down one of the Aviatics which fell vertically, and another he forced down out of control. The third made good his escape while Victor was engaged with the second.

This brilliant beginning brought to the American *Escadrille* the following complimentary citations from the French Army:

> Chapman (Victor). Corporal pilot of Escadrille 124 American citizen enlisted for the duration of the war. He is a pilot remarkable for his audacity, constantly hurling himself upon enemy aeroplanes without regard to their number or their altitude. On May 24th he attacked alone three German machines during which combat he had his clothing cut with many bullets and received a wound in the arm.

Unfortunately the enemy aeroplane destroyed by Chapman on this occasion fell too far within the German lines for its destruction to be verified and officially credited to him.

Another citation: The Military Medal has been conferred upon the following soldier: Rockwell (Kiffin Yates), #34805 corporal in Escadrille 124. Enlisted for the duration of the war and was wounded first on May 9th, 1915, during a bayonet charge. Passed into aviation and has proved himself a skilful and courageous pilot. On May 18th, 1916, he attacked and shot down a German aeroplane. On May 24th, 1916, he did not hesitate in attacking a large group of enemy machines during which combat he was gravely wounded in the face. This nomination carries with it the *Croix de Guerre* with one palm.

Signed, Joffre.

William Thaw was made an officer in the Legion of Honour with the following citation:

Thaw (William), #5503, lieutenant in Escadrille 124; enlisted voluntarily for the duration of the war; he is a pilot remarkable for his address, his devotion to duty and his contempt for danger; he has recently taken the offensive in 18 combats in the air, all within a short period. On the morning of May 24th, 1916, he attacked and brought down an enemy aeroplane. The same day he again attacked a group of three enemy machines and pursued them from 14,000 feet down to 7000 feet. Severely wounded during the course of the fight he succeeded, thanks to his energy and audacity, in directing his aeroplane within his own lines where he landed safely although the machine was badly crippled. (Already twice cited in the Order.)

On May 22, Bert Hall, then an adjutant, attacked an enemy aeroplane at 12,000 feet and worried it down to within 3000 feet of the ground, where he shot it down, causing it to fall within a few feet of the admiring trench soldiers who were gazing spellbound at the exhibition. On July 23rd he triumphed over another antagonist near Vaux. The following day he staggered home from a combat with his machine so badly mauled by enemy bullets that it could scarcely bear his weight. On November 6, 1916, he shot down an enemy machine over Buire, and on the ninth another, an L.V. G. two-seater, was destroyed by Hall over Sailly-Saillisel.

Bert Hall received the Military Medal and the *Croix de Guerre* from France, the Cross of St. George from Russia,—where he was sent to instruct the Russian pilots at the end of 1916, and the St. Stanislaus decoration and the *Vertu Militaire* were conferred upon him by Roumania. After the breakdown of Russia, Bert Hall returned by way of Siberia to the United States, where he still remains. He was born in 1880 and has reached the ripe old age of retirement.

Sergeant Elliot Cowdin was cited for the first time on June 26, 1915, for an exploit in which "he met and attacked simultaneously two German aeroplanes and forced them both to the ground. His aeroplane was badly damaged by the fire of the enemy and he received several bullet holes through his helmet."

On April 4, 1916, Cowdin while on patrol discovered a formidable formation of 12 L.V. G. machines cruising towards Verdun. Without a moment's hesitation he dived against this overwhelming force, shot down one of the twelve, and actually forced the others to beat a retreat. For this exploit Cowdin was given the *Médaille Militaire*.

Shortly after this brilliant exploit Elliot Cowdin was forced to retire from the service, owing to ill health. He returned to New York where he remained inactive until June, 1918, when he received a major's commission in the Air Service of the United States and again reported for duty.

Clyde Balsley of El Paso, Texas, did not finish his schooling and join his fellows at Bar-le-Duc until June fifteenth. There he found that daily combats had varied the monotony of life for those of the *escadrille* who yet remained on the active list. For some of the original seven were now far from active. Thaw and Rockwell were in the care of the medical authorities from injuries received in their combats on May 24; Victor Chapman had been wounded in the head on June 16, and though he refused to go to the hospital for treatment he was unable to stay aloft hunting the Boche with his usual vigour; and James McConnell had come a cropper in a bad landing and had been sent to Paris, together with his broken machine, for repairs.

Balsley arrived at the *escadrille* very young and inexperienced. He found many of his friends *hors de combat* and the others audaciously striving to fill their places by doing double time. The Germans appeared in thicker flocks than ever in their endeavour to hold the sky for the operation of their observation machines.

Balsley was taken across the front for the first time on the morning of the seventeenth of June. The next morning Captain Thénault, Norman Prince, and Kiffin Rockwell despite his wounds, accompanied Balsley to his first combat. A letter from Kiffin to his brother, Paul Rockwell, published in *La Guerre Aerienne*, gives the details of the extraordinary fight which followed:

> We were all four above the lines when we suddenly found ourselves in, the midst of about forty Boches who were united in a narrow sector but at different altitudes. At the height where we were there were about twelve or fifteen little Aviatic chasing machines which travel about as fast as we do, and moreover they carry a passenger. The pilot shoots straight ahead as we do while the passenger in behind is armed with a second machine gun which protects the rear and the sides.
>
> We were but four and were on the German side of the lines, but we remained grouped closely together and for ten or fifteen minutes we made evolutions around the Boches who fired at us constantly, some of the time from about fifty yards range. Finally we saw an opening. One of their machines crossed between us and the lines while all the rest were behind us. We plunged immediately upon this isolated Boche. A general *mêlée* resulted, for the whole swarm flew upon us from all sides and from above.
>
> I saw someone fall as though struck to death. "Was it Prince or Balsley ," I wondered to myself, " who had just

been killed?" Then I lost sight of another of our aeroplanes. There remained just the Captain and me. He signalled me and we drew away, and finally gained our field, convinced that the other two had been brought down.

Prince returned a little later. He had had to drop like a stone, for a Boche was on his tail and had already sent one bullet through his flying helmet.

It appeared that our poor Balsley had darted towards a Boche, got in close, and attempted to get his machine gun into operation when it jammed after the first shot.

He swerved off to adjust the gun when a bullet struck him in the stomach and *exploded against his backbone*!

Balsley fell vertically down, but fortunately he had kept his feet on the bar and was able to redress his machine and land it with his feet. He hit the ground not far from us and very near some trenches. His aeroplane was completely smashed in the landing.

First Kiffin Rockwell is wounded by an explosive bullet on May 24 and now Clyde Balsley was brought down by the same heinous and unlawful missile! The surgeons removed eleven fragments of this bullet from Balsley's interior the next day as he lay under ether in a hospital. Balsley kept them carefully arranged on the marble mantle by his bedside to exhibit to his callers this irrefutable evidence of German atrocity.

Captured Germans have insisted that the British pilots first used the explosive, small-calibre bullet in aerial warfare against the Zeppelins and therefore Germany was justified in employing them. The Hague Convention of 1909 agreed that no explosive projectile less than 37 millimetres in diameter should be used in war. This is the size of the one-pounder shell. The machine gun bullet is but .30 inch in diameter, and the rifle ball is approximately the same size. These small bullets were expressly and purposely excluded from use in "civilized warfare" in order to avoid "unnecessary human suffering." The German Government did not sign this agreement.

Early in 1915 when Zeppelin raids over London became a chronic habit of the Germans, aeroplanes were found to be the best defensive weapons against these destructive monsters. And the best method of bringing down the dirigible gasbags was by the incendiary or flaming bullet. Against these diabolical attacks upon defenceless women and children any effectual defence must be lawful.

But the German airmen claimed that British aviators filled their magazines with both incendiary and explosive bullets and that they used them not only against the Zeppelins but against German aeroplanes as well, whereupon the Huns retaliated by using them upon all occasions. Whatever may be the truth concerning the first appearance of the exploding machine-gun bullet in air combats, the dreadful missile came into fashion and apparently came to stay.

The fall of Balsley occurred on June 18, 1916. He left the hospital and returned to the United States two years later. He will never fly again. Incidentally Balsley's disaster led to the first supreme tragedy suffered by the American *Escadrille* or the *Escadrille Lafayette*, as it now was officially designated to avoid the remonstrances of the German Ambassador in Washington, who looked upon this organization of Americans as extremely unneutral. The wounding of Balsley and his pitiable state of suffering led to the death of the first of that gallant band of seven who formed the original *escadrille*—Victor Chapman of New York.

With bandaged head and impatient spirit, Victor Chapman remained at his aerodrome working over his aeroplane and gun after his wounding on June 16, when he should have been in the hospital. Every day he flew across to the nearby sickroom of Balsley, carrying to his wounded comrade champagne and oranges, for the nature of his injury prevented Balsley from taking ordinary food.

On June 23, Chapman went out on an uneventful patrol with the rest of his fellows. Returning to the aerodrome for lunch, Chapman filled a basket with oranges which he placed in his aeroplane, saying that he would follow the others over the lines for a little trip, after which he would land at the hospital and see Balsley.

Lufbery, Prince, and another started away without waiting for Chapman. Arrived over the lines they discovered a brace of enemy machines which they immediately engaged in combat.

Soon more of the Boches appeared on the scene, and after a short series of evolutions which accomplished nothing against such odds, the three Americans returned to their field. They landed and inquired for Chapman. It appeared he had gone to Balsley's hospital with his oranges.

An hour later a neighbouring French *escadrille* telephoned to 124 that one of their pilots had observed the retreat of the three Americans from the last melee, and that at the same moment a fourth Nieuport from the same *escadrille* was seen dashing at full speed into the midst of the enemy formation. It was Victor Chapman advancing to the support of his comrades.

Chapman was pursuing two of the fleeing Boches when his flashing Nieuport was seen to head vertically down and with motor full on it continued earthward at tremendous speed until it crashed some distance back of the German lines. Thus fell the first of that glorious seven.

Two days later arrived Chapman's nomination for the *Croix de Guerre* and his promotion to a sergeancy. The death of Victor Chapman attracted widespread public appreciation of his noble character and ideal devotion to France, both in that country and his own. His shining example won many enlistments to the cause he had espoused.

Chapman's loss was deeply mourned by the pilots of his *escadrille*. Miraculous escapes from death were recounted each night as these daring fighters returned one by one to their anxious mechanics. Chapman had always been the last to return. With their planes riddled with bullet holes, controls broken, and huge gaps in the fabric through which shells and shrapnel had passed, no unit along that great barrier lived through a more destructive storm than did this infantile yet glorious corps of American fliers at Verdun.

Baptized at Verdun! What more heroic beginning can be imagined! During the four months spent over this terrible battlefield the Americans had taken part in some hundreds of combats and had achieved sixteen duly verified victories. Doubtless three times as many German aeroplanes were shot down by the members of the *escadrille* during this period which were not credited, as they fell too far from the French lines to be observed by the authorities.

And the sole death in the *escadrille* during all these weeks of air combats was that of Victor Chapman!

By September, 1916, the German pressure at Verdun was sensibly lessened. Combats in the air became difficult to secure. The hunting was poor. Kiffin Rockwell had brought down his fourth official Boche on the ninth, and Lufbery had his eighth, but the game was getting scarce. Accordingly orders to vacate the Bar-le-Duc aerodrome and prepare for a change of scene were received on the eleventh of September with unanimous joy in the *Escadrille Lafayette*. This joy was little shaken by the further announcement that a week's leave in Paris was granted to the Americans. While they were enjoying a much needed rest their new machines would be prepared for them. Evidently they were going to the Somme. There were many rumours flying about concerning a French and British offensive on the Somme.

But instead of reporting along the Somme the Americans found themselves back at Luxeuil at the end of their week's holiday. An improved model of the Nieuport was being sent them, and they were to use them in protecting a gigantic bombing raid over into the enemy's country. Several bombing squadrons were gathering in Luxeuil, both British and French. The Mauser munition factories at Oberndorf were to be annihilated.

The improved Nieuports arrived slowly. Each pilot immediately set about adjusting the motor, instruments, and machine guns to his individual satisfaction. Raoul Lufbery and Kiffin Rockwell took their machines up for a try-out on September 23, the first flight they had made since leaving Verdun.

The enemy, suspecting some air offensive from this sector in

Alsace, had concentrated a heavy patrol force in the vicinity of Luxeuil. From this near vantage point in France many bombing expeditions were sent over to bombard the Rhine towns. Strong formations of Fokker fighting squadrons watched hourly for their appearance.

Rockwell became separated from Lufbery as they rose higher in the clouds, but both flew on deeper into the German lines, indifferent to their danger. These two expert duellists were the best in the escadrille. They had engaged in more combats, won more victories, and were conceded the most skilful tacticians of their unit.

Lufbery soon spied the game for which he was searching, and forthwith he made his customary attack. But his two-seater enemy was but a decoy. The American had no sooner appeared on the scene than he was himself attacked from every side by the hidden Fokkers. With some difficulty he made his escape without further injury than a few bullet holes in his new aeroplane. He landed at Fontaine, a field just back of his own lines. Upon landing he was told that Kiffin Rockwell, from whom he had so recently parted, had just been shot down and killed!

Rockwell too had found an antagonist, soon after he lost sight of Lufbery, in a German scout cruising alone over the French lines. It would be his fifth official victory and place him among the Aces!

Keeping his position above the Fokker until he turned back into the sun, Rockwell started his dive from 15,000 feet. The enemy plane, now aware of his approach, was at an altitude of 11,000 feet. With the coolness of a veteran Kiffin reserved his fire, keeping his target steadily in the centre of his sights. The enemy was headed towards him, sending forward a steady stream of lead from his two guns as he approached. Straight into this hail of bullets Kiffin Rockwell flew.

The attack took place just back of the trenches and was observed by many officers and troops. It was of short duration. The aeroplane of Rockwell continued on its course until but fifty yards separated the two combatants. Then the spectators saw the puffs of smoke from Kiffin's guns. The next instant a collision was narrowly averted by a quick swerve of the German. Rockwell's machine continued on its dive. One wing broke off and fell in the wake of the diving craft. The whole wreckage crashed an eighth of a mile behind the French lines.

Kiffin Rockwell was killed with an explosive bullet in the breast. Death had evidently been instantaneous.

The news was telephoned to the aerodrome, and his comrades brought his body home wrapped within the folds of the French flag. Two days later he was given a military funeral in which the British and French airmen joined. The second of the noble seven was gone!

Possessed of remarkable courage, endurance, and good judgment, Kiffin Rockwell had won the affection and respect of all the fighting airmen who had seen his attacks and heard of his gallant reputation. During July he had fought forty combats; in August thirty-four. Lieutenant de Laage de Meux, who was his usual fighting companion, stated that Rockwell had actually destroyed more than a dozen German aeroplanes in these combats. But as the great bulk of these duels occurred far behind the German lines, no official recognition of his frequent successes was possible.

There was a fineness of character in Kiffin Rockwell as in Victor Chapman that made their loss of especial bitterness to their comrades. Both had voluntarily relinquished the luxury of life common to rich men's sons and had stood shoulder to shoulder with the miserable misfits of life in the filthy trenches of the Foreign Legion. And even in this company both Chapman and Rockwell had won citations for conspicuous bravery. Both of these boys had estimated with disdain the sure approach of death. Victor Chapman had spoken of it with a friend but a day or two before his last flight. Kiffin Rockwell wrote to his mother:

"If I die I wish you to know that I died as all men should die—for that which is just."

And once he said seriously to a friend who attempted to remonstrate with him for his headlong bravery," I pay my part for Lafayette and Rochambeau!"

The great event for which the American pilots were waiting at Luxeuil—the aeroplane bombardment of the Mauser gunworks—at last was announced. It took place on October 12, 1916, and while its success was marvellous and complete, resulting in the utter annihilation of the German rifle factories, and while seven more enemy aeroplanes were brought down on that day by our American fliers, it marked the third tragic loss from the *Escadrille*—Norman Prince, its founder, organizer and patron.

The expedition planned was on a scale gigantic for that early day. Many tons of explosives were carried over by the French and British bombing machines, while a score of darting little patrols flew above and ahead of them to clear the path of obstacles. The latest arrivals found their bombs were superfluous. The works had been entirely destroyed by their leaders.

Prince and Lufbery, Masson and De Laage formed part of the escort, and each one of the four brought down one of the "obstacles" which attempted to bar the path. Late that afternoon they continued flying with their machines, hoping that two or three of their missing comrades might still be sighted coming in.

At last in semi-darkness they came down towards an aerodrome which they later discovered was near Corcieux. Lufbery and Prince were together, the others having already gone in.

Lufbery made his descent and landed safely upon the unlighted field. Giving him time to roll his machine out of the way Prince made a last circuit of the aerodrome, and coming around into the wind, cut off his motor and pointed down her nose. He was not familiar with the grounds and was unaware of a line of wires that extended across one end of the aerodrome. He crashed into them. His machine turned over, sending the pilot headlong from his seat. Prince fell, breaking both legs and sustaining severe injuries internally. On October 15, Norman Prince died in the hospital. His body was brought back to his comrades' camp and buried besides that of Rockwell.

Just before his death Norman Prince was given the honorary promotion of lieutenant and the Legion of Honour. He had conquered three enemy pilots in single combat and had already received from France the Military Medal and the *Croix de Guerre*, with the following citation:

> Prince (Norman), #939, Adjutant pilot of Escadrille 124, has served in *escadrille* for nineteen months and has been conspicuous for a bravery and a devotion beyond comparison in the execution of his numerous expeditions of bombardment and patrol. Was severely wounded October 12th, 1916, after having shot down a German aeroplane. Already possesses *Médaille Militaire*.

Two days after the death of Prince, his old *escadrille* left the Vosges to take its part in the great Somme offensive. Here again the *Escadrille Lafayette* played an honourable and conspicuous part. At the close of that campaign the American unit stood third in France with the number of its official victories.

The carefully selected experts of the Cigognes had then totalled two hundred German aeroplanes shot down—a full one third of the entire number destroyed by all France since the war began. N. 65 stood second with seventy-odd victories, of which nearly one half were won by its leading Ace, Lieutenant Nungesser. And third stood the *Escadrille Lafayette*, with a total of thirty-eight aeroplanes officially credited.

James McConnell was killed in combat on March 19, 1917, leaving only William Thaw to survive of the original group of seven. Chapman, Rockwell, Prince, and McConnell were killed in action; Cowdin retired by ill-health; Bert Hall was training pilots and cruising the air of Russia and the Balkans.

Others had taken the places of the absent ones, and the *Escadrille* was in a very flourishing condition. Over three hundred names were on its rolls at the time America declared war upon Germany! The example of this heroic seven had borne a glorious fruit.

McConnell had had a series of misadventures ever since his first flight with his *escadrille* over the Vosges, on which occasion he lost his companions and, after flying for two hours over an unfamiliar country, he was forced to land through the exhaustion of his fuel. Happily he landed in French territory and was soon back with his squadron.

Twice thereafter he smashed his machine upon landing and was both times severely injured. Consequently his fighting periods were considerably less than those of his comrades, and he lacked the experience and technique that their frequent duels taught the others.

Though he returned from the hospital to the aerodrome on the Somme a fortnight after its arrival there McConnell, then a sergeant, was still unable to take an active part in daily patrolling, owing to internal injuries received in his last accident. The air forces of the Allies were safely superior to those of the enemy at this time, and a huge score was rolled up in our favour during the early weeks of this campaign.

One of the newer pilots who had lately joined the American *Escadrille* was Edmond Genet of New York. He was a descendant of the French Citizen Genet who came to America during the administration of Thomas Jefferson to seek the aid of this country in behalf of the young republic.

McConnell and Genet left their aerodrome and flew north over the battle area beyond Ham about nine o'clock on the morning of March 19. Parsons accompanied them, but he soon became separated from his companions, who proceeded without him.

After an hour's cruise McConnell discovered three Boches back of St. Quentin and signalling to Genet to follow he darted in for an attack. In the fracas which ensued Genet received a bullet in the cheek and several severe injuries to his machine. Breaking off his combat Genet started for home, searching the adjacent skies in the meantime for a sight of McConnell. His comrade was not there.

That afternoon the *escadrille* was informed by telephone that an aeroplane of their squadron had fallen near Tergnier, a small village between St. Quentin and Chauny.

Three days later the victorious advance of the Allies had reached the spot where McConnell had fallen. His comrades flew over in their machines and hurried to the wreckage. McConnell was found beside his aeroplane, his body stripped of clothing by the Huns and every article of identification removed. His mangled form was unrecognizable, but the number on his machine served to identify him to his friends. His body was buried in the garden plot where he fell, his coffin consisting of the doors of a nearby house.

In a letter left on his writing table the morning of his disappearance James McConnell the beloved wrote:

> My burial is of no import. Make it as easy as you can for yourselves. I have no religion and do not care for any service. If its omission embarrasses you I presume I could stand the performance.

McConnell on the very day of his death was proposed for the *Croix de Guerre*. His melancholy death proved a sad blow to those comrades who had so long loved him for his happy fun-loving nature. The spirit of his devotion to the great cause is characteristically expressed in an entry in his diary on the date of his 29th birthday:

> This war will perhaps be my death, but in spite of all I owe it a profound gratitude!

Thus did these four intrepid Americans give their all to France. The honours they acquired, the losses they inflicted upon the enemy of their country, are perhaps trivial in comparison with the other stupendous upheavals of war, but it is safe to say that the imperishable glory of their example will long preserve their names in history as the apostles of America who pointed the way of liberty to their countrymen.

The Americans enrolled in original *Escadrille Americaine* on March 14, 1916.

William Thaw, 6 victories.
Victor Chapman, killed June 23, 1916.
Kiffin Yates Rockwell, killed September 23, 1916.
Norman Prince, killed October 15, 1916, by accident in landing.
James McConnell, killed March 19, 1917.
Elliot Cowdin, retired 1916 by ill health.
Bert Hall, retired to fight in Russia, December, 1916.

CHAPTER 2

Early French Heroes

In the beginning of the war it was difficult to carry on aerial warfare because aeroplane armament was, and remained through long months, very uncertain. The first encounters in air awakened no emotion in either of the rival pilots. On the contrary they exchanged a wave of the hand in greeting and continued their flight without swerving. It was the time when the most cautious fortified himself merely with an ordnance revolver. Later—great progress—the observers took a musket aboard, and it was not until the end of 1914 that some machines began to leave for the chase equipped with a machine gun.

It is well to remember that when Garaix was struck down by the German cannon, August 15, 1914, on the aerobus Paul Schmitt, he had on board a machine gun and two hundred cartridges. Moreover the Breguet 160-horse-power machine piloted by De Moineau was armed in the same way December, 1914. It was at this time that the first Voisins for bombarding made their appearance with automatic or machine guns.

The first of October, 1914, the German staff drew up a report on aviation which today seems prehistoric. One paragraph read:

> Thus as experience has shown, a real combat in the air, such as journalists and romancers have described, should be considered a myth. The duty of the aviator is to see and not to fight.

During the first weeks of hostilities the machines brought down were shot solely by the troops on the ground. This was made possible by the low altitude at which the machines flew.

It was September 8, 1914, when for the first time an aeroplane was struck down by another aeroplane. This occurred on the Russian front. In the course of a reconnaissance Captain Nesteroff met an Austrian machine which was flying above the cantonments, which he was preparing to bomb as soon as he saw it. Nesteroff hurled himself in the direction of the enemy, gained on him, caught up with him, and as he was not armed for an attack, deliberately, bravely, madly charged upon him, struck him, crippled him, and sent him in a summersault to the ground, himself entangled in the fall his courage had caused.

So died the Russian Nesteroff and the Austrian Baron Rosenthal. It was Nesteroff who was the first to loop-the-loop April 20, 1913, some days before Pegoud.

The honour of bringing down the first machine in a duel (which was not at the same time a suicide) belongs to Sergeant Frantz and to the mechanic Quenault; it was on the fifth of October, 1914. This success gained for one the Legion of Honour and for the other the *Médaille Militaire*. It seems of interest to recall the circumstances of this historic encounter as told by an eyewitness:

> At five minutes past ten there came over the German lines a Voisin biplane. We put our field glasses away for they would not be needed. A German machine is at about 1500 meters. The Frenchman charges straight upon him, holding himself a little above. From the French aeroplane came the bangs of the machine gun: ta-ta-ta . . . ta . . . ta . . . ta . . . The German passes under the Frenchman and tries to escape toward his own lines to the north. The Frenchman, taking care to keep above him, spins about in a circle of a very small axis, gains speed on the German, whom he overtakes, goes beyond, turns about, and comes back over the German, at whom he keeps popping his gun, while continuously planing above him. The German

makes some circles in the air while trying to escape the Frenchman. The German rises a little above the French plane, tries to rise still higher to take again his way toward the north. The French machine gun fires faster and faster: ta-ta-ta-ta . . . ta . . . ta- ta-ta-ta, a noise like the crackling of salt in the fire! The German loses his height, suddenly makes a short circle, and comes back upon the French biplane. The machine gun roars again. The Aviatic pitches forward three times on its nose, then falls in a spiral, the tail toward the sky. The conquering biplane swoops in circles in the air above the falling plane like a bird of prey above its victim.

We watched this marvellous spectacle from the terrace of the *château*. The Aviatic fell a thousand meters from us into a little wood; we ran towards it. The biplane had plunged into the marshy earth of the woods near a large pond covered with cat-tails and swamp grass; we went in over our ankles; the motor was almost entirely buried in the ground, the fuselage was twisted, and the wings were broken into a thousand pieces. One of the aviators lay quite dead three yards away from the motor.

The second, the observer, with beautiful hands exquisitely cared for and perhaps a great Prussian name, was caught under the red motor, now a wreck in flames. He seemed to us to attempt to pull himself out, but the movement was probably convulsive; he looked at us, clawed the earth with his hands, and died before our eyes; help was impossible.

At this instant an automobile arrived. The wheels began to sink in the mud, and the car stopped. The General and his staff came up to the aeroplane. They had witnessed the aerial combat. Directly afterwards came two young soldiers of twenty years, a sergeant and his mechanic, wearing the caps of aviators. They are the victors, the Sergeant Frantz and the mechanic Quenault, who have come to view their work. The General embraced them—we pressed their hands. An old woman gathered some flowers in the wood, which she offered them.

'What you have done here deserves the Cross; you shall have it. Count on me,' said the General. It was stirring. I imagined Napoleon there. He would have taken his own Cross, that of one of his Marshals and decorated the two aviators on the spot.

The fire of the German biplane was put out by some men. Nothing remained but the motor, a bomb which had not exploded, and the twisted fuselage. The two men, naked, their clothing entirely burned, lay some meters away, their legs and trunks burned, their arms stiff, only their faces preserved from mutilation. 'Boch faces,' said the men.

Above a whirring sound is heard! Two Frenchmen pursuing a German who is making at top speed for the north. If he has been able to see the ground, he will go home and tell them, 'This is what I saw an hour ago.'

It is a curious coincidence that the machine brought down by Frantz had already been the object of a fantastic pursuit on his part three weeks before. The vanquished German aviator himself tells of this in a letter which was found on him, in which he writes thus:

> These last days I have escaped beautifully. A Frenchman gave chase to me and it was only by good luck in having clouds to hide in that I was able to get away.

It is interesting to recall the text of the recompense of these two victorious airmen:

> By ministerial decision dated September 13th last the *Médaille Militaire* has been conferred on Sergeant Frantz, pilot aviator, for the aggregation of the services rendered by him from the beginning of the campaign. In particular Sergeant Frantz during the month of August last, under the fire of the infantry and artillery of the garrison of Metz, succeeded in dropping two bombs on the hangars

of the aero station at Frescati.

The fifth of October last, this same non-commissioned officer, accompanied by mechanic gunner Quenault, attacked a German aeroplane and succeeded in bringing it down while it was scouting above the French lines. The commander-in-chief confers on him the Cross of the Chevalier of the Legion of Honour, and awards to mechanic Quenault the *Médaille Militaire*.

In heroism it is only the first step that is hard. It had been necessary to wait three months for an aerial combat with a decisive result. It was enough. Frantz had opened the way for his comrades to follow.

Two days later, on October 7th, the civilian champion Gaubert enlisted voluntarily for the duration of the war, and Captain Blaise, on a Maurice Farman, surprised an enemy aeroplane from behind and flew along about twenty-five yards above it. The passenger, Captain Blaise, fired eight shots from his rifle. The German observer defended himself with a revolver, but the Boche machine soon fell inside its lines. The *Deutschen Nachrichten* announced soon afterwards that

> Lieutenant Finger, wounded in the course of an aerial combat on October 7, between Metz and Verdun, at an altitude of 2300 meters, died of his wounds October 9. The passenger was wounded in the crash of the machine which was destroyed.

This success, thus officially recognized by the enemy, did not, unfortunately, bring any reward to its author, Sergeant Gaubert.

October 25, 1914, Corporal Strebick and his mechanic David brought down a Taube east of Amiens. While regulating artillery fire on his Henry Farman, mechanic Strebick found himself in the presence of an enemy aeroplane and endured his fire for some time, but adroitly avoided the attack. Having no arms with which to return the fire, he finally had to return to earth to get a machine gun. With his mechanic he left again for the chase. At a short distance from the enemy aeroplane he permitted his passenger to draw a bead on the German machine. A few shots were heard and the aeroplane fell between the French and Boche trenches... And now comes the uninterrupted series.

On November 2, 1914, the famous pilot, Eugene Gilbert, with Captain de Vergenette as observer, saved Captain Morris when attacked by an enemy aeroplane equipped with a Mauser gun.

The Boche was about to fire at less than twenty yards when a whirring of a motor made him turn his head: fifteen yards from him a Morane-Saulnier approached. The German then put himself on the defensive, allowed Captain Morris to escape, and sought to avoid Gilbert, who resolutely pursued him. Captain de Vergenette fired three musket volleys, and the Boche aeroplane disappeared in the abyss and fell on to a field where it crashed. The pilot, no doubt, had been killed in the air.

Another victory for Gilbert on November 18. With his mechanic Bayle, he attacked an Aviatic between Albert and Bapaume. Ten balls from his musket, and the enemy machine fell near Rheims, where it was captured!

Then appears another champion. Sub-Lieutenant Mahieu on the 22nd of November had conferred upon him for a like exploit the Legion of Honour. Twice his observer had fired his machine gun without success. Lieutenant Mahieu then passed his adversary and forced him to turn back to the rear. Not having any more cartridges, Mahieu did not hesitate to charge on the Boche with the intention of colliding with him. But at some meters from the German machine, his passenger, attempting a last chance, fired his revolver. By an extraordinary chance, he killed the pilot, and the machine fell at once.

On the same day, an Englishman returning from a bombardment forced a German aeroplane to the ground inside our lines, and a Frenchman on a Morane-Saulnier forced an enemy bird to descend near the forest of Clairmarais, within our lines.

On December 18, one of our aviators killed with a rifle a German pilot whose machine crashed to the ground.

Third victory of Gilbert, January 10, 1915. "Near Amiens,"

declared the *communiqué*, a "German aeroplane was pursued by one of our Moranes and brought down. The machine fell in our lines. One of the officers was killed, the other wounded."

Gilbert was accompanied on this occasion by Lieutenant de Puechredon. They were returning from a reconnaissance when they saw an enemy aeroplane cruising over Amiens. They followed it, going very high in order to pass beyond it without being seen. Not far from Amiens they caught up with it, cut it off, and the observer fired four balls from his rifle. Two of these balls hit the enemy observer, Lieutenant de Falkenstein. The third hit the pilot Keller in the neck; the fourth pierced the radiator. The wounded pilot landed at once and was made prisoner.

> It is the third time that Sergeant Gilbert, who has already received the *Médaille Militaire*, has succeeded in bringing down enemy machines.

So was expressed an official communication. This victory gained for the heroes the red ribbon.

> The General Commander-in-Chief names Chevaliers of the Legion of Honour, Sergeant aviator Gilbert and Lieutenant *observer de* Puechredon who, on January 10th, brought down an enemy aeroplane with a carbine. In rewarding their bravery and skill, the General in Chief desires to encourage the pilots and observers who each day seek an aerial combat.
> The above award will be borne in mind by all the personnel of aviation.

January 25 an official *communiqué* pays tribute to the mastery of our pilots in these words:

> When the weather is clear and calm, our aviators frequently meet the enemy machines. There is not a single case where one of these enemy machines has not taken flight before a French aeroplane. Most frequently the Aviatic makes a half turn as soon as he sees the adversary. Less often he engages in battle.

Such was our biplane of the first period. We have seen the first attempts, noted the initial successes. We will now pass more rapidly over the victories, more and more frequent, at the same time reserving a special place for that king of the air, for that pioneer of the chase, for Garros.

Garros for some time had been perfecting an invention which eventually produced a revolution in the fourth arm of all the belligerent countries. It was a method of allowing the pilot to engage in battle without the necessity of being accompanied by an observer.

Homogeneity on board an aeroplane is extremely difficult to obtain. Moreover, the apostle of light aviation was of the opinion that the less dead weight an aeroplane was encumbered with, the easier to handle it would be, and consequently the better able to attack. It was necessary then to find a way to fire through the propeller without fear of breaking it.

After various experiments, many of which were faulty at first, Garros succeeded in finding a solution, thanks to a band of steel in form of a pyramid fixed on each blade at the spot passing before the gun muzzle. The balls that hit the blade were deflected so that the propeller was not damaged at all. This system was adopted by the Germans who later perfected it, basing it on a synchronization permitting the elimination of the bands of steel, and thereby increased the utility of the propeller.

While Garros devoted himself to these experiments, some other pilots distinguished themselves in combats.

Pegoud, on the 9th of February, 1915, accompanied by machine gunner Le Rendu, flew above the region of Grand-Pré, where he engaged in his first combat. Let him tell of the duel:

A Taube came in my direction, I attacked at less than 50 yards with my machine gun. It made a half turn. I followed it at 800 yards while my companion fired without ceasing. After a minute or so of pursuit, the enemy made a long glide on the left wing and fell; the front was enveloped in flames and smoke, fragments of fabrics detached themselves from the wings. It crashed to the south of Grand Pré.

In the same vicinity, I perceived then two Aviatics, of which one flew above the sector northeast of Montfaucon. I attacked the nearest. At the first burst of bullets he dived.

I charge upon him vertically, continuing my fire. I see him neatly hit by a tracer bullet, and he darts into space. I raise my machine to 5000 feet. I regain my altitude, pursue the second Aviatic which flies over the sector east of Montfaucon. I approach, firing my machine gun at him from about 40 yards below him. During fifty seconds, he sustains the combat by shots from his automatic rule, but soon he seems to be hit, and he falls in a spin. I charge in a vertical volplane, shooting my machine gun continuously. And the Aviatic, crippled in the wings and the tail, disappears into space.

Surrounded by the enemy's shells of all calibre, I safely came to the ground at Sainte-Menehould.

Such is the official account which Pegoud gave of this glorious exploit. One does not do better today! Unfortunately at that time they counted only those machines that fell in our lines.

On March 21, 1916, in the course of a reconnaissance, Sergeant Salze with Lieutenant Moreau brought down an Aviatic above the railroad track near Turckheim nineteen kilometres to the west of Colmar. He was scouting at long range when he was attacked above Munster by two Boches who found themselves below him. He dived on the first, placed himself in a favourable position, and Lieutenant Moreau opened fire at thirty yards. At the second charge, and with the fifth cartridge, the musket triumphs: the enemy pilot is without doubt killed, the Aviatic is crippled in one wing and crashes near Walbach. It falls astraddle a ditch.

Salze descends to 2000 feet to watch the fall, despite the artillery fire which has not ceased to rage during the entire combat, even at the risk of hitting the Boche. The French machine again takes the altitude and goes to attack the second Aviatic, more swift than the first. The two aeroplanes turn the one about the other. At the third turn the adversary flees, diving toward Colmar. Salze comes back above Walbach again to see his victim. A crowd of Boche soldiers are about the wrecked machine. Moreau fires his last cartridges on the group, then the conquerors joyfully return to Belfort, where they are feted as they so richly deserve. Lieutenant Moreau was killed later by a bomb, and Salze, having become Lieutenant and after having received the *Médaille Militaire* and the Legion of Honour, fell to his death in the trial of an aeroplane on August 22, 1917.

The first day of April was particularly glorious: it was especially notable as the day Navarre gained his first official victory. Navarre, then a sergeant, had left in a two-seater with Lieutenant Robert, when at 6.25 in the morning, after two hours of cruising, he met an Aviatic above de Fraisnes. He approached within thirty yards while under the enemy's fire, and Lieutenant Robert then fired three bullets from a carbine. All three hit, and the Boche was obliged to come to earth inside our lines, with his radiator riddled and the wing broken. The Frenchmen descended beside their victim and captured both pilot and passenger.

The same day Roland Garros, the "bird made man", who had again just taken his place at the front, left on his Morane-Saulnier for the bombardment of the shipyards of Bruges. He came down to less than 300 feet, according to his custom, to better assure himself of his target, and dropped his bombs. Returning, he met a Boche whom he attacked and dropped in flames into the French lines. He had placed himself behind and above the enemy, firing his machine gun at less than ten yards distance. He distinguished the sudden quivering of the back of the enemy pilot when the bullets struck, and this sight, he said, was particularly distressing.

The next day, Adjutant Pelletier d'Oisy, pilot, and the Lieutenant Chambre, observer, went aloft at five-thirty. An hour later they saw an Albatross, chased it, cut off its retreat, and opened fire at thirty yards. The Boche was struck and came down within our lines. Both passengers were captured but not until they had set fire to their machine.

Our aviation goes through a splendid series. The third of April Pegoud brought down another aeroplane. On that same morning an Aviatic flew above Sainte-Menehould and dropped on the line of the railroad nine bombs which fell in the fields. The champion hurled himself into the pursuit, but the German fled and could not be overtaken. Towards evening, as Pegoud was finishing his round, a Boche machine dived on him and engaged him in a duel. He crippled him above Somme-Bionne, obliging him to descend. They landed beside the wrecked machine and captured pilot and observer.

On April 13, Navarre brought down his second Boche. In the course of a reconnaissance in the region of Verdun, he attacked an aeroplane which he followed right into its own lines and succeeded in sending to the ground. The cannon tried to avenge their comrade. They made a hole in the propeller of the Frenchman, who succeeded in returning, but was obliged to come to earth at Sainte-Menehould before reaching his own territory.

Then it is Garros who recommences—alas! for so little a time—his glorious destructions.

The 15th of April, while crossing in the morning above Ypres, he saw two Aviatics regulating the artillery fire. He put the first to flight and brought down the second, which fell inside the German lines in view of the British trenches.

Three days later, on the eighteenth, at ten o'clock, he triumphed over an Albatross coming from Ypres, and made it fall a wreck between the Hill # 26 and Langemarck.

This hero, conqueror of five aeroplanes in eighteen days, was made prisoner the next day. French aviation has never experienced a more cruel loss. Garros disappeared, but his comrades did their best to avenge him. On April 28th, Lieutenant de Bernis, accompanied by Lieutenant Jacottet, brought down an Albatross above Muizon. The machine was captured.

Sergeant Mesguich, with Sub-Lieutenant Ferru, met an Albatross, attacked it at twenty yards, in spite of the abundant fire of the German passenger, followed it to less than 600 meters of altitude hi his lines, where it broke out in flames and where our artillery finished its destruction.

Sergeant Ortoli, future Ace of a *communiqué*, attacked with Sub-Lieutenant Menj a Boche who crashed between Miraumont and Beaumont-Hamelle.

Sergeant Mahieu, pilot, and Lieutenant Dunoyer, observer, triumphed at last over a fourth enemy who fell on the border northwest of Hisinger in the valley of Ancre.

As for Navarre, he attacked near Saint-Thierry-Brémont an Aviatic, which soon gave out a dense smoke and seemed to fall, overcome, to the earth.

It was a day admirable among all. Unfortunately it was marked by the first aerial victory of the enemy. On his return from the bombardment of the railroad station and the bomb factory at Leopoldshohe, Sergeant Caron was attacked and killed by a German pilot.

The seventh of May an Aviatic was brought down in a combat by one of our men near la Faloise.

The tenth of May, Adjutant David, on a Maurice Farman, was in an encounter with an enemy triplane, a type which had appeared for the first time, and which marked the initial effort of the enemy toward an aeroplane for the chase. Greatly to be feared, this type of machine was armed with two machine guns. More swift than David's machine, its tactics were to fly over him at thirty yards, firing two charges at him as it passed. Eight times in succession David endured this double fire. At the ninth passage he made a sudden turn and faced the enemy. His passenger fired two shots from his musket, hitting his mark, and succeeded in triumphing over the huge Aviatic, which burst into flames and vanished into space.

On May 20th came our first success with the aeroplane cannon: Sergeant Frantz, hero of the first aerial victory, and gunner Fralin, brought down an Aviatic with sixteen shots from their one-pounder gun.

A brilliant exploit on May 26th was due to the activity of

Sergeant Mesguich as pilot and Sub-Lieutenant Jacottet as gunner working together. They sighted an Albatross which had been signalled from the vicinity of Laon going toward Château-Thierry at an altitude of 10,000 feet. The two fighters hurled themselves into the encounter, rose above the enemy, and approached within thirty feet of him. The duel began.

In the very beginning Mesguich received a bullet in the shoulder. In spite of his suffering he continued his pursuit. The Boche tried to gain the advantage by colliding with him. Our aviators state that blood flowed down on the enemy fuselage. With the end of his gun almost touching his mark Jacottet fired a round of cartridges. The Albatross nose-dived and crumbled up, "rolling like a rabbit", according to the expression of the conquerors, on the side of the little hill where it fell.

The Frenchmen, descending in a spiral, placed themselves near the Germans. The pilot, thrown out of the aeroplane, was in mortal agony a few yards away; while the observer, a lieutenant of the Von Buelow Guards, was lying lifeless under the motor. In the cockpit they found ten large bombs and forty grenades.

June sixth a victory was registered by two heroes, both of whom later found death in aerial battle.

Maxime Lenoir, the future Ace, then regulator of artillery fire, was flying a Caudron when he was attacked by an Aviatic.

He returned the fire at once, all the while receiving some bullets in his own aeroplane, when Captain Quillien, accompanied by Lieutenant d'Anchald, as machine gunner, came to the rescue of his comrade, and opened fire against the Boche. Lenoir joined forces and prevented the adversary from escaping. At the end of ten minutes, the Aviatic crashed in our lines near Béthenain-Ville, at Sivry-la-Perche. The pilot, who had received a bullet full in the chest, was killed instantly. Another projectile had cut off the thumb that was pressing his automatic pistol.

The German aeroplane, freed from all control, had fallen, and the observer was thrown out of the cockpit. After a long search he was found in a forest, 1500 yards from the *débris* of his machine and the body of his companion.

On June 18th came a new success of Sergeant Gilbert. An aeroplane had been signalled in the direction of Aspach. Our hero rose and joined it in the clouds at the end of thirty minutes. The duel took place above de Weiller at 10,000 feet. The Boche, returning fire with a machine gun, hit first the motor, then the aeroplane, and finally hit Gilbert in the neck. Gilbert, flying above him, fired three charges. At the third he saw the enemy pilot raise his arm in a gesture of despair, and the machine fell instantly like a stone into our lines, a mile southwest of Weiller.

Gilbert had a lucky escape: his propeller was perforated, a cylinder was cut in two, the outside plate of the motor was riddled with shots, the fabric of the wings was torn into shreds by the explosive bullets, and he himself was wounded.

July boasts for us the success of two of our celebrated heroes, Captain Brocard and Adjutant Pegoud, and one other whose name may be surmised, Georges Guynemer.

On the third of July Captain Brocard, Chief of the famous Number 3, called "the Storks", pursued in his single-seater an aeroplane which had been bomb-dropping in our lines. He began the battle at six o'clock in the morning at thirty yards' range and finished the struggle at only 1200 feet above the trenches. He distinguished clearly the observer who first raised his arms to heaven and then controlled the fall of the machine near Dreslincourt, at less than a mile behind the German front.

The Boche was soon caught under the fire of our artillery, and his destruction was soon completed.

To give an idea of the heroism of Captain Brocard in this exploit it should be stated that his machine gun was put out of commission, and he finished this fight with his revolver. In this battle his Nieuport was pierced by five bullets.

On the eleventh Adjutant Pegoud brought down an Aviatic which fell in flames near the railroad station of Altkirch, in the enemy's lines. At once the German soldiers hurled themselves out of the trenches to bear aid to the machine, but at the same instant our 75's started action and obliterated the rescuers.

Finally comes the 19th of July which will remain famous in

the annals of French aviation. For on that day Corporal Georges Guynemer, accompanied by his mechanic Guerder, gave battle to a German aeroplane which caught fire and fell in its own lines.

The great Ace had arrived on the scene!

CHAPTER 3

Roland Garros, the First Air Fighter

As the name Wright is to America, so is the reputation in France of the celebrated aviator, Roland Garros.

Even before the war came to emphasize the importance of flying Garros occupied perhaps the most conspicuous position in French aviation. Every air contest of importance in Europe found him entered, and usually a victor. He had given exhibitions throughout the United States in 1911. He was the first to fly over the Mediterranean Sea. With Beaumont or Pegoud or Brindejonc de Moulinais he shared the prizes of the great European Circuit, the race from Paris to Rome, from Paris to Madrid, and in 1911 he won the Grand Prix d'Anjou.

At the mobilization of the air forces of France in August, 1914, Roland Garros was in Germany. Scenting the possibility of danger he did not wait even to collect his belongings, but evading his acquaintances took the first train to Switzerland and hastened on to Paris.

Upon his arrival he reported for immediate service and was attached forthwith to the squadron of notables containing besides himself Eugene Gilbert, Marc Pourpe, Maxime Lenoir, Armand Pinsard and Captain de Beauchamp—Escadrille M. S. 23.

The early months of war-aviation revealed many startling truths concerning the aeroplane. It could carry messages quicker than any other means where wires were not laid. It could fly over enemy positions and come back with the report of observations made in a manner that revolutionized modern warfare. It could drop bombs and literature into enemy camps, and shots from the ground were ludicrously ineffectual against its manoeuvring.

All these qualifications were immensely gratifying to Garros and his comrades, many of whom had for years been preaching to a deaf public the possibilities of aviation in commerce and in war. All these possibilities had been foreseen by the veteran Garros. But, one question undoubtedly had been settled in actual warfare that had previously been highly speculative—it appeared virtually impossible during the first month of the war to shoot down an aeroplane in flight either with guns on the ground or guns mounted on other aeroplanes. Bullets from the ground were wasted against the swiftly moving machines. Even if a lucky shot did strike them it passed through the wings without inflicting serious injury. This method of combating enemy machines might as well be abandoned.

There remained the possibility of mounting a machine gun on an aeroplane for the pilot's use in such a manner that the stream of issuing bullets would not hit the tractor propeller. To this problem Garros set his inventive mind.

In February, 1915, after many weeks of patient experimenting, Garros petrified his aeroplane enemies by suddenly appearing among them with his new invention. From the very nose of his aeroplane, hitherto considered the safest blind spot of all, deadly streams of bullets poured forth. In eighteen days Garros shot down five incredulous Huns. His success was instantaneous and complete.

France immediately set about duplicating the device of Garros on all fighting machines. It was a point of decided superiority over the German airmen. But alas! By a strange fatality, Roland Garros himself was brought down on the day of his last victory, April 19, 1915, and fell a prisoner into the hands of the Huns. Unable to destroy his machine before he was captured, Garros suffered the mortification of giving to his enemies the very invention over which he had so long laboured for their destruction.

His capture was due primarily to the very precise methods

ROLAND GARROS
Most famous before-the-war French aviator.
Inventor of shooting through the propeller

Garros adopted in his daring bombing raids. He had invariably returned home from these raids crowned with. success. Depots, bridges, factories, and supply stations he had repeatedly set on fire and destroyed, always by the same method.

Approaching his objective from a height of ten or twelve thousand feet, Garros would cut off his motor and descend through the defending but futile shells until his machine was within a hundred feet or so of his target. Then, pulling back on his lever, he released his bombs so near the roof that a miss was impossible. Switching on his motor again he would brave the shots from below and gayly make his way back into the French lines.

On April 19, he flew over into the enemy camp and descending low upon a freight train of supplies entering Courtrai, he dropped his bombs with his usual precision. He had descended with idle motor from a very high altitude. After watching for a moment the effect of the explosions Garros blandly turned on the spark and set his face towards home.

But the engine did not pick up! Not a single cylinder uttered a reassuring cough. The engine was cold or filled with oil, or perhaps the spark plugs were faulty. Every second the aeroplane was dropping nearer the earth.

Frantically Garros worked the throttle and nursed along his machine, endeavouring by every means to put some life into the stubborn motor. But in vain! His aeroplane dropped heavily to earth hi the very midst of his enemies, and he was captured even before he was able to wreak his vengeance, so richly deserved, upon his faithless engine. He was captured in a ditch where he had concealed himself at the last moment after hastily attempting to fire his aeroplane. The fire did not destroy the machine but was quickly extinguished by the Huns.

His great discovery was thus presented personally by himself to his enemies. And none too slowly did they turn it to their own advantage.

The "King of the Air" was in their hands. Twice before the newspapers of Europe had announced with fervid details the story of Garros' death. This time however his fate had been witnessed by several of his comrades, and France knew that her famous "bird-man" was indeed a prisoner in Germany.

For weeks no news came as to whether Garros was dead or wounded. His captors not only concealed all news of him but subjected him to many cruelties and indignities. He was confined for some weeks in the prison at Magdeburg, but later was liberated and given comparative freedom in the prison stockade at Cologne. So precious did the Huns consider this celebrated Frenchman, however, and so apprehensive were they of his ability to make his escape that they compelled Garros to sign his name to a register every thirty minutes of the day when he was not under lock and key!

For over two years this strict scrutiny was unrelaxed. In the meantime Lieutenant Marchal, the hero of the longest aeroplane flight in the history of the war—that from the French lines to Berlin where Marchal dropped leaflets into the German capital from his aeroplane and then flew onwards to within forty miles of the Russian frontier, a total distance of 750 miles without stopping—Lieutenant Marchal, through the exhaustion of fuel, had been compelled to drop into the German lines, where he was captured. He was sent to the same prison camp which contained Garros.

In January, 1918, France resounded with the news that Garros and Marchal had escaped from Germany and were in England. For military reasons the details of their escape cannot be given. Both airmen passed over into France and again entered into the service of their country.

In order to grasp the full measure of the service which Garros did to aerial warfare it is necessary to consider the position of the fighting aeroplane at the beginning of the war its-difficulties, its limitations, and the abnormal importance of the defensive power it was called upon to assume.

For since no manner of land guns could prevent the aeroplanes of the enemy from flying over to spy out the movements below, opposing aircraft alone could be entrusted with this function. And as yet even these armed defenders were of little value, owing to the awkwardness of shooting through the rushing air from the unsteady platform at the swiftly moving target ahead of or beside them.

Aircraft includes airships and aeroplanes. With airships we shall not be concerned beyond classifying them as comprising gas balloons or lighter-than-air conveyances, such as Zeppelins, dirigibles and observation balloons. They are all slower moving than aeroplanes, and offer a larger target to the enemy, hence they have occupied an insignificant position in air fighting as compared to the heavier-than-air machine—the aeroplane.

The aeroplane is either a pusher or a tractor, the propeller either "pushing" the machine from behind or "attracting" it from in front. Experience has shown that the tractor is swifter and more easily handled than the pusher, and thus of proved superiority.

With the tractor propeller buzzing rapidly before the face of the pilot, he finds himself in an awkward position when it becomes necessary for him to hurl bullets or other missiles at his enemy pilot. He can move his craft ahead but in no other direction. If his missile touches his own swiftly revolving propeller, the fragile slice of wood breaks. Even a handkerchief or a pilot's cap striking the whirling propeller has broken it upon occasions, compelling the aeroplane thus losing its motive power to glide immediately down to the nearest available landing place.

Yet if the pilot veers alongside his opponent and fires a broadside across the intervening space at the enemy, he but wastes his ammunition. He must steer his own machine while he is firing. The vibration of his throbbing engine as well as the rush of wind past him renders aiming sideways out of the question. He must shoot straight ahead, and his gun must be a fixed part of the aeroplane and sheltered from the wind to enable him to aim with accuracy.

If he carries another man in his machine to act as gunner this extra weight so burdens his aeroplane that the enemy in a single-seater machine can fly circles around him. He must fly alone then, and must devise some method of firing ahead without breaking his propeller.

Crude devices gradually gave way to more practical inventions. The earliest offensive armament consisted of:

August 4, 1914. (1) Short Cavalry Carbine. This weapon was of no value to the pilot, as the vibration of his aeroplane made aiming difficult, the swiftness of the enemy plane presented a target elusive and momentary at best, while the force of the wind against the extended barrel rendered steadying the rifle practically impossible.

(2) Bag of Bricks. This primitive weapon was used in obedience to military orders in France at the beginning of the war in the hope that close proximity to a hostile aeroplane might enable a pilot to hurl a brickbat into the enemy's propeller, thus breaking it and dropping the hostile craft to the ground. Strange as it may seem, two German aeroplanes were actually brought down by this "weapon." Its limited range however quickly caused its retirement as an aeroplane arm.

(3) Automatic Pistol. To this day the pilot carries a light automatic for defence and offense at close quarters, though its value during a flight is practically nil.

January 1, 1915.—Machine Gun Mounted on Upper Plane. The French Nieuport was the first aeroplane constructed to carry a rapid-fire Lewis gun weighing twenty pounds on the upper wing, where it fired over the top of the propeller. It was aimed by pointing the aeroplane itself, and it was fired from a string in the pilot's hand. German airmen quickly followed suit. They mounted their Parabellum light gun in the same way.

But while this invention was a decided improvement over previous methods the difficulty of reloading the gun from the pilot's seat limited its usefulness. When he fired one magazine of forty-seven cartridges the pilot had to descend to the ground to reload his gun.

February 1, 1915.—Machine Gun Firing through the Propeller. Roland Garros devised for France the first method of firing the gun from the fixed mount on the engine hood, straight ahead through the revolving propeller. Midway along each blade of the propeller a band of hard steel protected the wood from the bullets, deflecting the seven per cent, which hit it, the balance passing through without striking. The aeroplane itself was sighted at the enemy, and the gun was exactly in line with the sights. But this device, though extremely interesting, proved a not unmixed advantage, for the steel bands on the blades lessened considerably the efficiency of the propeller and the speed of the aeroplane was correspondingly decreased.

July 1, 1915.—The Synchronized Machine Gun. The German Fokker aeroplane first appeared with gun fixed atop the engine hood, the trigger synchronized with the propeller shaft so that bullets could issue from the gun only when the blades of the propeller were out of the way. If the two-bladed propeller revolves 1400 times per minute, the muzzle of the gun finds a blade in front of it 2800 times each minute. But there are likewise 2800 empty spaces each minute. As the gun fires only 400 shots per minute, the device is so timed that one shot issues through each seventh space.

This ingenious contrivance remains in full vogue to the present time, affording as it does ample convenience of reloading and perfect ease of operation to the pilot. Often two guns are synchronized to shoot through opposite sides of the revolving propeller. A push button on the steering bar fires guns simultaneously, while the pilot keeps his eyes on the enemy target through the telescope sights lined up squarely in front of him.

With the capture of the first German aeroplane so armed the secret was out, and soon both sides were provided with this great improvement in arming, thus balancing the scales again until something still more deadly could be devised. It was two years in coming.

July 1, 1917.—One-Pounder Gun. The celebrated Georges Guynemer, then Captain of the famous Cigognes, the elite fighting *escadrille* of France, used the first 37-millimetre *canon* on a tractor single-seater aeroplane. Its appearance marks a new epoch in the annals of aeroplane fighting.

Convinced that the 37-millimetre shell could not be safely fired between the blades of the propeller, Guynemer sought to evade this difficulty by shooting through the hollow hub itself. Any V-shaped engine lends itself to this style of gun mounting. The gun is built into the very crank case of the engine, fitting snugly down in the lower crotch of the V; its breech and feeding mechanism are within easy reach of the pilot's hand, while the muzzle of the gun extends ahead through a hollow revolving shaft on the far end of which the propeller is attached. This hollow shaft is driven by the crank shaft of the engine to which it is connected by gears.

The barrel of the *canon* protrudes two inches beyond the edge of the hub, so that the sudden shock of explosion will not injure the delicately poised balance of the propeller shaft. Some three inches in diameter, this shaft barely permits room for the free slide backwards of the gun barrel after each recoil. The recoil amounts to some eight or ten inches, depending upon the muzzle velocity with which the projectile is discharged and the amount of recoil force that is absorbed by the recoil chamber. Any tendency to "whip" upon discharge is checked by a sliding brace at the rear of the barrel.

This recoil force is utilized to operate the devices which eject the empty shell case and the next instant feed into the chamber of the gun a fresh shell. As the fresh shell is some seven inches in length the recoil must carry back the breech of the gun at least far enough to the rear to permit the fresh shell to drop into its place.

With this powerful weapon Guynemer brought down his forty-ninth, fiftieth, fifty-first and fifty-second antagonist, and its superiority over the smaller .30-calibre machine gun was incontestably established. His type of *canon* was semi-automatic in operation, that is, the recoil of the gun ejected the empty case, but the pilot himself had to fit in the fresh shell. This operation required two or three seconds, and in two or three seconds the adjacent enemy aeroplane had opportunity either to get out of range or possibly to reverse positions and become the attacker.

Therefore the full automatic *canon*, though necessarily weighing at least 150 pounds as against the 100 pounds weight of Guynemer's type of *canon*, affords the already overburdened pilot such valuable advantages that it is essential to provide him with this superior type of operation, seeking at the same time to reduce by a like amount the weight of some other commodity that the machine must carry.

Several types of projectile can be fired from this *canon*, including the solid shot; the impact shell, so called because it bursts into some score of fragments upon impact with the target; the grapeshot shell, a charge similar to a load of buckshot which scatters from the muzzle of the gun precisely like a charge of shot in duck shooting; and the fireworks shell, a name which may include a number of devices for releasing inflammatory and expanding projectiles.

Increased effectiveness may naturally be expected as this more powerful weapon is developed. Already automatic *canon* are being built into aeroplanes, relieving the pilot from any further effort in firing than merely pressing a button when his aeroplane is pointed on the target. The gun does the rest: fires, ejects the empty case and refills the chamber with a new shell, fires again, and repeats this performance if desired until the ammunition is exhausted.

Thus 120 shells weighing a pound and a half each are discharged each minute, making a total of 180 pounds delivered at the target each minute from the 37-millimetre gun as compared with 400 bullets per minute from the ordinary machine gun weighing approximately twelve pounds, a distinct advantage in amount of missiles delivered aside from the vastly increased effectiveness of each projectile that strikes the target.

The increased weight of the automatic one-pounder gun limits by just so many pounds the supply of ammunition or of fuel that the aeroplane can carry and still keep up with the enemy craft. To overload the machine means that your enemy can overtake you while you cannot overtake him; your advantage in gun power is quite useless to you unless you do overtake him. So speed must be preserved at all costs. Heavier armament may be added then only to the point where it begins to limit speed. The proper combination of speed and destructiveness spells the superior fighting aeroplane. Either factor without the other spells defeat. Two essential factors then must be supplied—speed and destructiveness.

Since there is no longer any secret as to what gives speed to an aeroplane it may logically be expected that Germany will always produce machines as fast and as quick in manoeuvring as our own. If we are actually unable to gain a decisive superiority in this particular there still remains the less explored field of destructiveness which American inventiveness may be safely trusted to develop until we gain and retain the paramount position over our less ingenious enemy that our duty to our brave airmen impels.

Not only in the weight and power of the gun does greater destructiveness lie, but in the character and effect of the projectile itself will be found the greatest opportunity for advance and improvement. To this end an understanding of the vulnerable spots on an enemy aeroplane is essential. What is the enemy target? Briefly answered, it is the pilot's head!

While an aeroplane may be roughly estimated as a target some twenty feet across and almost as deep to the end of the tail, bullets may strike this craft anywhere without inflicting serious injuries. Nonresisting over most of this surface, projectiles of the solid sort puncture this fabric but do not bring down the craft.

Though the fuel tank may be repeatedly struck with bullets it is not always punctured nowadays, as several devices have been perfected to prevent the leakage of the gasoline or its ignition.

The engine may be hit in a vital organ, or the indispensable propeller may be shattered by a lucky shot, but the enemy pilot can still glide miles back into his own lines without any other power than the pull of gravity. An aeroplane thus wounded can glide back more than a mile for each thousand feet elevation. Once landed within his own territory the pilot jumps into another aeroplane and returns to the combat while his mechanics busy themselves with repairing the damage received.

So we must eliminate one by one all these points of attack and centre our bullets against the pilot's person itself. And here arises another difficulty.

The pilot sits atop his fuel tank deep within the protective shelter of his cockpit which is armoured amply on the sides and bottom against the ordinary .30-calibre bullet, only the top of his head appearing above the rim. Over his head the top wing spreads its concealing shadow. Below him the pursuing airman cannot accurately select the exact point in the floor through which to direct his stream of lead. Conscious of the position of his pursuer the enemy pilot manoeuvres his aeroplane so adroitly that no opportunity is offered for an open target. Under these circumstances a victory seems impossible. The pursuing machine circles about him but is easily thwarted by a parallel move of the enemy. Too bold a venture results in a reversal of position, and the attacker becomes the attacked.

In such a common dilemma the heavy projectile becomes of prime importance. One or two hits by a one-pounder shell can demolish the structure of the enemy craft, and it collapses and falls to the ground. A one-pounder charge of buckshot scatters through the fragile upper wing and finds the pilot's seat. A "fireworks" shell bursts in the enemy's tail and sets his craft aflame. Other types of shell that are being devised to fit this canon will be found still more destructive.

At what distance from the enemy aeroplane does an experienced air fighter open fire?

This question becomes of great importance to the designer of the aeroplane gun, for upon the range, that is the distance of fire, depends many vital points. If the projectile must carry on a level flight for a mile after it leaves the muzzle of the gun, then more powder must be packed behind the missile than when half that range is desired.

If more powder is packed in, the force of the explosion is greater, and a stronger, heavier gun must be built to withstand this shock. Also the recoil is greater, and heavier contrivances to absorb this recoil must be provided. These additions of course add many pounds weight to the load of the aeroplane. It is essential, as we have seen, to cut down this load to the lowest possible point so that an abundant supply of fuel and ammunition may be carried and still enable our machine to keep pace with the light enemy aeroplanes.

The writer in a recent visit to the front secured the opinion of a score or more of the French and British air fighters on this important question of range. It was an interesting discovery.

While various diverging opinions were collected, varying from fifty yards to three hundred yards, it was noticeable that the more experienced airmen saved their ammunition and waited for the most favourable opportunity of a bull's-eye, while novices at the game were not so daring as to await the precise instant for opening fire but preferred a comparatively long range.

Among the phenomenal citations of the French army may be noticed that congratulating the marvellous Guynemer for bringing down an aeroplane on one occasion with a single shot! And before the expiration of the next sixty seconds this incomparable pilot turned upon another plane and brought it crashing to the ground with two more shots!

"Père" Dorme, the "Unpuncturable" as he was called by other members of his *escadrille*, had brought down ten enemy machines before receiving more than two bullet holes through any part of his own plane. And the modest young René Fonck on April 3, 1918, was announced to have brought down thirty-two German aeroplanes without having permitted his enemies to place one single bullet hole in his well-manoeuvred fighting plane!

Thus it will be seen that the finished pilot coolly waits his opportunity for a victory at close range, handling his aeroplane in the meantime so adroitly that the enemy cannot bring his weapon to bear upon him.

Obviously it is more difficult to hit a target at two hundred yards range than at fifty yards. Pilots opening fire at this long range naturally waste much of their ammunition. But even accepting two hundred yards as a minimum range we have no demands made upon the muzzle velocity of the projectile that cannot be supplied within the weight of the automatic canon above designated—150 pounds.

This problem of muzzle velocity is bound up with the speed of the aeroplane as well as with the proper range for firing. An interesting table of speeds has been compiled by a British writer (O'Gorman) which is appended here for comparison.

Table of Comparative Speeds

Man walking	4 miles per hour
Man racing	20 " "
Horse racing	30 " "
Bicycle racing	32 " "
Steamship	42 " "
Motor boat	62 " "
Railroad train	90 " "
Automobile	120 " "
Aeroplane	150 " "
Pistol bullet	600 feet per second
Machine-gun bullet	1000 " "
Sound	1100 " "
37-millimetre gun	1600 " "
Largest gun	3000 " "
Light	186,300 miles per second

The 37-millimetre gun, credited in this table with a muzzle velocity of 1600 feet per second, refers, of course, to the field gun where a range of a mile is requisite. For the aeroplane gun no such length range is desirable. If we cut down the muzzle velocity one half, to 800 feet per second, we will get a flat trajectory of approximately 500 yards, which as we have seen is more than will be required even for emergencies in a fighting aeroplane.

Now an extreme aeroplane speed of 150 miles an hour means that the machine is moving 220 feet through the air each second! If fired upon when fifty yards away by a projectile having a velocity of 800 feet per second, it requires only three sixteenths of a second for the projectile to reach its target. During that three sixteenths of a second the target has moved onwards forty-one feet. Now if we increase our muzzle velocity to one thousand feet per second, we necessarily incur an increased recoil force, besides adding some thirty pounds weight to the gun's equipment—two serious disadvantages. And the sole benefit received is a saving of three eightieths of a second of time in the projectile's flight—far from a commensurate advantage when both results are analyzed.

Other methods of arming aeroplanes we will not consider here. The rear pivotal gun to defend against pursuing aeroplanes; the flight formation of a squadron of planes which enables several pilots to aid in repelling attacks on their comrades; the construction of the fighting aeroplane so as to leave the minimum of "blind spots" for enemy attack—are all topics which deserve individual study.

Thus Roland Garros, the "King of the Air", through his first invention of mounting the fixed machine gun on the engine hood of an aeroplane, acquired another title, "The Father of Air Duelling."

After four years of war in the air, through which several thousand conquerors of the air have met their deaths by means of this invention, it still remains in full vogue among all the fighting nations of the earth. Some valuable improvements and additions have been added to its design, but in principle the first synchronized aeroplane gun of Roland Garros remains the same. To his device will Germany owe her banishment from the skies of France.

CHAPTER 4

The Cigognes

A finished pilot or an infallible sharpshooter is not so infrequently met in these exacting days of war; yet a combination of the two interesting accomplishments in one slim lad of twenty or thereabouts is odd enough to win him more than casual attention.

Add to these qualifications characteristics of courage, of energy, of judgment and intuition, all developed to an unusual degree, and the human product becomes so remarkable that he may be confidently expected to tower high above his fellow mortals in this contest between flying matadors.

Among all the groups of comrades who are fighting shoulder to shoulder for life and country in this stupendous world conflict now raging, there is one organization in France which stands conspicuously ahead of the others in individual brilliancy as well as in squadron efficiency. This group is that French *escadrille* popularly known as the Cigognes, by reason of the flying stork painted as their *escadrille* emblem on the sides of their aeroplanes.

Officially it is known as the N. 3 (Nieuport 3), but from its recent substitution of Spad aeroplanes in place of the Nieuports of 1917, it will in the future be designated as the Spad 3.

So extraordinary has been the success of this group of French pilots, so brilliant have their personal exploits proved, it is no wonder their names are household words in France, and their methods of attack have established the air-fighting tactics of the

French Air Service.

It is perhaps needless to observe that victory or defeat of the air campaign hangs upon these *avions de combat* or fighting planes. Bomb-dropping aeroplanes, observing and photographing aeroplanes cannot venture forth when opposed by faster enemy fighting planes. The sole means of clearing the air of these enemy fighting planes is by superior and preponderating fighting planes of our own.

Thus the intense popularity of this most spectacular arm of aviation is well founded; upon its encouragement and success depends the very existence of our air force as an implement of warfare.

It is for this reason, primarily, that a recital of the air exploits of the famous Cigognes is of importance. Aside from the interest we feel in these thrilling adventures, their perusal affords us a definite clue to the human characteristics essential to a continued success against an unscrupulous and intelligent enemy.

Painstaking preparation and excessive caution will be found ever present in the daily fights of these heroic knights of the air—most conspicuously present in the survivors of them.

One moment's relaxation spells oblivion to the pilot and an irreparable loss to his comrades and country.

The *escadrille* of the Cigognes was formed on April 1, 1915, with ten fighting pilots. To date this wonderful corps has brought down over three hundred German aeroplanes. Its membership includes the greatest air fighters in France, and enrolment under the insignia of the Flying Stork is the highest honour that can be conferred upon those ambitious airmen who constitute the finest of the fighting men of France.

Since its birth the glorious Cigognes have lost twenty-two fighting pilots, killed in combat or missing, and twenty-three have been wounded more or less seriously. Their captains have been Commander Brocard, the founder, wounded and retired to Aviation Section of the War Office in Paris, Captain Auger, killed July 28, 1917, Captain Heurteaux, wounded September 3, 1917, and Captain Guynemer, killed September 11, 1917.

Lieutenant Raymond, one of the only two surviving pilots of the original membership of this famous N. 3, is now in command of the *escadrille* during the convalescence of Captain Heurteaux.

In April, 1915, Captain Brocard, commander of the brilliant N. 3, then a reconnaissance *escadrille*, was commissioned to transform his squadron into a fighting unit. Brocard, twenty-nine years of age, had learned to fly long before the war broke upon France. His *escadrille* had taken a conspicuous part in scouting and bomb-dropping expeditions up to this tune, and Brocard had distinguished himself as a pilot of rare courage and reliability. His heroic example and his extraordinary ability as a leader had established throughout the War Zone of Europe the fame of his brilliant Cigognes. The bluest of the young blood of France was now in the Air Service. Their highest ambition was membership in the famous N. 3. Thus it was that Captain Brocard was able to select the *élite* of the *élite* in organizing anew his beloved *escadrille*.

The success of his Cigognes has been wonderful, and the result of Brocard's inspiration has amply justified the concentration of so many exceptional sharpshooters of the air in one fighting unit.

Out of the five hundred sixty-seven German aeroplanes shot down before January, 1918, by all the Aces of the two hundred odd French *escadrilles* now in service, this single corps was credited with over two hundred of this total!

Captain Heurteaux succeeded to the command of the Cigognes in December, 1916. Before he entered aviation, Heurteaux had served from the first days of mobilization as a lieutenant in the French cavalry. Twice in one month he received citations for bravery and heroic conduct in this arm of the service.

At the beginning of 1915, Heurteaux was breveted a pilot and was attached to the celebrated Escadrille N. 23 with Roland Garros, Eugene Gilbert, Marc Pourpe, Pinsard, and others. Here he served brilliantly, and as observer and *bombardier* took part in many expeditions against German factory cities in the interior. Upon its organization as a fighting squadron, he became a pilot in N. 3. Modest, trustworthy, and simple, his extreme conscientiousness soon made him a leader, and his repeated successes marked the young officer as exceptional even among his audacious comrades and superior officers of the Cigognes. It was his habit to spend several hours in his hangar before day light every morning personally examining and testing his guns and ammunition as well as his machine and armament before starting aloft.

At this time Heurteaux had already achieved the unique feat of bringing down an enemy aeroplane with one solitary bullet! Subsequently Guynemer duplicated this extraordinary sharpshooting and splendidly surpassed it by bringing down another enemy a minute later with two more shots! Truly a royal pair of air fighters for one small squadron!

Heurteaux amused himself in the midst of a battle by politely bowing and waving ironic greeting to his encircling enemies. This open contempt for them increased their hatred, he explained, and. tempted them to shake their fists at him in reply, thus often exposing them in their blind fury to his superior adroitness in manoeuvring and attack. His combats have usually been victorious, although he has been three times wounded. His disdain for danger and his positive confidence in his aeroplane and armament were powerful factors in his continuous successes.

Between Heurteaux and another Ace of the Cigognes, "Père" Dorme, an exciting rivalry existed in Escadrille N. 3 as the weeks passed and their "scores" increased side by side. Heurteaux had a safe lead, when in one week Dorme shot down eight of the enemy and jumped ahead of his rival. This lead he held to the day of his disappearance, May 25, 1917.

Each night upon returning to headquarters, these valiant heroes nonchalantly watched their new victories chalked up, and as tranquilly received a few days later the official recognition and thanks of their Government for their deeds of prowess. Each well deserved citation entitles the pilot so honoured to sew another palm on his ribbon, from which is suspended the *Croix de Guerre*.

Heurteaux hotly pursued five enemy planes on the morning of May 5, 1917. He succeeded in overtaking them and dived in upon one, which he cut away from the group. Suddenly he discovered he had been led into an ambush. From behind a cloud above him, two waiting Boches descended, firing as they approached. Captain Heurteaux received one ball in the arm and one in the leg. His machine dropped like a stone for five or six thousand feet until the enemies, believing he would crash to the ground, relaxed their pursuit for an instant.

Seizing the expected opportunity, the heroic Heurteaux rallied superbly from his suffering and quickly straightened out his whirling machine despite his crippled muscles. With wonderful pluck, the wounded pilot successfully eluded his pursuers for the entire thirty miles' flight back to his aerodrome.

Within two months after his injury, Heurteaux had left the hospital and was back in his beloved *escadrille*. On July 9th he was the recipient of the Medal of the Legion of Honour. In less than twelve months of fighting, this painstaking Heurteaux has brought down officially twenty-one enemy planes besides a large number not verified.

On September 3, 1917, Heurteaux went aloft to try a new gun. At twenty thousand feet he encountered an enemy biplane and swept in to the attack. His bullets unaccountably missed, due, as he believed, to faulty adjustment of the sights. Again and again he fired, until finally his gun jammed and could not be further operated.

He descended in a spin to avoid pursuit, but even as he was whirling he felt a succession of shocks and found he had been shot by his foe through the thigh. Suffering intense pain and almost fainting with loss of blood, Captain Heurteaux succeeded in landing within the English lines, from which he was tenderly removed to their hospital.

Upon this unfortunate absence, the command of the Cigognes fell to that prince of French Aces—Georges Guynemer. His term, alas! expired with his death only eight short days later. Before describing the marvellous career of Guynemer, it may be well, to look first into the achievements of some less famous but equally extraordinary comrades of his in this celebrated escadrille.

Lieutenant Peretti learned to fly in Pau long before the war. In January, 1912, he began his flying practice and on the day he was shot dead over Deauvillers (only to come down mechanically and unconsciously on to his own field with an almost faultless landing), he was credited with the record total of almost eight hundred hours flying for France, two hundred seventy-three hours of which were spent over the German lines.

Every machine that leaves the hangars is timed in its flight by the waiting mechanics, who are responsible for the life of the engine. Incidentally this span of life of the aeroplane engine does not exceed one hundred hours at the Front. Then it is "scrapped."

Peretti was sent to Morocco in October, 1912, where he passed his first two years in war aviation. Returning to France when Germany declared war, Peretti was one of the few veteran aviators in the world. He was naturally looked upon as a leader in aviation circles, and his services in the Cigognes as bombarder, observer, and fighter were conspicuously successful and distinguished, bringing him many citations and decorations.

On April 28, 1916, after a combat with an enemy Fokker far aloft, Peretti was seen to return to his aerodrome. No one believed he was hurt. His light Nieuport circled down toward the field with its customary cleverness, and as his mechanics ran forward to meet him, they saw the aeroplane suddenly turn on its wing and crash. Upon lifting the fallen hero from the ruins, it was discovered he had been mortally hit by several bullets.

Two of his comrades immediately went aloft in their machines, seeking vengeance on his slayer. Soon they perceived the enemy Fokker still free-lancing high in the heavens west of Verdun, With inflexible purpose they launched themselves in his pursuit—overtook him—and within the hour of their dear comrade's death, dropped his conqueror crashing to earth in No Man's Land.

Captain Albert Auger was given command of the Cigognes upon the retirement of Captain Heurteaux, when he was wounded May 5, 1917. Born in 1889, the son of a famous General of France, Auger had an ardent love for flying and above all, for military aviation. Poet and artist, sportsman and soldier, this gallant youth had obtained several citations for exemplary conduct in the 31st Infantry before entering the Air Service.

Of remarkable audacity and coolness, Captain Auger became noted for his repeated narrow escapes in his desperate attacks upon enemy aeroplane formations of overwhelming numbers. Time and again he received citations for victories against terrific odds. Generous, lovable, and entirely devoid of self-appreciation, he was grievously mourned by his command, when on July 28, 1917, he was finally overcome in combat by four enemy aeroplanes. He had brought down seven Germans and had received ten *palms* with his Legion of Honour and *Croix de Guerre*, when, shortly before his death, Captain Auger wrote his mother that he feared the unusual strain under which he had been living had so injured his health that he "could not hold on to the end." Over his grave his old commander spoke these words:

> The sorrowing Cigognes, who have so often flown by your side, have come to bid you *adieu*! Already fifteen of us have preceded you to the tomb, and they await you there on High, more numerous than we who remain. Tell them we will not fail in our duty; that in the heavens, where now you dwell, we will continue to faithfully guard our sacred trust; tell them to bless our flights and to prepare us a place among them when our turn will come!

Noble, glorious sons of France! Is it possible the savage Huns can extinguish this devoted spirit from the earth?

One of the most romantic careers of all these gallant Cigognes is that of Lieutenant Armand Pinsard. Twenty-seven years of age when war was declared, Pinsard had already served nine years in the Army, the last two of which were in the Air Service.

Today he ranks third in the Cigognes and seventh among all living French Aces, with his score of twenty German aircraft shot down. On June 12, 1917, he was seriously injured in rising from his flying field, and but recently returned to his command.

It is hoped that the coming season will find him healed of his hurts and again at his irresistible stride. He is now commissioned captain.

Modest René Dorme was a pilot of only twenty-three years of age. Dorme possessed all the medals that France could bestow, but these he carried in his pocket and rarely exhibited.

He was a dead shot with machine gun, and above all the Aces of his remarkable corps, he was the most accomplished and polished pilot. Even Guynemer himself proclaimed Dorme the greatest of them all. Dorme's tactics it was, which originated the useful "wing slip" as a favourite escape from sudden attack.

His name, "Père Dorme", was painted on the side of his fuselage. The nickname "Père" was given him for his sober and thoughtful manner towards his fellows. He was about to begin an attack on an enemy plane, July 30, 1916, when in diving at his foe he unconsciously crashed headlong into another enemy aeroplane which had suddenly swerved in under him. Happily, his plane was staunch and was not broken by the shock, while the German fell in pieces to the ground.

Dorme's machine held together, and although he himself was knocked unconscious in the aerial collision, he recovered his senses in tune to bring his aeroplane safely into French lines.

Dorme arrived July 6, 1916, at the front as a pilot.

Since the beginning of the war he had been in the 7th Artillery. Before the end of the month he had brought down two enemy machines. During August he shot down six more aeroplanes officially, but in reality he had eight actual victories, besides three additional victims whom he had seriously injured.

The following month, after six days' leave in Paris, he returned and piled up nine more successes, of which four were official—that is, four were witnessed by at least three French officers who reported them to head-quarters.

In October he won six more victories, of which three were official, making a total in four months of twenty-six enemies actually overcome, of which fifteen were certified successes.

In a furious air battle one early morning in midsummer, Dorme brought down a German triplane, which; as he puts it, looked like a flying fortress alongside his baby Nieuport. The enemy machine carried two gunners besides the pilot, and all three guns at times were pouring separate streams of lead into his tiny aeroplane.

For ten minutes or more, Dorme tenaciously clung to the Goliath, diving at the monster through the hail of bullets and firing into him again and again. Finally the huge enemy broke and sank behind the French lines. Over and over he rolled as he fell, Dorme circling above him until the final crash.

Under the piled-up *débris* in the woods at the edge of Fromezey, the awe-struck *poilus* quickly found the three Germans and their three guns. Each of the enemy airmen had been shot dead before the machine fell.

Upon landing, Dorme discovered his own aeroplane wings were splashed and dyed with the blood of his enemies—so close a hand-to-hand combat had been fought. He himself had not been scratched, but his aeroplane on this occasion was made a sieve.

Lieutenant René Dorme left his aerodrome at six-thirty on the morning of May 25, 1917, accompanied by another Ace of the Cigognes, Lieutenant Deullin. Both were in Spad machines. They soon were attracted by white smoke-bursts in the air, denoting enemy aircraft pursued by French anti-aircraft shells.

Getting swiftly through some cloud banks, the two knights flew unobserved to a point above the hostile aeroplanes, then they dropped upon them from above. Guns below ceased firing. A running combat ensued, and the two comrades were separated, Dorme pursuing the Germans over their own lines.

Deullin brought down his man and, the other enemies having disappeared, he dropped down to his flying field to learn how Dorme had fared. Dorme had not been seen. All day they waited, but no news came. To this day René Donne's fate is unknown.

Dorme's loss was mourned by France with extravagant sorrow, second only to that occasioned three or four months later by the crushing loss of Guynemer, their idol.

The air tactics of these two remarkable pilots were strangely different. While both were lads of excessive modesty, Guynemer's tactics were far more spectacular than those of Dorme. Guynemer was perhaps the better marksman of the two, but Dorme, he conceded, was the more finished pilot. Guynemer's machine returned riddled with bullet holes, while Donne rarely permitted his to be struck. His dodging manoeuvres were celebrated throughout France.

Guynemer brought down fifty-three enemies in seventeen months; Dorme officially accounted for twenty-four in nine months, while in reality he had shot down as many more which fell too deep within German territory to be recognized by his own officers. When his superior officer once told him regretfully that he could recognize only eight victories out of the eleven claimed by Dorme in one week, the hero replied:

"The enemy know it is eleven, and I am content."

Always sent where trouble was thickest, always found facing the most dangerous fliers of the enemy, always a step or two in advance of the styles in war aviation, this incomparable squadron of Flying Storks will go down in history as the most celebrated band of comrades that ever died for France. Rivalling in romance and in affectionate comradeship *D'Artagnan and the Three Musketeers*, Guynemer and his Aces who led this band at the zenith of its fame set a new notch on the heights of human achievement for the youth of the world to attain.

Now over Verdun, now along the Somme, now hastily summoned to meet the threatened attack on Paris, no period of idleness ever cooled the ardour of the Storks' enthusiasm.

On August 7, 1916, four Aces of the Cigognes, Guynemer,

Pinsard, Heurteaux, and Deullin, devised and inaugurated a new function for the already overworked aeroplanes of war. Leaving their aerodrome at break of day, with two machine guns each, and with an abundance of cartridges in the belt-feed ammunition boxes, the four daring pilots descended low over the bivouac of the German infantry behind the third line of trenches.

Flying at scarcely one hundred feet above ground, the four scouts suddenly appeared over the startled Teuton regiments as they were massing and preparing for duty in the trenches.

Swooping back and forth over the German formation, the four Cigognes poured into the frightened troops a steady hail of bullets. German machine guns and artillery were brought to bear upon the aeroplane warriors but immediately directing their attention to these defences, the Cigognes quickly scattered the gunners and completed their rout.

The Fritzes fled in terror to their dugouts, and the four aeroplanes finally were forced to give up the attack for lack of a suitable target. Continuing their flight, they swept down a road filled with advancing automobile lorries, and these vehicles they riddled with bullets.

Discovering then a distant train of coaches loaded with troops, they dashed over to meet it, and flying so low on either side of the cars, that at times they could *see each other's machines through the windows of the coaches*, they raked the entire length of the train, killed both engineers in the locomotive, and expended their last cartridges through the windows on to the seats under which the German troops had hidden for shelter.

Their ammunition exhausted, the four Cigognes flew homeward together and landed safely without one having received even a scratch! No wonder the sign of the Stork brought terror into the Teutonic breast!

The individual scores of the Cigognes at this writing are as follows:

Lieutenant René Fonck	59
Captain Guynemer (missing Sept. 11, 1917)	53
Lieutenant René Dorme (missing May 25th, 1917)	23

Captain Alfred Heurteaux (wounded Sept. 3, 1917)   21
Lieutenant Deullin   20
Captain Armand Pinsard (wounded. accident June 12, 1917)   20
Lieutenant Jean Chaput (killed in combat May 18, 1918)   16
Lieutenant Frank Baylies   12
Lieutenant Tarascon (wooden leg)   11
Lieutenant Mathieu de la Tour (killed in comb. Dec. 12, 1917)   11
Captain Albert Auger (killed in combat July 28, 1917)   7
Lieutenant Gond   6
Lieutenant Borzecky   5
Adjutant Herrison   5
Adjutant Sanglier (missing May 10, 1917)   4
Captain Brocard (retired December 1, 1916)   3

Six of these consummate heroes will, unhappily, never serve their country more. But their memories will be revered and glorified by the people of France as long as that nation endures.

CHAPTER 5

Georges Guynemer the Miraculous

France, the land of poetry and legend, the shrine of Roland and Jeanne d'Arc, whose sorrowful soil has for four years borne the devastating imprint of an invader's heel, has taken time to pause in her heroic struggle to worship and adore the superhuman prowess of this one of her sons, this fragile boy of twenty-two, whose daily combats against the enemy became as familiar to the very children of France of the twentieth century as were those of Roland to the people of an earlier day.

Eight times shot down from on high! And seven times miraculously saved from a certain death!

He stopped an enemy's bullet with his fingers on one occasion, and it was during the same combat that two or three other bullets passed through the framework of his aeroplane on a straight course towards his heart, only to be deflected at the last instant by a trifling obstacle!

On the very morning of his decoration as an officer of the Legion of Honour by General d'Esperey he went aloft on a cruise for enemy aeroplanes and had two encounters; upon his return, and after the conclusion of the ceremony, the general desired Guynemer to show him his fighting aeroplane. Straight across the floor of the fuselage upon which the pilot's feet must rest while they touch the rudder bar, a line of bullet holes was traced—received in one of the combats of the morning.

"How was it that your feet were not struck?" inquired General d'Esperey, pointing to the row of bullet holes.

"I had just moved them, my General," replied Guynemer simply.

Returning almost daily from his chases with his aeroplane and often his clothing riddled with bullets; hurling himself with absolute abandon against three, ten, fifteen, or twenty enemy machines in formation, among which he usually succeeded in bringing down one or more; exulting in the number of wounds which his faithful planes brought home as if to bear witness to his charmed life, and encircling them with red paint to make them more conspicuous; on two occasions shooting down an enemy machine with one single bullet; on May 25, 1917, bringing down four enemy aeroplanes in one single day—at that time the record—all these extraordinary exploits coupled with the very extraordinary energy of this slim boy soon placed him upon a pedestal which raised him high above his comrades; and by reason of his many miraculous escapes from certain death, eventually surrounded him with a halo of fame unknown to the French populace since the day of Jeanne d'Arc.

Conqueror in fifty-three aerial combats wherein the result was officially established by the verification of three or more eye-witnesses, Guynemer brought down as many more German aeroplanes quite as effectively if less officially. His comrades in the *escadrille* knew this and respected their chief accordingly.

Possessed of every decoration that a grateful nation could officially bestow upon him, conscious of a position in the public esteem that, tinctured as it was with the legendary, illumined him with more glory and worship than was accorded even to a Joffre or a Foch, Georges Guynemer fulfilled the expectations of his fellow countrymen, when on September 11, 1917, he disappeared from the eyes of the world while in the full exercise of his duty. The heavens swallowed him up, and to this day no reliable clue to his disappearance has been discovered. Small wonder then that the people of France in contemplation of this last exploit of their adored hero place his memory with one acclaim alongside the niche so long occupied by that last youthful miracle of France, Jeanne d'Arc!

Guynemer's parents were well to do. His boyhood was spent at the family home in Compiègne and later at Stanislas College. Two older sisters, his father, and his mother guarded him carefully against sorrows and ills, fearful of his feeble health which upon several occasions interrupted his course of studies and sent him home for rest and convalescence.

Before war had threatened France this young schoolboy, enamoured with the thought of flying, had cultivated the friendship of aviators and had actually made several flights with them. His desire to enter aviation knew no bounds. He haunted the flying fields whenever he found himself in their vicinity. He studied their motors and parts. He imagined and gave utterance to improvements which amused his expert friends exceedingly. Later on not an aeroplane constructor in France but gladly listened to the suggestions of this boy.

First attempting to enter the infantry and being twice rejected because of his slight figure and extreme youth, Georges one November day met an army aeroplane pilot and suddenly learned of the new importance of aeroplanes in war. He set off again for the recruiting office and pleaded once more for admission into service, this time in the aviation branch. Again he was refused.

Arming himself with such recommendations as seemed most important to his success, he returned a few days later and applied for a position as mechanic, as labourer, as office boy—any work would be suitable so long as he might be near his beloved aeroplanes. His passion and perseverance conquered all objections, and he was accepted as a labourer and put to work in the aerodrome at Pau.

Once admitted to the sacred precincts, the rest was easy. The boy did his required work and found time to learn all that the mechanics knew. Then he pestered the pilots until they took him up for flights. Quickly he mastered the machines himself, and in February of 1915 he earned his pilot's certificate.

The same intense desire led Guynemer through the humdrum activities of reconnaissance and bombardment aeroplane

Captain Georges Guynemer with his father
The idol of France, conqueror in 53 aerial combats
brought down by the enemy September 11, 1917

duties to the more daring and more individual excitement of the chase. Before he graduated into the fighting pilot's class he had already brought down his first enemy aeroplane from his two-seater bombing machine on July 19, 1915. He had met his baptism of shell fire over enemy lines with a coolness that marked him even then among his fellows. He had undertaken several special missions which included the landing in enemy's lines with a spy, returning a day or two later in his machine to bring him back, and had received several citations for his energy, coolness, and fearlessness.

The *escadrille* in which Guynemer made his debut was the Cigognes. It already contained, besides Captain Brocard, Vedrines, Deullin, Dorme, Heurteaux, Auger, Raymond, De la Tour, a galaxy of stars that with Guynemer's aid made the Cigognes the greatest fighting squadron in France. And among these carefully selected champions this boy, Guynemer, was to become the chief!

The famous Nieuport fighting machine made its appearance shortly after Guynemer scored his first victory, and the Cigognes were the first to be equipped with this fast single-seater. Armed with a machine gun firing straight ahead through the revolving propeller, the pilot must be not only a good shot and a master in the art of attack, but he must at the same time keep himself out of the range of fire of the enemy while at close quarters. Thus adroitness in manoeuvring and accuracy of aim become the two prime requisites for the fighting pilot.

With characteristic fervour Georges Guynemer, the corporal, set about mastering these requirements. Finding himself frequently embarrassed while in the midst of combats by the jamming of his machine gun, Guynemer studied the mechanism of the gun until he devised methods of correcting these defects. Patience, perseverance, and tireless labour conquered for Guynemer every problem that confronted a pilot. These very labours, which were easy for him since they were part of the passion for flying which captivated him, go far to explain the extraordinary successes which attended his duels in air for the two years following.

Before every flight Guynemer spent an hour over his aeroplane and gun, examining every wire, screw, and turnbuckle, oiling his gun, greasing each separate cartridge, leaving no detail to the exclusive care of his faithful mechanics. His motor, his propeller, his controls he knew so intimately that he could demand from them the last ounce of their strength without overstraining them; thus secured in the perfection of his implements he went aloft to use the same painstaking thought in the details of the combat that ensued. Thus we reduce the miraculous element in Guynemer's career to those frequent occasions when his impetuosity in combat carried him full into the enemy's fire regardless of consequences, and to those several escapes from an expected death when his machine was shot down completely out of control. Seven times this miracle happened, and he landed without a scratch. The eighth—no one can say how the miracle operated on that occasion, the eleventh day of September, 1917, for no one has been found who witnessed it.

In September, 1916, occurred one of his most miraculous escapes. Guynemer, while in combat with seven enemies far within the German lines, received a shot in the radiator of his engine. Suddenly his motor stopped. He was some twelve thousand feet in the air and more than fifteen miles distant from his lines. He pointed his aeroplane towards home on as level a slant as safety permitted, and turned his attention again to his pursuers. Fortunately they were unaware of his predicament, and with wholesome respect for the French "Ace of Aces" they immediately welcomed this unexpected opportunity to save their own skins, and hastily dived to their aerodrome.

Guynemer, in his crippled aeroplane, necessarily descended lower and lower as he approached the trenches. His engine was dead, and he glided only by the pull of gravity diagonally towards his lines.

The German anti-aircraft gunners, discovering the identity of the famous Cigogne, literally filled his path with bursting shrapnel. His machine was repeatedly struck by pieces of shell, and the fabric was torn into fluttering bits.

Barely maintaining headway, it was a question of life or death as to the machine's ability to reach the French lines. Guynemer had frequently said he would never surrender to a German, vowing that as long as he had a cartridge remaining he would direct it against his foes, whether in the air or from the wreck of his machine in their lines.

As Guynemer crossed the German trenches, he was scarcely fifty feet above the heads of the eager Huns, who were standing up in their trenches, firing desperately up at the crippled and tattered Cigogne. A hundred yards beyond, Guynemer saw the French *poilus* hanging recklessly over their trenches to watch his uncontrolled descent through this furious hailstorm of bullets. He realized he could never reach his goal!

Suddenly the *poilus*, blindly determined to rescue their hero, leaped over their embankments and charged headlong upon the Boches. Guynemer's aeroplane dropped heavily into a shell hole in No Man's Land, forty yards from his lines. The Nieuport smashed into bits, but by a veritable miracle the pilot was thrown free from the wreck and escaped absolutely unhurt. Guynemer was instantly surrounded by the devoted *poilus*, picked up, and borne hastily away in their protecting midst to the shelter of the trenches, whence he was rapidly carried to the rear.

Upon rejoining his squadron, the audacious Guynemer remarked coolly, "I was born on Christmas eve. They can't hurt me!"

Nineteen of his enemies were brought down by Guynemer on one Spad machine. "Old Charley" was the nickname he gave this faithful thunderbolt, and "*Vieux Charles*" painted in square black letters along the white fabric of his aeroplane informed the scores of his victims of. their doom before they fell.

Fighting six, eight or ten combats a day, returning to his aerodrome with his machine a sieve, his propeller mowed off with bullets, a dozen shrapnel holes received from anti-aircraft guns through his wings, Guynemer on his small fighting plane piled up victory after victory during the Battle of Verdun. Regardless of his comrades' counsel for caution and prudence, Guynemer would fly in weather so stormy that there was no possibility of finding the Boches in air. His passion for combat fairly devoured him.

One morning in July he attacked an L.V.G. of the enemy as was his custom, full in the face. As he approached a bullet from his enemy struck between his thumb and forefinger of his right hand, as it lay encircling the trigger of his gun. The bullet had traversed his engine, the oil reservoir, the gasoline tank, the cartridge box, and his glove, *and came to rest between his fingers!*

The pain of the impact made him lose his aim, and he came home to find another bullet in the edge of his seat; one had penetrated the revolution counter in a direct line for his heart but stopped after bulging out the brass towards him, another had flattened itself against the projection of his Vickers gun, directly opposite his chest, and others had riddled the rudder, the propeller, and his garments.

Forced to land a scant hundred yards behind the trenches he "got for dessert", as he put it, some hundred shells from 3-inch, 4-inch and 5-inch guns, which demolished his machine into splinters.

In September, on the Somme, after shooting down two enemy machines during the forenoon of Saturday, the twenty-third, he was in pursuit of a third when a shell from his own batteries caught him in full flight when he was at 10,000 feet altitude, breaking his left wing and tearing away part of his radiator. With half his air support missing, his mangled aeroplane started down like an onion peel. Guynemer calmly steadied the disabled machine as best he could with his controls and the weight of his body, finally bringing her into a glide but was unable to lessen her speed.

The troops below watched the catastrophe, knowing full well whose crash they were witnessing. Utterly unable to reduce his speed or to prolong his course for a single foot, Guynemer landed less than a hundred yards from the battery which had unwittingly fired the very shell which had struck him. His Spad hit the ground headfirst and buried its nose so deep that it could not be budged. The soldiers ran to get his remains. Upon arriving, they found Guynemer standing by the side of his wrecked machine, regarding it with so deep an interest that he did not observe their coming.

The men picked him up and carried him away on their shoulders despite his protests. They deposited him before the quarters of their general, half a mile away. Embracing him while he ordered his men to prepare for review, the general then led him before their motionless ranks, while from the neighbouring crowded dugouts came boisterous cheers which soon merged into a swelling chorus of the Marseillaise.

On January 25, 1917, was enacted one of the crowning dramas of war aviation, with Guynemer again playing the leading role. Again the miraculous power of this youthful warrior was hailed throughout France for he had *brought down and captured without arms of his own, a two-seater machine of the enemy's.* While recognizing in this very extraordinary feat some of the fabulous strength of will for which the gentle Jeanne d'Arc was so famed, the details of this exploit give us but another view of the determination and passion of Guynemer, a view which helps to explain the secret of his wonderful success.

He had up to this time scored twenty-nine official successes. The Cigognes were still flying over the cities of the Somme valley, and their *escadrille* had accounted for a total of almost two hundred of the Boche machines in single combat. Guynemer had been unusually active, but the bad winter weather had somewhat lessened the sport of which he was so fond, and he had taken this opportunity to send his Spad to Paris to have certain improvements added at the factory.

The previous day he had lain idle at camp. The morning of the twenty-sixth, he borrowed a machine from one of his men and went aloft after game. His distaste for the mediocre fittings of the borrowed aeroplane in comparison with the perfection of his own was so vexing that he could not suppress an allusion to it in an entry in his diary the next day—the same entry which describes his capture of an enemy aeroplane by sheer will power:

> The 25th I watched the others fly and itched. The 26th Bucquet lends me his taxi. Gun sights a deplorable emptiness. What a layout! Line of aim worse than pitiful.
>
> 12 o'clock saw a Boche at 12,000 feet. Up went the lift. Arrived in the sun. In tacking about was caught in nasty tail spin. Descending, I see the Boche 400 yards behind, firing at me. Recovering I let go ten shots. Gun jams. Completely jammed. Finished. But the Boche seemed to feel some emotion and dived away full south with his motor wide open. Let's follow him!
>
> I do not get too close to him, for fear he will see that my gun is played out. Altimeter drops to 5000 feet above Estries-Saint-Denis. I manoeuvre my Boche as nicely as I can, and suddenly he redresses and sets off towards Ressons and lays it off stiff.
>
> I try a bluff. I mount to 2000 feet over him and drop on to him like a stone. Made an impression on him but was beginning to believe it did not take when he suddenly began to descend. I put myself 10 yards behind him; but every time I showed my nose around the edge of his tail the gunner took aim at it. We take the road towards Compiègne—3000 feet—2000 feet again I show my nose, and this time the gunner takes his hands from his machine gun and motions to me that he surrenders. *All Right!*
>
> I see underneath his machine the four bombs in their resting place. 1500 feet. The Boche slows down his windmill. 600 feet. 300 feet. I swerve over him while he lands. I make a round or two at 300 feet while the men come up from the aerodrome to get him. But not having any gun or cartridges I cannot prevent them from setting fire to their taxi, a 200 H. P. Albatross, magnificent.
>
> When I see they are surrounded I come down and show the two Boches my disabled machine gun. Some headpiece!

They had fired 200 shots at me. My ten bullets that I fired before I jammed had struck their altimeter and the revolution counter, hence their emotion! The pilot told me that my aeroplane I shot down day before yesterday at Goyancourt had gunner killed and pilot wounded in the knee. Hope this unique confirmation will be accepted by authorities. It will make my 30th.

Other instances of aeroplanes surrendering in air have been known, but never, I believe, has any other conqueror with useless gun so imposed his determined will upon an armed enemy that, like the famous coon of Davy Crockett, it begged to come down and give itself up. Who can deny to Guynemer the place that will be accorded him in history and legend for his unparalleled victory of January 26, 1917?

Guynemer's frequently expressed ambition was to get his fiftieth Boche aeroplane. On May 25th the record-breaking bag of four aeroplanes in one day brought him the following citation, together with the Legion of Honour Rosette:

> Office of the *élite*. Fighting pilot as skilful as he is audacious. Has rendered striking services to his country not only by the number of his victories but by the daily example of his sustained ardour. In his never-failing mastery of his conflicts, he, unmindful of danger, has become for the enemy through his sureness of methods and manoeuvring, the adversary feared above all others. He accomplished on May 25th, 1917, the most brilliant exploit in bringing down in a single minute two enemy aeroplanes and in adding to them on the same day two other victories. By these exploits he has contributed to exalt the courage and enthusiasm of the troops in the trenches who witness his triumphs. 45 aeroplanes shot down; 20 citations; twice wounded.

On July 5th he received his Rosette, and on that day he also received something for which he was far more eager than his decoration. This was the new Spad aeroplane in which was mounted a 200-horse-power Hispano-Suiza motor which drove a propeller from the end of a hollow shaft. And through this hollow propeller shaft a light one-pounder gun fired straight ahead, without the risk and danger attending any attempt to synchronize its shells between the blades of his propeller.

It was his own idea! For months he had argued and pleaded with the authorities to give him a more deadly arm. Finally forced to succumb to his desire, the new fighting machine was built according to his directions.

And now he had a weapon that would send ahead of his meteor-like craft explosive shells of an inch and a half diameter instead of the trifling little machine-gun bullets of one sixth that diameter. One fair shot at the fleeing enemy was all that Guynemer desired with such a gun.

On July 27th Captain Guynemer took Lieutenant Deullin with him for a hunt across the British lines. His *escadrille* was now stationed at Dunkirk, and the Battle of Flanders was on. Hovering over the British trenches was a group of eight German machines. The two Cigognes climbed high above them and selecting his victim, the nearest, which was a large and powerful two-seater Albatross, Guynemer dived upon him. At two hundred yards he fired one shell from his 37-millimetre gun. The Albatross burst into flames and fell on the instant, a flaming mass, some distance back of its own lines. It was for Guynemer a gratifying victory, and his forty-ninth.

Three more victims were added to his score with this new and powerful weapon before his customary recklessness again imperilled his life and filled his new aeroplane with bullet holes. It must be sent to Paris for repairs, and in the meantime Guynemer must content himself with hunting Boches on his old out-of-date war charger.

Suddenly a new Guynemer revealed himself to his friends and comrades. He became nervous, sick and irritable. The most envied man in France found himself discontented and unhappy. Was it because he had attained his mark of fifty? Because he had seen the fulfilment of his desires in his new fighting plane which he had proved to be a success? Because the pent-up passion and determination which had so miraculously carried a human body safely through so many almost inevitable annihilations was at last beginning to devour the slight vessel which contained it? Such was the opinion of Commander Brocard, his early mentor and close friend.

Throughout August, 1917, Guynemer fought even more furiously than was his wont. His fifty-third and last victory was gamed on the twentieth. But his miraculous instinct seemed deserting him. Deprived of his own machine, his pet, he cruised far into the German lines over Flanders in his "*Vieux Charles*" or in another of his comrades' machines.

He made several visits to the factory in Paris and to his father's home in Compiègne. Parents and friends urged him to rest, to give up the chase now that he had attained "his fifty!" to teach his new pilots the tactics and manoeuvres that had brought him such wonderful successes over the enemy pilots.

To all such suggestions Guynemer replied impatiently: "They will say that I stopped fighting because I have received all the decorations France can give me." He burned with the desire to show "them" that he would work harder now to bring down aeroplanes than he had ever done before.

And he did work harder. He took even greater risks. He flew seven hours one day, engaged in several combats, but was unable to score a victory. Evil luck pursued him. On September tenth he used up three different machines, each one refusing to properly function and forcing him to land.

That night his comrades, unable to control their captain, telephoned to Paris, informing their old commanding officer, Brocard, that Guynemer was sick and in no condition to fly and imploring him to come to the aerodrome to take their captain away for a much needed rest. Commander Brocard promised to come and telegraphed Guynemer to expect him the following morning at nine o'clock.

Guynemer, undoubtedly suspecting the intrigue of his friends, ordered out his aeroplane next morning at eight o'clock and directed Lieutenant Bozon-Verduras to accompany him. Brocard arrived at the Dunkirk aerodrome in automobile shortly before nine. Guynemer had departed on his last flight at eight-twenty-five.

The mystery of Georges Guynemer's disappearance is truly so baffling that one wonders little at the superstitious belief held by the French peasants that he did not come down but on the contrary ascended straight to heaven—a last miracle!

The facts are these: Lieutenant Bozon-Verduras reports that northwest of Ypres he and Captain Guynemer discovered a two-seater Aviatic at 12,000 feet. Guynemer went in for the attack, leaving the lieutenant above him to guard against a rescue. A distant formation of enemy fighting planes was sighted by the sentinel, and he went forward to intercept them. They swerved off to the east without seeing him.

Returning to his station he searched the skies for the captain's aeroplane. It was not in sight. Believing Guynemer had downed his opponent and had followed him close to earth to witness the crash, Bozon-Verduras volplaned down and circled about at a low level for a considerable time without discovering any sign either of Guynemer or his victim.

Somewhat disturbed Bozon-Verduras ascended again and made wide cruises around the point of rendezvous, searching the distant skies in every direction with his glass. Finally, after two and one half hours of fruitless probing, his fuel was exhausted, and he flew back to camp. Guynemer had not returned.

All day they waited, sending frequent inquiries by telephone to the neighbouring aerodromes. Guynemer had not been seen.

It has always been the German custom to announce promptly the fall of any enemy aviator. If the pilot has fallen from his machine and his identity lost, the number and name of his aeroplane is published and sent abroad. In the case of a German victory over a Guynemer, whose name and exploits were frequently published in the German press, the news would certainly flood the entire world. But for ten days after September 11th, not a word came from Germany concerning Georges Guynemer.

The French had maintained a strict silence on their side, hoping that Guynemer had dropped uncaptured within the enemy lines, and that unaware of his presence the enemy's chance of apprehending him would be lessened. But a London newspaper on September 17th printed the story of his disappearance. The enemy now must know of his loss.

Four days later, about the time required for a London paper to reach Germany through Holland, the *Cologne Gazette* printed the casual information that a Cologne fighting pilot, one Wissemann, heretofore unheard of, had written to his mother in Cologne informing her that he had shot down Guynemer, the French Ace of Aces, and that hereafter he need fear no one. He dated his victory *September 10th*. Guynemer disappeared the eleventh.

Necessity for secrecy removed, application was made through Geneva Red Cross directly to Germany for information about the body of the French aviator, Georges Guynemer. An immediate reply was given the Red Cross to the effect that Guynemer was shot down in combat back of Ypres on *September 10th*, and that he was given a military funeral and his body was buried in the cemetery at Poelcappelle in Flanders.

A few days later Poelcappelle was captured by the British. Diligent search was made for the grave of Guynemer, but none was found.

An official request was thereupon made by the French Government through Spain to the German Government for definite facts concerning the disposition of Guynemer's body.

The extraordinary reply came that Guynemer had been killed on the eleventh, and not the tenth (full particulars having been published in the meantime of Guynemer's disappearance on the eleventh), that Guynemer had been killed by a bullet in the forehead, that his aeroplane had broken its right wing in the crash so that its number could not be ascertained and published (when as a matter of fact the number is stamped on the fuselage and the broken wing could not affect its discovery), and that finally, Guynemer's body could not be removed and buried owing to the violent artillery fire that was directed against the spot by the British, which fire eventually obliterated and destroyed every trace of both aeroplane and pilot!

Consider the incredulity with which this astonishing official contradiction from Germany must have been received by a people already anxious to believe that their hero was immortal, that he had accomplished his miraculous tasks by a power superhuman, that his unrivalled wings had at last carried him into the infinite where no manmade machine could follow, where no human mind could soar!

Thus shrouded in mystery we must leave Georges Guynemer, a marvellous if not a miraculous human being. What he might have accomplished had he consented to devote his impetuous ardour to the training of other air duellists after he had "made his score" will never be known.

But one or two of his observations concerning his well mastered science may well be remembered.

"My aeroplane," he said one day, "is nothing but a flying gun. My work begins every day with the most minute inspection of every implement upon which the combat depends.

"It is more than adroit manoeuvring that wins a victory. It is determination to last longer and hit harder than the Boche."

CHAPTER 6

Raoul Lufbery

What immortal spark did Raoul Lufbery fan into life during his combats in foreign lands to make his name a household word? Lufbery, unknown to fame in his own land, goes abroad and dies a soldier's death. And with that taking off, America discovers the name Lufbery is as familiar to its ears as is the name Pershing, the name Sims.

Even so did France discover that a Guynemer had taken his place in the popular mind along with a Joffre, a Clemenceau. And the great British public turned to wonder in its contemplation of a youth named Ball, who rivalled at twenty-two the prominence of a Lloyd-George or a Haig. And in unimaginative Germany herself, von Richthofen, their famous Ace, was worshiped with a fervour that only a von Hindenburg or the All-Holiest Kaiser himself might be expected to occasion.

What is this fascination that the heroes of aviation exercise over the minds of mankind? Let us look at the details of Raoul Lufbery's life and see where this extraordinary claim on human appreciation begins.

The beginning of Major Lufbery's career, even in this land of democratic tastes, would scarcely recommend itself to the average American parents of today. Perhaps this very absence of home training but the better illustrates the native ability of precocious American childhood, permitted to shape its own powers. Tor at seventeen years of age this boy ran away from his father's home in Wallingford, Connecticut, and set off by himself to see the world. He spent three years wandering over the cities of France, the home of his maternal ancestors, working at any job he could find just long enough to give him funds with which to carry him to the next haven of his desires.

From Marseilles he sailed for Algiers, which he visited to his heart's content. Thence to Tunis, to Egypt, thence through the Balkan States to Germany, thence to South America, and finally, after three years' absence from home, he returned in 1906 to Wallingford, only to find that his father had likewise departed for a similar bit of globe-trotting.

After a year at home Lufbery again set out. This time he went to New Orleans and enlisted in our regular army. He was sent to the Philippines where he served two years. And here we find the first item that helps to explain Raoul Lufbery's ultimate position as the American Ace of Aces. In the Philippines he won all the prizes for shooting. He was the best marksman in his regiment.

Quitting the army at the completion of his service he again set out to see the world. He ran through Japan and China. Then he went to India. Here he found employment as ticket collector in the railway station of Bombay.

One day a tall native presented himself before the ticket taker.

"Do you want a ticket?" asked Lufbery.

"Say 'sir' when you speak to me," replied the Indian. Lufbery, with ready decision, caught the native by the small of the neck and deposited him outside the station. A few moments later he was summoned before the authorities, and in the course of the brief interview that followed learned that he had assaulted the richest and most powerful merchant of Bombay.

Leaving Bombay, Lufbery found himself after a few weeks at Saigon, in Cochin China. And here, early in the year 1910, he saw his first aeroplane.

Marc Pourpe, the famous French trick flier, was giving an exhibition in the far East. He tells of his first meeting with Lufbery. He had lost his mechanic there at Saigon, and all further exhibitions must wait until he could secure another. In utter despair he had urged native after native to lend him aid, but none would attach himself to such a perilous occupation.

"I had spent several days in the place, when one morning a young man detached himself from the circle which surrounded me and approached me. He said he would like to have a few words with me. About my height, well put together, eyes frank and loyal, with a perpetual smile on his lips, he struck me at once as being honest.

"'You want a mechanic?' he asked me.

"'Certainly,' I said.

"'Do you want me?'

"'Are you a mechanic?' I demanded.

"'No.'

"'Do you know anything about an aeroplane motor?'

"'No.'

"'Then why do you bother me? Are you trying to be funny? I have other things to do than to amuse people. Goodbye.'

"'Just a moment,' he replied. 'You, yourself—the first time you ever saw a motor—were you competent? No. But you learned it. Why can't I do the same? I am not afraid of work. You show me a thing once, and I will remember it always. I know you will never regret it if you take me.'

"His reasoning was full of logic. His method was original. I agreed, and I will say that never have I seen a person more devoted, more intelligent and more useful. He is already better informed about a motor than most of the so-called mechanics of Paris. Moreover, this boy has hung his hat in every country in the world. He is not a man, he is an encyclopaedia. He can tell you what the weather is in a given season in Japan, in Egypt, in America, or in France. He observes everything and once he has noticed it, it is engraved on his memory.

"He told me that in all his travels he had never been more than a week without working. He was hospital interne at Cairo, a stevedore in Calcutta, station master in India, a soldier in America. I am glad he is now a mechanic.

"If he likes it, I will take him back with me at the end of my tour and will keep him with me. It is rare to find a good mechanic. His name is *Raoul Lafberg*, and he spent his childhood in the vicinity of Bourges. If I return with him, you will see what a sympathetic character chance has thrown in my way. So once more in my life everything goes well."

Raoul Lafberg! In the fear that Pourpe would not take him as mechanic if he thought him a foreigner, Lufbery, who spoke French like a native, told him his name was Lafberg!

During the summer of 1914 Pourpe and Lufbery were again in France where they were to accept a newly designed aeroplane. Before they left, war broke upon Pourpe's distressed land. He at once enlisted with his new aeroplane and was sent to observe and report upon the movements of the inpouring German troops through the valleys of Luxemburg.

Lufbery wished to enlist with his friend, but was declared to be an American, and found he must first join the Foreign Legion. This accomplished he was eventually permitted to accompany Pourpe to the front as a mechanic.

But their long and loyal friendship was soon to be ended. On December 2, 1914, Marc Pourpe was killed. Lufbery burned with the desire to avenge his friend. To his great joy his application for admission into the Air Service of France was granted, and within a few weeks his knowledge and experience gained under his long apprenticeship with Pourpe gave him his brevet. He was sent to the front with the celebrated Escadrille of Bombardment, the V. 102. Following is his account of one of his early bombing expeditions translated from *La Guerre Aerienne*:

> In January, 1916, I piloted a 140 H. P. Voisin and was a member of Bombing Escadrille 102. One clear afternoon about 1.15 o'clock we received orders to hold ourselves in readiness to leave on a mission. As is customary, our objective was not at once designated. Nevertheless, basing our conclusions upon the quantity of gasoline we were ordered to carry and the direction of the raid, we all guessed that it would be the railroad station at Metz. All the available aeroplanes were to take part in the raid,—a total of

forty machines half of which belonged to my group, the other half forming a part of Group 101 commanded by the dauntless Commander Roisin.

At the extremity of the field the machines are drawn up in a single line facing the wind. The mechanics take a last look at the engines; the gunners test the functioning of their arms and place the projectiles in the bomb racks. They are shells of 10 kilos that make, it seems, as much damage as the ordinary 155. For my part I took 6; some of the others took 8, 9, and even 10, the number varying according as to whether the engine was working well, the machine perfectly tuned, etc....

We are ready; we only await the last instructions. They distribute to us the maps on which the route we are to follow is marked out.

All the pilots set their watches by that of the chief of the expedition. Fifty minutes after the departure of the first aeroplane we must all be above Saint-Nichola-du-port and at a minimum of 2000 meters of altitude. From there and according to the signals which would be given by the Commandant we were to advance toward the lines or we were to return to the flying field. This last case would be determined by the bad weather, the wind, the clouds, or again in case of defective grouping.

The purring makes itself heard from the extremity of the line on the left. An aeroplane advances, rolls on a few seconds, then leaves the ground. A second follows it, then a third. I have Number 7. I turn toward my observer, Marechal des logis Allard, and ask him if he is ready. On his reply in the affirmative, I make contact and give it all the juice, then like my comrades I roll along a few seconds and take the air.

Before leaving, my passenger-bomb-dropper warned me that he would try to get a little sleep while I was getting my elevation, saying that he would be ready to study his map when we got on the other side of the trenches. This

I found entirely natural and I made no objection as he could not be of the slightest use to me in making my machine mount up. I turned around several times during our climb. Allard had his eyes closed, but I doubt that he slept. Certainly he had a right to, for he would soon have need of all his coolness and energy.

2.20 p.m. I am exactly on time at the rendezvous. The machine of Soudain, leader of the squadron, is recognizable by the little red flags placed at the extremity of his planes. I see the signal for departure. There remains nothing for me but to follow the group.

Crossing the trenches, the faster machines make one or two spirals to permit the slower ones to catch up. When the formation has become more compact we continue our advance, greeted here and there by bursts of shrapnel. No one is disturbed by this harmless firing; it is a question of chance or a lucky shot. To be dangerous a shot must hit the pilot or a vital part of the machine. One or even many holes in the fabric are of no consequence.

I occupy myself with the country that unrolls beneath my feet. To the right the Seille, a river scarcely recognizable at this season, its banks washed out by floods. It has the look of a great necklace of pools and ponds. To the left, the Moselle and its canal which form two beautiful silver lines which lose themselves at the north in a cloud of vapour. That which I mistook for a cloud of vapour is nothing but the smoke from the chimneys of Metz.

Getting nearer I distinguish through this curtain of smoke the groups of houses and churches, the long buildings covered with red tiles which are probably the barracks. The whole is surrounded with a girdle of small green parkways which are the famous forts. From aloft they appear quite inoffensive.

Only a few minutes and I shall be above the small freight station which is my objective. Those of the machines who find themselves in front, make at this moment a half turn to permit the laggards time to catch up with them. Lacking some ten horse power myself, I do not take part in this manoeuvre but I make straight for the goal, where I am the first to arrive.

Our coming must have been announced. Many enemy machines are about, cruising around at various heights ready to receive us. And here comes one of them to give me welcome. I quickly look around to see if my observer is on the lookout. His machine gun is trained on the enemy, his fingers caress the trigger. Good. Everything ready. At 150 yards the Boche biplane makes a sudden turn and presents us its right flank to permit its gunner to fire. Today such a manoeuvre is unnecessary as the two-seaters carry two rapid-fire guns, one fixed and the other mounted upon a pivot at the rear. I do not lose sight of the enemy machine. Very clearly the black iron crosses stand out on the fuselage and rudder. The fight begins.

The two machine guns begin to spit fire. The Boche dives away and seems to have had enough. I do not think it worthwhile to follow him. Besides, the road ahead is now clear, and I have an important mission to accomplish. Through the opening in my floor I see the forking of the railroads, some trains at a standstill and others moving, the depots containing the freight and munitions.

My observer touches my left shoulder and motions me to keep straight ahead. Another slap satisfies me that his bombs have been released. It is finished. I have nothing to do but make my half circle and return to the landing field.

The Boches become more and more numerous. We must redouble our vigilance. But in spite of all our care we are surprised by a Fokker fighting machine. He fires a volley into us and escapes before we have time to confront him. Two or three little 'spats' indicate to me that he has aimed well and my machine is hit.

Nevertheless the motor roars on regularly, and the fuel

tank, which my comrade hastily examines, does not seem to have been injured. The wind which blew from the north assisted our quick return. In a short time we found ourselves back again above the trenches. Without knowing why, I laughed aloud. I turned my head and saw that my observer was laughing also. We were happy and radiant. Now that we were out of danger we wanted to exchange expressions, to discuss the success of our raid, but the noise of the motor was too great. We could not hear ourselves speak; we had to be patient and wait until we had landed.

Slowing down and taking the descent, my machine glided sweetly above the valley of the Meurthe. We came down in a volplane gently towards the ground. My comrade, who had the happy thought to light a cigarette, passed it to me for a few puffs which I found delicious. Little by little everything took on more of an aspect of reality; the beautiful green moss became the forests; the black ribbons, the railroad lines; the white ribbons became the roads and highways; that which I had taken from a distance to be a curtain of black smoke grew into enormous proportions, and I recognized the lovely city of Nancy.

Now we are at 800 feet altitude above the aerodrome. A last spiral and we land.

My first care is to examine my machine. 'I find that the fabric of my planes is riddled with bullets. Many of our comrades have not yet returned. It is said some will not return. Several of our Voisin machines were seen descending in enemy territory.

They come in, one by one, a white speck in the skies. 'That must be the one I saw at a distance behind me,' says one. 'No, it is one I met as I was coming back,' says another.

Now have all returned of our formation, and the face of our Captain suddenly changes its grave expression. He cannot conceal his satisfaction in seeing his whole squadron intact.

Alas! It is not the same in all the squadrons. Although there is still time to find ourselves mistaken, it is to be feared that at some of our messes black bread will be eaten this night.

Six months later we find Sergeant Lufbery transferred from the Bombing Squadron to the newly organized *Escadrille Lafayette*. Here began that list of heroic exploits in the air which gained for him the title of the American Ace of Aces, and which demonstrated beyond all question Lufbery's superiority as an aerial duellist over any of his fellow Americans—as well as over some two-score of his antagonists.

Officially credited with eighteen victories in single combat, Lufbery brought down, in fact, something over twice this number of enemy aeroplanes. Many of them were shot down far inside the German lines where none but his comrades observed their fall. Others fell in such a manner that it could not be definitely said that they were destroyed. Judged, however, in strict accordance with the rules of the French Air Service, Lufbery's victories placed him at one time fourth from the highest in France in personal superiority.

On July 30, 1916, he brought down his first victim over Etain. Five days later he triumphed again over his Boche, this time in company with Adjutant Sayaret. These successes brought him his first citation from the French Government, in these terms:

> Model of address, of coolness and of courage. He has distinguished himself by numerous long-distance bombardments and by the daily combats he has had with enemy aeroplanes. On July 30th, he unhesitatingly attacked at close range a group of four enemy machines. He shot one of them down near our lines. Succeeded in bringing down a second on the 4th of August, 1916.

On August 8th another fell before the expert marksmanship Lufbery had acquired during his service in the Philippines; and four days later he brought down his fourth official enemy plane.

This continued increase of victories brought Lufbery a promotion to the rank of adjutant.

His fifth victory, on October 12, 1916, consisted of a huge three-seater Aviatic which he shot down in flames, during a bombing expedition against the munition factories at Karlsruhe. It was during this same expedition that Norman Prince received his mortal wound upon landing. Victor Chapman and Kiffin Rockwell had already fallen, and Clyde Balsley was lying a helpless cripple in a Paris hospital.

Lufbery with his fifth official victory became an "Ace", and in accordance with the French custom, was given a citation for each succeeding victory.

The *Lafayette Escadrille* was transferred from Verdun to the Somme at this juncture, and ere Lufbery continued his long list of uninterrupted successes over the German airmen. On December 27th he shot down two in one day, but one of which was credited to him. During one of these combats he narrowly escaped death, returning to his aerodrome with his flying jacket torn with bullets. For these exploits he was rewarded with the Legion of Honour. Already decorated with the Military Medal, he was the first American to receive from England the British Military Cross, which was conferred upon him on the following June twelfth.

On that same morning he had brought down his tenth enemy aeroplane. Flying alone at some 18,000 feet altitude, Lufbery saw at a distance a formation of seven Boches. Two of them were two-seater observing machines, the other five constituting an escort for their protection. Lufbery flew into the sun and awaited his chance for a surprise. At last he observed one of them cut off from the others and unsuspicious of his presence. He dived upon him, firing as he approached. Twenty-five or thirty shots—and his machine gun jammed. But it was enough. The Boche wavered a moment, then began a chute. Over and over it fell, both wings tearing themselves away in the violence of its motion. As the victor volplaned away to his own flying field, he saw his enemy crash into the German trenches and vanish in a cloud of lifting dust.

But Lufbery had very narrow escapes as well as brilliant victories. Here is his own simple story of one of his combats which nearly ended his career, translated from *La Guerre Aerienne*:

> My altimeter marks 2000. Below me a marvellous panorama! the Vosges! The beauty of the country makes me forget for an instant the object of my voyage: the chase of Boche! In order to get a further view of this beautiful spectacle, I decided to make a little curve to the left which would permit me to fly over Ballon in Alsace.
>
> On the turn to the north at the far end of the narrow valley I perceived a tiny silver mirror. The temptation was too great. Why not admire for a few moments the delightful view? Weakly I allowed my aeroplane to turn in spirals, seeking, but in vain, its reflection on the tranquil silver surface of the lake.
>
> The little diversion might have lasted some time longer if my motor had not interrupted my enjoyment by throwing out some discordant notes. It made me uneasy. I listened attentively: it seemed to me to beat more and more irregularly. I anticipated a treacherous breakdown, and a forced landing on the edge of one of those precipices whose wild aspect I had been admiring a moment before and where I could not count on any immediate assistance.
>
> Instinctively I increased my speed. I wanted to fly away from these places. Always I notice that the nearer I approach the level the better my 'mill' seems to get into its turning. And now it began to breathe perfectly; it is probable that it had been so all along and had never had the slightest intention of playing me a bad trick.
>
> Who knows but that it was I, the pilot, who had just been the victim of an unpleasant illusion, not to say the small beginning of a fear. A little ashamed of this weakness I lectured myself severely, with the thought that within a short time, perhaps a very short time, I would have to confront a Boche and fight him.

Like a tired horse who droops his head after a long race, my machine, which had mounted to 4600 meters, commenced to fly horizontally of its own accord with a slight tendency to nose dive. It is an indication that he has attained his maximum of altitude.

Almost at my feet the great city of Mulhouse. At a few kilometres to the right in a clearing the German aviation field of Habsheim.

A glance at my map showed me that I had passed over their lines without knowing it. That was not a matter of much importance, and besides it happened often enough, especially where the lines of trenches are straight as is the case in the sectors where there have been no important operations.

There was rather a strong wind blowing from west to east, which was unfavourable for the chase in this region. Besides I did not think it necessary to penetrate any farther into the enemy's lines and turned about to the north. At this moment the artillery of *'Deutschland ueber alles'* sent me a few volleys to show that I had not eluded their vigilance. Their aim was poor, so I thought it unnecessary to manoeuvre with turns and changes of altitude which I usually employ to get out of the way of a more exact fire.

A mountain whose summit differed from the others by its brick-ed colour attracted my attention. It is Hartmanswillerskopf celebrated for the heroic defence of the little French mountaineers. There as at Verdun *They shall not pass.*

A half turn to the right, another half turn to the left, permits me to take a cautious view over the landscape about me.

Nothing unusual! Reassured I continue on my way, and coming nearer and nearer to Hartmanswillerskopf I search my memory to recall where I had seen anything as beautiful as the view which met my eye at that moment.

I have it—it was in the photographs of the moon! Exactly,

of the moon in its most marked aspect. Creased, scarred, weather-beaten, this peak stands out in singular fashion from its neighbours which are for the most part covered with verdure. Nevertheless I am all the tune on guard. My glance searches the skies for possible enemies.

This time the precaution is not useless. At this moment appears an enemy, a little below and behind me. It is a little one-seater biplane of the Fokker or Halberstadt type. A glance around assures me that he is alone. I am surprised at this, for it is certainly the first time that a machine of this sort has deliberately placed itself in a position so disadvantageous for fighting. Perhaps it is a trap. One never knows! If it only may prove to be a beginner, lacking experience, who listens to nothing but his courage in his purpose to become one of the great Aces of his country.

However that may be, the wind keeps blowing from the west and carries me farther and farther into the lines. It will not do to allow the Boche to have this advantage too long: I decide to begin the attack without losing another second.

An about face, followed by a sudden double spin, carries me a little behind my adversary. Profiting by this advantage I dive upon him, but with a remarkable skill he gets out of range of my machine gun. He has anticipated my manoeuvre and parried the blow before it was struck. I am now aware that I have to do with a master of his art. This first encounter has proved it to me.

Making my machine tango from right to left, I saw him again below me but much nearer than before by at least forty yards.

Suddenly he noses up as if to begin a looping, and in this awkward position fires a volley at me which I dodge by a half turn to the right. A second time I attack but with no more success. The wind carries us to the north of Mulhouse, and I begin to ask myself if I am not playing my adversary's game for him in delaying longer.

At this moment I chanced to glance in the direction of Belfort which was about twelve miles within our lines. I perceived in the air little white flakes. Evidence of the presence of a Boche.

A lucky chance! I had now an excuse for abandoning without loss of honour the match, which I confess I am not at all sorry to leave. Only before leaving my adversary I feel that I must show him that I appreciate that he is a valiant foe and respect him as such. Drawing my left arm out of the fuselage I wave him a sign of *adieu*. He understands and desires to show courtesy on his part, for he returns my farewell.

All my attention is turned toward him whom I already consider as my new prey, a big white two-seater of very substantial appearance.

I draw nearer and nearer to him. Good luck! For the first time since I have been a chaser I am going to have the good fortune to battle within our lines. Also this increases my confidence until it makes me disregard all measures of caution and even the science of tactics.

Another motive impels me to take more than ordinary risks. I am determined that he shall not escape me, and I make up my mind to shoot at him until I have won the victory.

What joy if I can only lodge a ball in his motor, or in his gasoline tank, which would oblige him to make a landing on French soil! Then I should be able to speak with the conquered and ask them their impressions of the aerial duel in which they had just taken part. But there is an old French proverb which says *You must not sell the skin of the bear before you have killed him*. I had occasion that day to prove the wisdom of this as you shall soon see.

Enough of dreaming! The moment for action has arrived. Quickly I place myself in the rear and on the tail of my enemy from whom I am separated by a distance of about fifty yards. Then I open fire with my machine gun, and continue firing up to the moment when my plane, his superior in speed, arrives so near the big two-seater that a collision seems inevitable.

Quickly I pull up, leap over the obstacle, and fall in a glide on the right wing. Increasing my speed I re-establish my equilibrium and prepare to tempt fortune a second time. Curse the luck! It is of no use. The motor, the soul of my aeroplane, has received a mortal wound and is about to draw its last breath.

Turning my head I discover that the ailerons are also seriously injured. My enemy fortunately does not seem to wish to profit by the situation. He continues his flight in the direction of his own lines. Perhaps I have wounded him very seriously. I hope so. Anyway, his flight leaves me master of the field. But that is a very small consolation. And also of short duration; for I am coming down faster and faster. At last I safely take the ground on the nearest flying field within gliding distance.

Pilots, observers, mechanics surround me and besiege me with questions. They have seen the fight and want the details. For the moment I do not explain much but that I have encountered a Boche who does not understand joking! Besides, I was in a hurry to examine the wounds of my little aeroplane. It is very ill, poor thing! Three bullets in the motor, the gasoline tank ruined, a strut out of commission, many holes in. the hood, finally the left aileron was cut and broken off by the bullets. It had made its last flight! Poor Coucou!

To recount all the aerial successes of this American champion is but to repeat the usual details of his sober inspection of his aeroplane and his arms before dawn; his calm scrutiny of the skies for the black crosses of the enemy planes; his adroit manoeuvring for the best position from which to surprise the foe; his determined and patient attack; his exactness in machine-gun marksmanship; his jubilant return to his comrades with another certain victory on his score.

During months of his service in France Lufbery suffered from acute seizures of rheumatism which frequently necessitated his return to the hospital. Quiet and unassuming in his conversation, Lufbery won universal respect from the mechanics and affectionate loyalty from his comrades. Everyone who met him felt as Marc Pourpe wrote, *He is not a man, he is an encyclopaedia.*

When America entered the war and began her preparations for her own Air Service in France, certain of the experienced fighting pilots who had been fighting for France were given charge of the new American *Escadrilles*. Lufbery and William Thaw, both original members of N. 124, the Escadrille Lafayette, were commissioned majors. To them fell the task of organizing the eager youths who were to assist in clearing from the skies of France the invading Hun.

Possessed of all the honours that his army could bestow upon a noble soldier, and wracked with physical pains that were daily increased by inclement weather, an ordinary man would have been satisfied to seek his ease and fill his required duties with the instructions to his pilots. But Major Lufbery instructed by example, not by speech. Not unmindful of his value to his comrades as their mentor and commander and impelled by an ardour that knew no rest, Lufbery continued his active patrolling, exposed himself to every risk.

On Sunday, May 19th, the American Ace of Aces went aloft over Toul with his fighting squadron. Enemy fighting machines were flying over the American line. The latest designed Fokker aeroplane, a single-seater triplane, appeared deep enough within our territory to be cut off before he could escape. Lufbery darted swiftly to the attack.

Exact details of any air combat are known only to the combatants. Fighting machines of today move with a speed of 140 miles per hour. Approaching each other they lessen the distance between them at the rate of over *400 feet each second*. Let someone calculate the fraction of an instant given to the pilot in which he plans his manoeuvre, alters his position, takes his aim, and presses the trigger!

Lufbery's machine fell in flames. He was seen to jump from the blazing mass when 2,000 feet from the ground. A parachute attachment might have saved his life as his body was found to be uninjured from the enemy's fire. A non-inflammable fuel tank might have permitted him to continue his attack until the Fokker triplane dropped as his nineteenth victory.

Deprived of these improvements, Lufbery died. With his lamented loss the title of the American Ace of Aces passed to Sergeant Frank L. Baylies, of New Bedford, Massachusetts, who after eight months at the front had amassed a total of twelve enemy machines. Upon the gallant death of Baylies, Lieutenant Putnam of Brookline, Massachusetts, with ten official victories, headed the American list of Aces.

CHAPTER 7

The British Aces

> SONG OF THE BRITISH AIRMEN
> (To the tune of "My Old Tarpaulin Jacket.")

The young aviator went stunting,
And as 'neath the wreckage he lay—he lay,
To the mechanics assembled around him
These last parting words he did say did say:

> Chorus

Take the cylinders out of my kidneys,
The connecting rod out of my brain—my brain;
From the small of my back take the crankshaft,
And assemble the engine again.

CAPTAIN ALBERT BALL

The first great English Ace whose name will go down to posterity was Albert Ball, born at Nottingham, August 21, 1896, killed in combat by von Richthofen the younger on May 7, 1917. He was not yet twenty-one and had received all the greatest decorations. He was, we believe, the only Englishman to receive the Military Cross, the D. S. O. with two bars, and the Victoria Cross, not to speak of the Legion of Honour and other orders of the Allied countries.

At the beginning of the war Albert Ball enlisted as a private in the Sherwood Foresters. Soon after he became a non-commissioned officer in the Nottinghamshire and Derbyshire regiment, and then within a few months he requested to be transferred to aviation. He obtained his pilot's certificate—number 1898, on a Caudron at the Ruffy-Beaumann school at Hendon on October 15, 1915.

Sent immediately to the French front, Ball became distinguished from the first through his judgment, his audacity, his fearless courage, and his unusual skilfulness. When he was killed Major-General Trenchard wrote to Ball's father, a former Mayor of old Nottingham, the lines which follow and which admirably portray the hero of the day.

"He was the most audacious, the most skilful and the most marvellous pilot in the Royal Flying Corps. Every pilot in the corps considered him a perfect model and all strove to imitate him. He was a most popular officer. His zeal was an example for everyone. I have never met a man greater than your son and one who became great in so short a time yet who remained so modest and so simple."

Ball presented a striking appearance: small, nervous, his nose, a little snubbed, giving him the look of a boxer, his hair always long and wavy. He laughed easily, and his piercing eyes quickly changed their expression from sternness to amusement.

One could not fail to recognize in Albert Ball the true sportsman. He lived only for aviation. All his spare time when off duty was spent in the hangars, verifying his instruments, his armament, his motor, and every detail of his equipment. In this particular he resembled Guynemer and likewise Donne, his two great contemporaries in the French Air Service. In combat Ball was still more like Guynemer. He rushed into action with an impetuosity that usually carried all before it, disdaining danger.

Bail dashed out in all kinds of weather, forcing a fight wherever possible and by preference fighting alone. When he sighted an enemy he darted into the attack with the ferocity of a maddened eagle. He would throw himself into the midst of a compact enemy formation and break it up through their sheer fear of collision. Then with contempt for the enemy's timid nerves Ball would attack them one after another, until all were vanquished or fled.

Whether the opposing formation consisted of ten, fifteen, or twenty enemy aeroplanes this young hornet appeared equally indifferent. Like a Lilliputian he struck this way and that, darting with the suddenness of a serpent at an unsuspecting enemy, keeping always a wary eye out for ripostes, and alert as a fox, always evading at the last instant the furious assault of an enemy.

Invariably this small youth remained master of the field. If he had enough exercise for one flight—and this was usually not until the moment that he ran out of ammunition or when his machine was so severely injured that it threatened to drop, he returned tranquilly, made his report, and recounted his exploits, often minimizing them; that is to say, he often did not mention his victories because his victims had been destroyed too far within the enemy's lines. He quickly filled up his tanks with gasoline and oil and set out once more to look for game.

When he was killed he had to his credit forty-three aeroplanes and one balloon.

Before describing any of his exploits let us recall some of the citations he received with his decorations:

June, 1916. Having been unsuccessful in an attempt to destroy an enemy balloon with incendiary bombs, he went to fetch ammunition with which he shot down the balloon in flames. A distinguished chaser; on one occasion he attacked six enemy aeroplanes, brought two of them down and put the others to flight.

September 16, 1916. Remarkable bravery and skill. Observing a group of seven enemy aeroplanes in battle formation, he attacked one instantly at less than fifteen yards and brought it down. The others took flight. Continuing his patrol he saw five machines; he approached one of them until he was less than ten yards distant and brought it down. He attacked another of them, riddled it with bullets and brought it down. Then he went back to the nearest aerodrome for more ammunition. He set out again, attacked three new enemy aeroplanes and brought them down out of control. Having no more gas he returned with his machine riddled with bullets.

September 26, 1916. Remarkable courage and skill. While escorting a bombing squadron he perceived four enemies in battle formation. He dived down upon them, separated them and brought down the nearest; to assure himself of the destruction of this one Ball descended to less than 200 yards from earth. At another time observing twelve enemy planes in battle formation, he swooped down upon them and brought one down. Many others coming up, he fired three bands and brought down another. He returned to his aerodrome, passing over the lines at very low altitude, with a seriously damaged aeroplane.

It is to be noted that this exploit was revealed by an observer in Ball's company. Ball had not mentioned the matter on his return!

King George personally decorated Captain Ball on November 18, 1916, with the Military Cross and the D. S. O. for having at this time brought down twenty-nine enemy machines.

Another citation:

November 23, 1916. Remarkable courage and skill. Attacking three enemy aeroplanes he brought down one of them. He had brought down eight enemy machines in a very short time and had forced many others down out of control.

On February 19, 1917, in recognition of his distinguished services, Ball received the "freedom" of the city of Nottingham. The Mayor in his speech recalled the fact that in four months the Ace had engaged in more than one hundred combats, brought down thirty aeroplanes, and that he had himself been brought down six times without any serious consequences.

Apropos of his many combats Ball told the following anecdote:

I have never met but one German aviator who really had

courage. This one gave me the most sporting combat of my career. The duel lasted half an hour. Then both of us having exhausted our ammunition we came side by side to express our mutual admiration. I hope to encounter that adversary again; he is a real sportsman.

After this function at Nottingham Ball was made instructor in a flying school. He would have been invaluable as a trainer of pilots, but he soon grew restless; the combat was his life, and he was homesick for the front. He asked to be allowed to go back. He added a few more victories to his score, but a few days later he met his death.

During the last week of April Ball attacked two two-seater Albatross machines: one flew off, the other crashed to the earth. A few moments later he saw five Albatross above Cambrai. He brought down the nearest one at the very end of his gun. The others fled. The next morning on patrol at 14,000 feet elevation he observed an enemy formation which was rising from its aerodrome. He hid in a cloud and waited for the Boches. When they were at 8000 feet he dropped down upon them and accounted for one of them in a twinkling. He realized that the others formed a barrier between himself and his own lines. What was he to do? He tried to force a passage. In vain.

Then he made a loop but the enemies followed him. That was what he wished. Now that the Huns were separated from one another, he turned about for the attack and brought down two of them. Then, short of ammunition, he returned, laughing, to his camp. Another time, when he was engaged in a struggle with two Halberstadts, he brought down one of the Boches. The other, mad with rage, rushed upon him, trying to cause a collision. A brave idea—almost too heroic to be German. The Englishman realized the situation. By a quick turn he avoided the collision, freed himself, came back upon the enemy and shot him down. The two enemies one after the other were so badly disabled that they fell to the earth where they crashed.

Before giving the details of the tragic end of this great Ace it is fitting to cite the text of the last official homage that was

CAPTAIN ALBERT BALL
The first great English Ace, killed on may 7, 1917,
in his twentieth year, after shooting down 43 German planes.

rendered him:

> For his unfaltering and brilliant courage: from April 25th to May 6th he took part in 26 combats, destroyed eleven enemy aeroplanes, made two fall out of control, and forced down many others. In all these encounters Ball flew alone. On one occasion he attacked six enemy aeroplanes, he fought twice against five and once against four. At another time with two other pilots he attacked an enemy formation of eight aeroplanes. In each of these cases he triumphed over an adversary. All together Captain Ball has destroyed forty-three German aeroplanes and one balloon. In many encounters his machine was seriously injured; once to such an extent that it required the most marvellous skill not to crash, all the wires of his controls having been cut. Each time he returned with a damaged aeroplane he at once set out again on a new one, giving always the proofs of the most extraordinary courage, of determination and skill.

A few days before his death Albert Ball wrote to a friend the following letter which will give an idea of his character:

> You will learn with pleasure that I have brought down ten more Huns and that my total is now forty, two more than my French rival.
> Oh! I am not wasting my time. Today or tomorrow I am to be presented to Sir Douglas Haig. I am really very happy about it. I shall try to bring down some more if I can!

Such was the boy who reposes today in the enemy territory at Annoeullin.

On the evening of May 7, 1917, Ball left with a companion on his patrol. They encountered an enemy aeroplane which they attacked and brought down. Then there came upon them a group of four Huns: the two English pilots flew directly at them. Ball's comrade found himself in so unfavourable a position that he seemed to be completely at the mercy of the enemy. He went into a tail spin to get out of it, withdrew, gained again a good altitude, and returned to the combat. He dived upon one of the enemy and brought him down. Then he turned to attack another when a bullet fractured his wrist and another ball broke the steering lever. Overcome by the pain, he could no longer continue to fight. Moreover, further manoeuvres were rendered extremely difficult, but in spite of his pain he succeeded in regaining his own lines where he came down in his own territory. Once landed he fainted.

What happened after this pilot left the field of combat for some time remained a mystery. Ball was left alone against three. But that was not too many for him. Just the day before he had brought down two enemies who had fallen about three hundred yards apart. The 6th of May he had hurled himself against four Boches, had triumphed over one and had vainly attempted to force the rest to fight. His comrades never feared for Ball's safety, no matter against what odds he fought.

Wolff's agency accounted in these terms for the end of the British hero:

> On May 7th two English aeroplanes were destroyed by our aviators. Lieutenant von Richthofen brought down a triplane piloted by Captain Ball. This was the 20th victory for the German.

After the death of Captain Ball the King of England sent the following letter to his father:

Buckingham Palace, May 28, 1917.

It is for me a cause of sincere regret that the death of Lieutenant (with the temporary title of Captain) Albert Ball, D. S. O. and M. C. of the 7th battalion of the regiment of Derbyshire and of the R. F. C., has deprived me of the honour of myself giving to him the Victoria Cross, the highest of all the honours awarded to courage and to devotion to duty.

George R. I.

One might say of Ball, the English Guynemer, as of that great French Ace, that he had in reality many more victories than those which were officially accredited to him.

Ball is mentioned for the first tune September 11, 1916, and at that time one might have been pardoned a certain scepticism in reading in the *London Daily Mail* that:

"Lieutenant Albert Ball, eldest son of the former Mayor of Nottingham, has brought down 22 enemy aeroplanes. In a letter he tells that he has had 84 aerial combats and that one night upon being attacked by four enemy machines, he brought all four of them down."

It seemed then that this Ball, of whose exploits no one had ever heard, must be a fraud. But the British have never followed the practice of the other belligerents: they do not cite in their *communiqués* the names of their Aces. The information concerning Ball was entirely true.

Ball first made himself known in June, 1916. Having set out to attack a balloon with bombs he failed to bring it down. Furious at this disappointment he returned for a new supply, went a second tune to the attack, and this time was successful. The citation which this exploit earned for him recounts that at one time, when giving battle to six enemy planes, he brought down two and put the others to flight. Such were the first combats of the young hero who had been at the front only during the month of June.

In September, sighting a group of seven enemy machines, he rushed upon one of them, opened fire at less than ten yards and brought him down. The others did not wait for their turn, and when Ball was ready to take them on he saw them flying away in the distance. He continued his chase. Soon he found himself in the presence of five other Boches. He fired on one from eight yards, and the Boche exploded in the air. He turned toward a second who attempted to avenge his comrade. Ball triumphed anew and saw him crash on a roof in the village. Then Ball left the field to reload his machine gun. This done, he returned to attack the three other aeroplanes, one of which he crippled and forced to descend. As his gas was almost gone he at last was compelled to return with a machine riddled with bullets.

On another occasion in September, he was escorting a bombing *escadrille* when suddenly a group formation of four enemy aeroplanes presented itself. He flew toward them, broke through their line, and brought down the nearest which fell in a nose dive; then he went down himself to 150 yards to make sure of its destruction.

Some days later he fought single-handed against twelve enemies swooping down upon them with contemptuous boldness. All the tune under the incessant fire of his adversaries, he turned his machine upon first one and then another, bringing down the nearest German and obliging three others to make off without any control over their machines. He himself returned to a very low altitude with a much damaged machine.

Such are some of the exploits of this Ace of nineteen, who in six months had placed to his credit twenty-nine aeroplanes and one balloon. A marvellous model of audacity and devotion to duty was this young Albert Ball of Nottingham to the pilots of the Royal Flying Corps!

COLONEL WILLIAM A. BISHOP OF CANADA

But one living man can rightfully claim to be the conqueror of seventy-two enemy aeroplanes. This marvellous record is held by Colonel William A. Bishop who won a host of friends in America during his brief visit here in the fall of 1917. Modest, unspoiled, and gifted with a rare wit, this young Canadian tested some of the joys that his prowess so richly merited when throngs of his fellow men crowded about him to gaze upon the great champion of the British Flying Corps and to listen to his vivid narration of his exploits, which had netted him at that time forty-seven victories.

Returning to his fighting squadron in France after his brief furlough, during which Bishop was married, the youthful captain entered again into the furious air fighting above the heads of the advancing Huns and in three weeks accounted for twenty-five more aeroplanes—a total of seventy-two.

Now he has been retired by a wise commanding officer and attached to the British Air Board with the rank of colonel. In this office the great champion is now organizing all-Canadian units of air fighters and at the same time is giving the authorities at home the benefits of his vast experience in action. But one human being ever exceeded his score. This was von Richthofen, the German, who was called upon by his hard-pressed country to undertake one too many flights and who fell in combat within the British lines, thus depriving the Huns of his sorely needed services as an instructor.

Bishop entered the war first as a cavalryman and served in this capacity for several months before securing his transfer into aviation. At the end of 1915 he began his flying experiences as an observer. He spent four months in the passenger's seat, regulating artillery fire by his wireless messages and vainly waiting for his opportunity of getting a shot at an attacking enemy aeroplane. Finally in May, 1916, Bishop was injured in a bad landing and was compelled to spend several months in a hospital. Upon his return to his squadron he learned with much satisfaction that he was to become a fighting pilot, and for the balance of the year he applied himself to the study of the various types of fast scouting machines and experimented in trick flying, night flying, and target practice.

On March 7, 1917, the new fledged pilot flew his own machine across the Channel and landed at Boulogne. He had been selected as a member of the most celebrated fighting squadron in the Royal Flying Corps—that commanded by the English champion, Captain Albert Ball.

The Battle of the Somme was on, and the German invaders were just beginning their retreat to the famous Hindenburg line. Air combats were plentiful and could be had for the seeking, but for a few days the new pilots of the squadron were cautioned against taking part in single combats in which their inexperience would be a perilous handicap against the expert fighters of the enemy.

But on March 25th, Bishop went aloft on a cloudy morning with three of his comrades, and when some distance behind the German lines they espied three Albatross machines which seemed desirous of a tourney. The four Britishers were mounted on Nieuports carrying synchronized machine guns. Their leader and one other pilot in their formation were old hands at this game. Bishop and the fourth, who was his chum, were novices.

In a moment the fight was on, and every man was for himself. With a feeling which Bishop later described as "savage elation" the young Canadian picked out his target and throwing caution to the winds descended upon him. The Boche fell. Fearing a ruse, Bishop opened up his motor and followed him. Ah! It was a ruse. The enemy pilot, after dropping some thousands of feet and feeling he was safely out of the *mêlée*, redressed his machine and looked about him. To his utter astonishment Bishop's Nieuport was again immediately behind his tail, and tracer-bullets were cutting through the fuselage about him. He dived again with the British pilot still on his tail. The next instant the Albatross turned over and fell 2000 feet to a crash.

Bishop descended low to assure himself that this latest move of his enemy was not another ruse. One glance at the wreckage however satisfied him that he had shot down his first enemy machine. Rather numb from the discovery of his own superiority, the victor turned on his spark and looked about him to ascertain his position. Then he received another shock. His engine would not function!

Descending lower and lower over the strange terrain, Bishop felt his spirits sink with his machine. He knew he was in enemy territory and he knew he was compelled to land. His first victory would then be his last!

Gliding southward as far as his powerless aeroplane would carry him, he landed gently behind a ruined village. Soldiers came running up to capture him. Bishop leaped out of his machine and took refuge in a shell hole. From behind his defences he gradually became aware of a strange familiarity in the accents of his pursuers. They were speaking the purest Tommy Atkins.

Colonel William Bishop
Canadian. The premier Ace of the Royal Flying Corps, who brought down 72 enemy planes

When safely back in his own aerodrome, Bishop received the laconic compliments of his comrades with feelings somewhat mixed. It was true that he had brought down his first enemy; but the narrow margin which had saved him savoured a little too much of the miraculous. For he had brought his dead engine to earth just one hundred yards behind the English trenches without knowing it. Even a contrary wind would have delivered him a prisoner into the enemy's hands!

From that time on Lieutenant Bishop's successes steadily increased. Fighting daily behind the German lines and engaged in combats without number, the young pilot little by little acquired that sense of air fighting which enabled him to anticipate the movements of the antagonist and to choose the precise moment for an attack that was most propitious. On April 7th he shot down an observation balloon and its defending aeroplane. For this feat he was awarded the Military Cross and a citation.

During the Battle of Arras late in April, Bishop was the hero of a singular exploit which endeared him to the infantry troops who witnessed it. His own description of this incident in the *Saturday Evening Post* is so vivid I will quote a few paragraphs of it.

> On the fourth day of the battle I was flying about five hundred feet above the trenches an hour after dawn. It had snowed during the night and the ground was covered with a new layer of white several inches thick. No marks of the battle of the day before were to be seen; the only blemishes in the snow mantle were the marks of shells which had fallen in the last hour. No Man's Land itself, so often a filthy litter, was this morning quite clean and white.
>
> Suddenly over the top of our parapets a thin line of infantry crawled up and strolled casually towards the enemy. To me it seemed they must soon wake up and run. They were altogether too slow. They could not realize the great danger they were in.
>
> Here and there a shell would burst as the line advanced

or halted for a moment. Three or four men near the burst would topple over like so many tin soldiers. Two or three other men would then come running up to the spot from the rear with a stretcher, pick up the wounded and the dying and slowly walk back with them.

I could not get the idea out of my head that it was just a game they were playing at. It all seemed so unreal. Nor could I believe that the little brown figures moving about below me were really men—men going to the glory of victory or the glory of death. I could not make myself realize the full truth or meaning of it all. I seemed to be in a different world, looking down from another sphere on this strange uncanny puppet-show.

Suddenly I heard the deadly rattle of a nest of machine guns under me and saw that the line of our troops at one place was growing very thin with many figures sprawling on the ground. For three or four minutes I could not make out the position of the concealed German gunners. Our men had halted and were lying on the ground, evidently as much puzzled as I was. Then in the corner of a German trench I saw a group of about five men operating two machine guns. They were slightly on the flank of our men and evidently had been doing a great deal of damage.

The sight of this group woke me up to the reality of the whole scene below me. I dived vertically at them with a burst of rapid fire. The smoke bullets from my gun smote the ground about them and it was an easy matter to get my aim accurately on the German guns, one of which had turned its muzzle towards me.

In a fraction of a second I had reached a level of only thirty feet above the Huns, so low that I could make out every detail of their frightened faces. With hate in my heart I fired every bullet I could into the group as I swept over it, and then I turned my machine away.

A few moments later I had the satisfaction of seeing our line again advancing and before the time had come for me to return to my formation our men had occupied all the German positions they had set out to take.

On the 20th of April, 1917, Bishop was promoted to a captaincy. He had shot down his fifth machine and had established a reputation for skill and judgment that had won the approval of his superiors and the esteem of his comrades. Captain Ball at that time had shot down his thirty-fifth aeroplane and stood prominently above his fellows as the most brilliant knight of the air. Bishop was to survive to more than double the score of his old commander.

Following the natural custom of all the belligerents, the best of the British air fighters were sent to the sectors where the best of the enemy aeroplanes were stationed. Captain Bishop therefore had few green freshmen of the enemy forces with whom to engage in single combat. On the contrary his most frequent encounters were with the members of the von Richthofen Circus whose identity was distinguishable by the red noses of their machines. Several of this group fell before the superior tactics of the Canadian. With equal disdain for concealment Bishop had his own fighting plane painted a bright blue so that his enemies would know whom to thank for the steady decimation of their fighting squadrons.

Day after day Bishop sought out and offered combat to his famous rivals of the German air force. He did not share the feeling of admiration and terror for the von Richthofen Circus that these champions thought they inspired. Frequently Bishop sailed over their very aerodrome and sat tranquilly above them single-handed, daring them to come aloft in any number and try their luck. More frequently he met them in the sky and vainly manoeuvred about them, looking for an opening for an attack which they were too skilful to permit and totally unable to surprise out of their watchful antagonist.

Bishop's Nieuport was a faster climbing machine than the fighting Albatross flown by the German champions. When caught with a gun jam the Britisher, instead of flying homewards with the pack at his heels, invariably climbed over their heads and proceeded to free the jam and manoeuvre from his superior height for another attack.

It is impossible to ignore the very large element of luck which attended the fighting career of Captain Bishop and the extent to which his heedless-determination to overawe his opponent served to win him his victories. Bravery, skill, judgment, and experience he utilized to a marvellous degree. His stupendous score of successes and his numberless encounters with the best air fighters of the enemy testify to Bishop's ability. But his impatience, his lack of caution, and his supreme confidence in himself often subjected him to risks from which only his lucky star could save him.

Time and time again he returned from his expeditions with his aeroplane riddled with bullet holes, his engine out of commission, and shrapnel holes through his wings. Frequent engine failures far back in Hunland threatened to drop him a rich prize into the hands of the enemy, when by some miracle his engine recovered its senses and carried him home.

One of the most brilliant stunts Bishop ever carried out was a solo attack on an enemy aerodrome some fifteen miles within the German lines one early morning in June, 1917. Single-handed and alone, Captain Bishop flew over at daylight and hung around the aerodrome until the enemy airmen awoke and prepared their machines for the day's work. Becoming restless at their laziness, Bishop finally flew down and sprayed their barracks with machine-gun bullets. This had the desired effect. In a few minutes machine guns, anti-aircraft guns, and aeroplanes were directed at him.

Ignoring the former, Bishop continued circling a short distance overhead, tempting his numerous enemies to come up and get him. Soon the first volunteer was ready. Bishop watched him leave the ground, then with one swoop he was upon him and nailed him with the first shot. The Boche crashed on his own field just as another of his comrades left the ground. This one shared the same fate. Another and then another came up, and half a dozen more were ready to support their attack on so audacious an intruder.

Bishop had left before breakfast and was growing hungry. Moreover his ammunition was nearly exhausted

Swooping down upon the nearest enemy, he shot into him with such effect that the Albatross slipped sideways and fell into the trees. Then continuing his straightaway course, the intrepid Britisher flew home and sat down to his breakfast. He had brought down three enemy machines before breakfast, but being unwitnessed they could only be added to that invisible score which without doubt would more than double the official number of seventy-two victories that is now credited to this heroic Canadian of the Victoria Cross—Colonel William A. Bishop.

Captain J. L. Trollope

Captain J. L. Trollope of the Royal Flying Corps, who was reported missing on March 28, 1918, and later was heard from in a German detention camp where he was under medical attention for slight wounds received in combat, established a world's record a few days before his disappearance in shooting down six enemy aeroplanes on one day's hunt. Lieutenant René Fonck of France duplicated this feat of six victories on May 8, 1918. The account of Trollope's extraordinary performance was given out with the subsequent news of his capture.

Captain Trollope was out with a formation of British aeroplanes when they saw four German planes trying to interfere with the investigations of some British observing machines. Captain Trollope dived into the four, caught one of them by surprise, and with the first rounds from his machine gun sent the first in pieces to the ground. The other three made good their escape.

Five minutes later he saw two enemy two-seaters far below him and alone dived down upon them, engaging them one after the other. Both dashed to earth within one minute, and so near the ground were they that their bursting into fragments was clearly visible.

The victor climbed up to rejoin his formation which was in the thick of another *mêlée* far above him. He took a hand in this fight, shot away all his ammunition, and was forced to return to his aerodrome to replenish it. Three victories were thus won in one flight.

Starting aloft again with fresh ammunition, the captain saw a distant formation of three enemy aeroplanes crossing his lines. He got between the sun and the last of the enemy machines, darted in with complete surprise, which is half the victory, but just as he was sure of his victim his gun jammed and he had to withdraw while he freed the jam.

This accomplished he returned, taking on another of the enemies, and attacking him point-blank from the front, sent him on his last chute to a point back of the British lines. The fourth!

Without waiting to see the end of his last enemy, Trollope opened up his throttle and pursued the nearest of the survivors. Overtaking him less than a mile away he poured bullets into him as he approached. The German caught on fire and fell ablaze within his own lines. The fifth!

Trollope turned home quite satisfied with his day's work. But on his way he observed a combat going on below him between a British two-seater and an enemy scout. He descended upon them, darted upon the enemy fighting plane, and with the first round sent him down spinning. He returned to camp to find all his victories had been witnessed by other pilots of his squadron.

Captain Noel William Ward Webb

Captain Noel William Ward Webb, M. C. (and bar), Flight Commander, R. F. C., reported missing on August 16, 1917, and since reported killed, received a commission in the R. F. C. in March, 1916, obtained his wings in June, and on July 4th went to the front.

On July 19th he brought down his first Fokker, and by September 17th he had brought down his third German machine; it was a Fokker monoplane this time.

He was appointed Flight Commander (temporary Captain) in October, 1916, and shortly after received the M. C. for a service performed under conditions so perilous that all the officers of his squadron shook hands with him and his observer at their departure, never expecting to see them again. His description of this expedition is dated September 2, 1916:

> Yesterday the clouds were very low, only about 3500 feet, and in the afternoon a notice came round asking for volunteers to go out and strafe Hun kite balloons. Of course, I offered, and as Flight Commanders and a married man were the only other ones to offer, I got the job.
>
> Our orders were to cross over in the clouds; if we saw any German balloons, drop down and strafe them, then get into the clouds again and come back.
>
> We started off, and when we got near the lines I saw three German balloons up, so I got into the clouds and went over. I went on for as long as I thought would get us over them, and then came down.
>
> Unfortunately, I had gone a bit too far, and was quite a long way back from the lines. However, we turned round, and there were the balloons, about two miles away. We had then dropped to 2000 feet, and could see everything quite plainly. We passed over one town and could hear them firing at us with machine-gun and rifle fire.
>
> Well, we chased on to the balloon, firing hard, and came to within about fifty yards of the first, and I could see the fabric sort of quiver as each bullet hit it. Of course, they were pulling it down the whole time, and when it got too low we moved off to the next. They had been Archieing us, and the shells were bursting almost on us the whole time; they could not have been nearer without hitting us, and they were using machine-gun fire as well. I was swerving and dodging for all I was worth. Well, we got to the other balloon, and got within under 50 yards of it, firing like anything, and they pulled that down as well. Unfortunately, neither of them caught fire. I then tried

twice to climb back into the clouds, but each time I got straight for climbing they Archied us so badly that I had to give it up. So, finally, I made a dash for the lines. It was a good long way to go, and they Archied and machine-gunned us the whole way, and as we crossed the trenches at 1000 feet we had a pretty hot time of it.

When we got well over, I had a look back, and saw that both the balloons were up again, though not so high as before, and I was going back to repeat the performance, when I saw that one of my petrol tanks had been hit, and the petrol had all leaked out. We found afterwards that the other one had been hit in two places, but neither shot had pierced it. If either had, I should be in Germany now. Well, after that, I went home, and we found that, besides the petrol tank, one strut had been smashed to bits by Archie, and the planes were absolutely riddled with bullets.

Early in October Captain Webb was invalided home, and on recovery was posted to a squadron in England, where he acted as instructor and during the latter part of the time as Squadron Commander. On June 21, 1917, he returned to France to a Scout Squadron, and soon after his arrival won a bar to his M. C., with the following exploit:

Out alone in a single-seater machine on a practice flight he saw "white Archie" bursting a short distance away and above him. He climbed up towards it, and found at 17,000 feet an enemy two-seater and immediately engaged it in fight. He wounded the observer, but the pilot continued the combat until he was wounded himself, upon which he made for earth, followed by Captain Webb. They landed together on a British aerodrome, and as a memento of the occasion he was permitted to retain the clock from the German machine. This was subsequently mounted in the boss of his propeller, which had been shot through during the fight.

Captain Webb had proved himself a brilliant pilot, and had brought down twelve enemy machines. On August 16th, when leading his flight on patrol, he encountered a large formation of enemy machines, and was last seen diving on two hostile aircraft.

Through news obtained from Geneva, it appears he was killed the same day, a heroic ending to a brilliant career.

Major James Byford McCudden

The Royal Flying Corps suffered a melancholy loss on July 9, 1918, when Major McCudden, then the highest ranking Ace in the world in active service, crashed to the ground near a small village in Northern France and was killed. He had just flown his machine across the Channel from Scotland, where he had been spending a short leave, and was on his way to the front to take over his new command. Forced to land in strange ground through engine trouble, McCudden made his repairs and again set out. He had risen but a few yards from the ground when something went wrong with his aeroplane and the valiant conqueror of fifty-eight German airmen crashed down to his death.

Since the death of the German champion on April 21, 1918, McCudden had held the world's championship in his specialty of air duelling. Bishop passed his lead while McCudden was absent from the front on furlough and topped his rival with a score of seventy-two.

The story of James McCudden's life somewhat resembles that of the American Raoul Lufbery, and illustrates the fact that fame and honours are won not alone by the university graduate but by any aspirant who determines to seize them.

McCudden's father was a warrant officer in the Royal Engineers. His mother was Scottish. He was born in the barracks at Chatham in March, 1895, and entered the British army as a bugler when he was but fifteen years of age.

When the first British Expeditionary force went to France young McCudden enlisted as a private. During the retreat from Mons his ability as a mechanic was pressed into the service of one of the British aviators, and a week later he began flying over the front as an observer.

His remarkable coolness and good judgment recommended him to his aviator friends, and the accuracy and intuition revealed in his reports as an observer quickly brought him the coveted permission to learn flying. From sergeant he became lieutenant, and once launched into air in his own fighting plane he immediately began to pile up his victories.

Cool and precise in his manoeuvres and a sure shot, the young lieutenant became invincible. He was never wounded despite the furious combats which ensued and which at the end netted him so prodigious a score of victories. On two occasions McCudden shot down four enemy aeroplanes while alone on his hunt back of the German lines. Three combats were fought with Immelman without result, as both airmen were too clever to give the other an opening.

He became captain of a fighting squadron, and under his direction and by reason of his extraordinary protection of the fledglings under his charge, this squadron piled up some two hundred victories in eleven months.

One day in the course of his patrol McCudden attacked a two-seater Albatross which made but a feeble attempt at defence. He dived in to deliver the *coup-de-grâce* when, to his surprise, he saw the observer raise his two hands in surrender. Motioning the German pilot to direct his course towards the British aerodrome McCudden dropped in behind and exulted within him-self at the surprise his homecoming with a captured aeroplane would occasion his comrades. This feat of capturing an enemy in midair and bringing him home as a prize was an exploit frequently contemplated but seldom realized.

As McCudden was happily grinning to himself, he suddenly perceived a stream of flaming bullets passing his head from the rear of the Boche machine. The treacherous Huns had repented their surrender and were trying to shoot down their captor.

In a flash McCudden was beneath them and with one burst from his Lewis gun the Albatross plunged sideways and began to tail-spin. With rage and disappointment McCudden followed the doomed aeroplane down until he saw his coveted prize crash into pieces just back of the German trenches.

Of slight build, democratic and amiable in disposition, and always a fastidious dresser, this famous airman was popular both with his comrades and with his superiors.

"This officer is considered," said the official *London Gazette*, "by the record he has made, by his fearlessness and by the great service he has rendered to his country, deserving of the very highest honour."

This eulogium was occasioned by the feat above referred to in which this boy of twenty-two had in one hour and thirty minutes totally destroyed four German aeroplanes and their crews—costing Germany some $250,000, as the value of aeroplanes and trained pilots is computed for this hour and a half of young McCudden's time.

Already possessed of the Distinguished Service Order, a bar to the same, the *Croix de Guerre*, the Military Cross, a bar to the M. C., and the Military Medal, James Byford McCudden, the bugler boy, received from his King as a last reward the highest mark of valour and distinction that a mighty nation can confer—the Victoria Cross.

This glorious citation accompanied it:

> As a patrol leader he has at all times shown the utmost gallantry and skill not only in the manner in which he has attacked and destroyed the enemy but in the way he has during several fights *protected the newer members of his flight*,[1] thus keeping their casualties down to a minimum.

Truly it calls for courage to bring down fifty-eight armed aeroplanes. But that courage becomes conspicuous and deserving of the very highest honour when it includes shielding from danger the inexperienced fellows who are devotedly following their daring leader.

Captain Philip F. Fullard

With the retirement of Bishop and the death of McCudden

---

1. The italics are the author's.

Philip F. Fullard, the intrepid leader of Squadron Number 1, became the ranking Ace of the British Air Force. On December 18, 1917, he shot down his forty-eighth enemy aeroplane and in the afternoon of the same day severely fractured his leg in a game of football on his own aerodrome, and was invalided back to Blighty.

Born at Hatfield in 1897, Fullard was educated at Norwich Grammar School; he was a brilliant student and stood well among the leaders in his class. Slight and delicate in figure and of excessive modesty Philip Fullard would not have been selected at the beginning of the war as a likely candidate for the first position in his country's air service.

He was offered a commission in an Irish regiment, but having set his heart on the aeroplane service, he declined it and betook himself to a flying school. Here he passed his tests, secured a commission, and was sent to the front in April, 1917. In nine months this boy of twenty made the almost incredible record of forty-eight enemy aeroplanes destroyed!

Before breakfast one morning Fullard and a comrade shot down seven aeroplanes, of which Fullard got three. For three months he worked with a flight of six pilots which he led, and during this period they brought down more German machines than any other squadron in France—and themselves suffered but a single casualty. His unit had accounted for two hundred enemy machines up to October 1st, and at the time of his unfortunate accident the number had passed two hundred and fifty.

On one occasion his goggles were shot away by a German scout, and his machine was set afire, but with cool judgment this great airman returned to his own lines for a safe landing.

Early in May, one month after his appearance in a fighting aeroplane, Fullard shot down four enemies, and the following morning three more. The extraordinary ease with which this wonderful pilot won his successes seems almost miraculous. Conscious of his superiority Fullard avowed that when he attacked an isolated aeroplane he felt that he was committing murder. He admitted no risk to himself, and the stupid manoeuvres of the enemy to escape his certain aim scarcely interested and never delayed him.

On another occasion however Fullard had cause to alter his opinion. The unknown antagonist that he had chosen for a victim displayed such unusual tactics that the young Englishman came off a bad second, much to his disgust and alarm. He escaped gladly to his aerodrome and announced seriously to his mechanics, "I just found a Boche better than me." This lapse of grammar in the brilliant schoolboy might be attributed to the depression of the moment, but more likely it originated in the retelling by the stunned mechanic.

His comrades of the squadron which he commands adore their captain and follow closely in his wake. One by one Fullard has received the list of decorations which Great Britain confers upon her most distinguished soldiers, and among the numerous citations which his gallant victories evoked the following was selected, engraved upon a plaque and placed in his bedroom by one of his devoted comrades:

In numberless occasions he has shown the greatest courage and absolute contempt for danger, invariably attacking enemy aeroplanes wherever he finds them; he officially destroyed eight enemy machines in one period of ten days. His determination and his gallant spirit in attack have always brought disaster to the enemy.

Captain Andrew Edward McKeever

Captain Andrew Edward McKeever, of the Royal Air Force, is of Irish-Scotch descent and, like Bishop, is a Canadian. McKeever was born on August 21, 1895, at Listowell, Ontario, Canada.

He first entered the war as a member of the Queen's Own Rifle Regiment in Toronto, but secured his transfer to the Flying Corps and began his training at the School for Military Aeronautics at Oxford, England, in January, 1917. Early in March he received his first actual flying instruction at Northold, and the latter part of April he graduated as a pilot at Honslow.

With the unusual distinction of having completed his training without a single smash McKeever, who had already passed his gunnery tests with credit, was selected for service in France on May 15, 1917, when an order came for one pilot who was needed to fill a vacancy in an aviation camp back of the lines.

On May 29th the future Ace received his chance. The Photographing Squadron # ... was in need of a pilot. McKeever was at once sent to the aerodrome. He was to fly a two-seater Bristol Fighter and take photographs of enemy positions with some twenty other pilots who formed the membership of this unit.

The quality of this young flier may be judged from the extraordinary record he made in air duelling while part of this photographing squadron. In five months McKeever shot down and destroyed twenty-nine enemy aeroplanes. During this same period (from June to November) his gunner, who sat behind him in the two-seater machine, destroyed eleven more Hun machines. One gunner, L. F. Powell, shot down eight of these eleven. Powell subsequently quitted his position as gunner and was sent to flying school to perfect himself in the piloting of a fighting machine.

Andrew McKeever brought down his first Hun on June 20, 1917, and his second fell the following day. On the 26th and 27th he accounted for his third and fourth victims.

Three Germans crashed to earth from his bullets on one day, July 10th, and twice he repeated this triple performance of three-in-one-day, on September 28th and on November 30th.

Captain McKeever's story of this last encounter is extremely interesting and is almost unique in the annals of aviation. Its narration had to be drawn from him piecemeal. This boyish Canadian captain with the Distinguished Service Order on his breast is not reluctant to talk about his exploits in the air; in fact, no other topic is so fascinating to him as aviation. But he is absolutely without conceit when talking about his adventures over German lines, and his utter absence of fear and the fact of his exceptional superiority over his fellow pilots in combat does not seem to him to be a matter of self-congratulation or of wonder.

Hence the amusing aspect of being caught alone by nine Hun aeroplanes when sixty miles from home arouses more glee in him than do the circumstances of his heroic and successful combat against such desperate odds.

McKeever is frank and generous in his conversation and manner. Fastidious in habits and in dress, keenly alert in mind and in movement he impresses one with an efficiency that is becoming typical of every great air duellist.

"I do not drink and I quit smoking," he told me, "because I thought I could get along in this business better without it." Captain McKeever has on more than one occasion found himself absolutely alone in the midst of an attacking squad of eight or nine German aeroplanes—a squad through which he has each time fought his way to safety and at the same time incidentally brought down two or three of those antagonists who sought to bar his road. In such positions a pilot undoubtedly needs all his faculties sharp and true. McKeever's brilliant successes, coupled with the fact that he has never received a wound in the air, indicate that his policy of avoiding stimulants while engaged in this delicate "business" may be worth imitating.

The Bristol Fighter of 1917 flies at a speed of one hundred and thirty miles per hour. At high altitudes of twelve thousand or fifteen thousand feet it can be manoeuvred by a skilful pilot with an agility and speed unequalled by the best single-seater fighting aeroplane of the Huns. It has in fact one more point of superiority over the German chasing machine. The Bristol carries a gunner in the rear seat who covers the sides, top and rear of the tail, while the pilot aims his forward machine gun at any enemy target ahead.

Thus the Bristol, while primarily a reconnaissance machine and though used by Captain McKeever mainly in photographic work, still is a formidable fighter. These observations are necessary to an understanding of the story of McKeever's "big show" which he unwittingly entered five miles beyond the enemy's lines on the morning of November 30, 1917. Surprised by nine enemy aeroplanes while he was alone, McKeever downed three of them single-handed, his 27th, 28th and 29th victories, while Powell, his gunner, destroyed a fourth and shot down a fifth in a badly damaged condition.

"Early that morning," began Captain McKeever, "the commanding officer called for a volunteer to do a special reconnaissance sixty miles south of the aerodrome where a big battle was raging. It was a wet rainy day, and clouds hung down to within three hundred feet of the ground over the aerodrome. No aeroplanes would be out on such a day, and we thought it would be useless to try to see any important positions in such weather. But somebody had to go; it was ordered from Headquarters, so I volunteered and got the job.

"I called my gunner and we set off in the rain. We went up through the thick clouds, and at about eight thousand feet we burst through and came out into the warm sun. There I set my course by compass and kept on south for about sixty miles over the clouds until I judged we were over the spot we wanted.

"As I emerged below the cloud ceiling, I found they were much higher up here than at the aerodrome. The weather had cleared at this particular point, the rain had stopped and the clouds were floating at about fifteen hundred feet above ground. All of which goes to show that you can't always judge of the reasons for orders that are sometimes sent you.

"We covered our area thoroughly and finished the reconnaissance without seeing another aeroplane in the sky. I kept so near the ceiling that even the Hun batteries failed to spot us. We were six miles inside Hunland. Sometimes we got down to about twelve hundred feet, but not lower.

"We had just finished our observing when I noticed a big explosion followed by a huge blaze of fire about five miles to the south. The British trenches ran north and south along here, and the blaze was the same distance inside

Hunland as I then was. I knew at once that a British shell had struck an ammunition dump of the Huns and set it afire. As I got nearer the spot I saw several thousand German soldiers running about the stack of burning material trying to remove as much of it as possible to prevent the spreading of the fire.

"We went down low and took a good look at the thing. And then it occurred to me that it would be a good stunt to fly around close to the ground and sprinkle a few belts of bullets among the Huns who were working about the pile. This usually has the effect of 'putting their wind up' and taking all the heart out of the poor Hun.

"I turned around to notify Powell to get ready for action when all of a sudden I saw four Hun machines coming right at us. They were not one hundred yards away from my right wing. And five more were coming at us from back of my tail. Two of the latter group were the two-seater type and were painted a bright red. There were nine of them, all nicely grouped to prevent my turning back towards our own lines. And I was only a thousand feet up.

"Instead of turning to the left to escape them I instantly whirled to the right into the midst of the four coming at my right wing.

"The first one passed over me, not expecting me to turn so quickly. The second Hun was smack in front of me. Why we didn't collide I could never explain, but even while I was expecting a collision I let him have a burst of about ten rounds and zoomed up over him. He fortunately went down. I saw him somersault in a mass of flames.

"Inside the following second I let go another burst of a few bullets at the next machine which was coming at me head on. He staggered a bit in the air, then went over sideways instantly and fluttered down a total wreck to the ground. At the same time my gunner, Powell, made another hit, and the last of the four fell. The whole round was over in half a minute, and three Hun machines were actually falling through the air at the same moment. The first one which had passed over us had joined the five at our rear.

"Instead of flying north as they expected I flew on deeper into the German lines. When they discovered I had no intention of running away from them, they spread out and came for me again. Again I turned to meet them, and this time I got my sights on one of the bright red two-seaters and dropped him with one burst. As we went through Powell riddled another single-seater so badly the Hun had to glide away in a damaged condition.

"Five of the nine Huns were thus accounted for, but the others had me in an uncomfortable position after my last dive through them. They all came down on me, firing as they came. I wondered why Powell didn't defend our rear, and I glanced over my shoulder at him.

"Powell's gun had been hit and was completely out of business. He simply stared back at me with the air of a man who thinks it's all over. I turned back and made one more 'about face' at the pursuers. Then I got my surprise.

"The first bead I got on a Hun I fully expected to see him drop. I had him dead in my sights. I pressed the trigger-and nothing happened! My gun had been hit almost exactly like Powell's in their last firing bee. Later I found the C spring had been broken.

"The surviving Huns were shooting at me from every side. One bullet cut through my flying boot and grazed my leg. That was the nearest to a wound I ever got.

"Without looking around I pulled over my stick and my aeroplane fell on to her wing and dropped straight towards the ground in a side slip. We fell like a stone, giving the Huns the impression that their last volley had been a winner. I had no idea we were so low down when I began the drop, and I almost overdid it. I passed some treetops. That looked bad. I flattened out and found we were not twenty feet above the ground!

"The enemy aeroplanes were directly over me but they had been completely taken in. I suppose I was under their floor where they could not see me, and besides they were certain I had crashed. When I picked up again I immediately turned south instead of towards home, and if they took pains to watch for me at all they would have looked in the other direction.

"The trees behind which I had fallen bordered a main highway running north and south. I flew for five miles down this road behind the trees. Finally when I was satisfied they had not suspected my ruse I zoomed over the trees, turned west and made for our own lines.

"We crossed a big encampment of the Huns the other side of the trees and it was a calamity not to have a gun aboard that was working. The Huns let us have it with rules and machine guns and *minenwerfers* but we were too low to give them time to aim. I have always noticed that their bullets cut the air at least thirty to forty feet behind my tail under such circumstances. Frequently they fire tracer bullets and one can see them go past.

"Old Powell had lost his sense of direction completely with all this manoeuvring after our fall behind the trees. As we were crossing the Hun camp he tapped me on the shoulder and yelled: 'We are still over the Huns. They are shooting at us.'

"I waved my hand to him that it was all right and pointed my hand towards our trenches which were dead ahead. And just as I did so I noticed a superb new Hun aeroplane sitting in No Man's Land very close to the British trenches. I learned later that McCudden had shot it down not half an hour before. It hadn't yet been destroyed by the artillery of either side. It had not even been credited to McCudden, but the report we made of it when we got in soon settled that.

"When I reached my aerodrome (and the shells of the Huns followed us for five miles inside our lines), I found that the report of my downfall had preceded me. British officers had seen me drop behind the trees and hadn't seen me pick up and fly south. They knew who I was, and they telephoned I had fallen in German lines. But the old bus brought us safely in with four more victories to her credit besides the one which Powell had crippled. All of them had been witnessed by our officers back of the trenches."

It was McKeever's twenty-ninth accredited success. On December 4, 1917, he shot down a German observation balloon for a lark and gained his thirtieth victory.

Since the retirement of Bishop to the Air Board of Great Britain and the lamentable death through accident of McCudden, Captain Andrew Edward McKeever, wearer of the Distinguished Service Order and the Military Cross with Bar, stands second only to Captain Philip Fullard among the active Aces of the Royal Air Force. And if one computes the amount of tune in the air in connection with the number of victories secured, McKeever's record is absolutely unique.

Flight Commander C. P. O. Bartlett

Flight Commander C. P. O. Bartlett, of the Royal Naval Air Force of Great Britain, won a bar to his Distinguished Service Cross on March 28, 1918, by one of the most remarkable manoeuvres that has been recorded during this furious war in the air.

Returning from a distant bombing raid in the late afternoon of this day Commander Bartlett suddenly found himself hemmed in by three fast triplanes of the enemy air force. He was at a height of 2500 feet and was piloting a heavy two-seater machine that was wholly outclassed by the swift fighting machines that circled around him.

While manoeuvring warily about with an eye upon each of the swooping enemies he saw five more German fighting planes coming in to assist in his obsequies. Suddenly changing his tactics he boldly dashed into the newcomers, and with his first shots from his machine gun he had the satisfaction of seeing one of them fall to the ground badly hit. His passenger at the same time brought down another of the five and sent it down out of control with a burst from the rear gun.

The next instant Commander Bartlett observed two of the German triplanes diving steeply down upon him from a great height. They were on opposite sides of his machine and were hurling themselves down on converging lines, firing ahead as they dived.

With cool, calculating precision Bartlett maintained his course until the last necessary fraction of a second, then suddenly he turned his machine over into a quick side slip. The two pursuers dashed headlong into each other; their wings interlocked as the two triplanes met and embraced. In one whirling mass they fell until they struck the ground with a crash. As Commander Bartlett passed over the spot on his way home, he saw the flames destroying the last vestiges of the wreckage of the two triplanes. The others had disappeared.

Lieutenant Alan Arnett McLeod, Royal Air Force

The priceless Victoria Cross was never more fittingly bestowed than when on May 1, 1918, the King was graciously pleased to confer this honour upon Second Lieutenant Alan Arnett McLeod, in recognition of the following outstanding performance.

While flying with Lieutenant A. W. Hammond as his observer Pilot McLeod passed over the lines to attack with bombs and gunfire the massed formations of German troops pressing towards Amiens. At a height of 5000 feet his machine was suddenly set upon by eight fast fighting planes of the enemy. They surrounded the heavier aeroplane, diving into it from all sides and subjecting it to a murderous fire from their forward machine guns.

By manoeuvring with almost incredible skill McLeod evaded them time after time. Never forgetful of the opportunity to destroy one of his more agile antagonists the pilot during each attack placed his own machine to such good advantage that his gunner, Hammond, succeeded in shooting down three of the attacking party, one after the other. The remaining five circled about them with more caution, awaiting an opening for another attack on the Britishers with less risk to themselves.

At this juncture Hammond discovered that his pilot lay swooning in his seat. McLeod had been struck five times during the combat!

Another rush from the enemy came, and another volley poured through the British machine. Instantaneously a burst of flame swept back from their engine. A bullet had penetrated the fuel tank, and their aeroplane was ablaze 3000 feet above ground!

Keeping his gaze rearward where he covered the swooping Boches with his machine gun, the doomed gunner waited for the flames to reach him. Finally, looking to the front, he discovered that McLeod, wounded and suffering as he was, had crawled from his seat and was balancing his weight on the left-hand lower plane, thus side-slipping his aeroplane so that the flames were fanned by the wind away from the gunner. Thus Hammond was enabled to devote his attention to the pursuers behind him who did not leave off shooting until within a few hundred feet of the ground. The British aeroplane crashed a blazing wreck in No Man's Land.

Hammond too had been wounded six times during this horrible descent. With the last crash of the machine Hammond was flung unconscious to earth, almost within the grasp of the enemy trench soldiers, part of the burning wreckage on top of his body.

McLeod, who had suffered no further injury at the landing, threw himself into the midst of the fire and dragged his unconscious companion away. The German trenches opened up a hailstorm of bullets upon the gallant pair, as McLeod sublimely staggered towards his own lines with his burden. Again he was wounded and sent to the ground, but he recovered his feet and with a last heroic plunge he dragged Hammond to the top of the British parapet and fell down into the trenches, with Lieutenant Hammond on top of him.

When the Tommies picked them up both airmen were still unconscious from exhaustion and loss of blood. They were removed to the rear and later to London, where McLeod received his Victoria Cross and Lieutenant Hammond, the gunner, was rewarded for his share in the exploit by the Military Cross.

Lieutenant C. P. O. Tadmow of the Royal Air Service was given the Conspicuous Gallantry Medal in July, 1917, for a somewhat similar exploit in air. During a combat his two-seater aeroplane received a bullet hole in the radiator, and he perceived his engine would soon overheat and stall, dropping him a prisoner in Hunland. With great bravery he climbed out on to the front wing, steadying himself with one hand by gripping the hot metal of the engine, while with the other he laboriously plugged up the hole in the radiator.

For fifteen minutes he remained in this perilous position while his machine was rushing through the sky 6000 feet above ground. Fortunately he had shaken off his enemy and was not interrupted in his fearful task. His observer directed the machine until Lieutenant Tadmow, with scorched and bleeding hands, climbed back to his seat and succeeded in landing the aeroplane within his own lines.

The British authorities do not publish the names and scores of their Aces, and it is only upon the occasion of the decoration of these heroes with the Distinguished Service Cross or some other medal that the number of their victories is made public. For this reason the list of British Aces in the Appendix is far from complete.

In this British list twenty-five pilots have been mentioned in *communiqués* as having brought down "many" enemy aeroplanes. Estimating this "many" as at least five victories (for the *communiqués* make a distinction between "many" and "several") twenty-five pilots have accounted for one hundred and twenty-five enemy aeroplanes, and probably more.

With the fifty-three British Aces named who have a total score of six hundred and thirteen enemy aeroplanes destroyed, and the twenty-five additional fighting pilots who are officially credited with "many", Great Britain has Today at least seventy-eight living Aces of aviation. Germany at present writing has but thirty-seven.

Chapter 8

René Fonck

The most polished aerial duellist the world has ever seen is Lieutenant René Fonck of Spad 3, conqueror of fifty-nine enemy airmen up to July 15, 1918.

René Fonck was born at Saulcy-sur-Meurthe in the Vosges, March 27, 1894. He was preparing to pass his examinations for mechanical engineer when smitten with a passion for aviation; he decided to qualify for his pilot's license so that he could go into the aero-nautical branch of the military service. He had made his first trial flight on a Blériot before war was declared.

A young conscript of the class of 1914, Fonck was called to the colours August 22, 1914, and sent to the second group of aviation at Dijon. He had been here less than a month when, without any reason being given, he was transferred to Epinal to finish his training in the 11th Engineer Corps then stationed there. When this was completed he returned to his former branch and was sent to Saint-Cyr as pupil-pilot on a Caudron. His preparation finished he passed his examinations for a commission at Crotoy in April, 1915.

He was then assigned to Escadrille C. 47 which he joined at the front on June 15, 1916. He had at last attained his great desire—he was placed in a squadron on the Vosges front near his native heath, where he knew every stick and stone. He was delighted to find himself detailed for aerial photograph work and thus he was occupied in the operations at Metzeral and afterwards at Linge.

His first citation from the aeronautical division of his army was expressed thus:

> Fonck (René), Corporal pilot in Escadrille C. 47 and Wiest (Georges), Sub-Lieutenant Observer. Being given the mission to discover the enemy batteries which embarrassed our attacks went out in spite of the most unfavourable atmospheric conditions, flying low above the enemy to gain the desired information, in spite of a terrific fire by which their machine was riddled with bullets.

Escadrille C..47 was then sent to Champagne to prepare for the September offensive. During the attack it formed a liaison with the infantry. This unity of action between infantry and airmen was inaugurated there. Fonck had here the perilous distinction of being brought down by fire from the ground, his machine made literally a sieve, but he succeeded in getting out of this bad plight uninjured.

On November 25, 1915, following this offensive, Fonck was cited in the order of the army with several of his comrades in the *escadrille*.

> Fonck (René), Sergeant pilot of Escadrille 47. Has rendered the most important services during the period of preparation, flying daily for reconnoitring and regulating artillery fire; on the days of September 25 and 26, 1915, he succeeded in the service of surveillance in spite of the most unfavourable atmospheric conditions and despite the greatest dangers.

On the Oise, where the C. 47 was sent shortly after, each one of his reconnoitring expeditions was the occasion of numerous and bitter combats. He bravely confronted these dangers during seven consecutive months. The persistent bravery of the pilots had been affirmed for a long time and had been proclaimed in glowing citations issued in Alsace and Champagne; their experience and skill were now to receive official commendation. Fonck among them was credited with an exceptional mastery of his profession. He gave proof of this mastery on August 6, 1916, in the region of Moyenville, where he accomplished a feat that earned for him the Military Medal, which his citation recounts thus:

> Fonck (René Paul). Adjutant pilot of Escadrille C. 47. Remarkable pilot, brave, skilful, and alert, having already taken part in a large number of aerial battles. August 6, 1916, he resolutely attacked two enemy aeroplanes strongly armed. He gave chase to one and by a series of bold and skilful manoeuvres compelled it to come down intact within our lines. (Already twice cited in orders.)

What the citation does not mention was that there had been no combat. The German aeroplane had been continually out-manoeuvred by Fonck and he kept it in such a position that it was impossible for it to use its guns, it had to dodge and descend and finally save itself by making a landing within our lines. All this occurred without Fonck or Lieutenant Thiberge, his observer, firing a single shot from their machine guns. The enemy aeroplane was a Rumpler of one of the latest models. It was intact, and its passengers uninjured. At 10.30 in the morning they were prisoners.

The captured observer, an officer, fumed with impotent rage. He had in his pocket a permission for leave that afternoon at two o'clock!

The German pilot questioned by Commander du Peuty could only say:

"I was outmanoeuvred in such a way that I could do nothing. My adversary pressed me, kept always the mastery over me; no matter what I did he kept me continually at his mercy. I could do nothing but come down."

One must admit that such a victory merited the Military Medal.

The *escadrille* was sent immediately after this to the region of the Somme. Here battles were thick, and the French and English gave each other mutual aid. It was at the Somme that Fonck first came to the attention of the Allies who later accorded him the signal honour of bestowing upon him two military decorations.

At the end of the year 1916 Escadrille C. 47 returned to the Vosges to prepare a new attack in the region of Linge. On March 17, 1917, in the course of a photographic mission, Fonck was attacked by a group of Boche aeroplanes. After a quarter of an hour's fighting he succeeded in bringing one down in flames and putting the rest to flight. He was cited in an order of the army March 30, 1917, in these terms:

> Fonck (René), Adjutant-chief, pilot of Escadrille C. 47. Pilot remarkable for his skill and bravery.
> March 17, 1917, in the course of a photographic mission he gave combat to a large group of the enemy chasers and brought one down in his lines.

As a result of this second victory equally glorious with the first, Fonck, besides his fourth citation, received the reward that he desired most of all: he was detailed to make part of a fighting group. And then, after a few hours' flying on a Nieuport, he was intrusted with the most perfect French fighting machine, the Spad, which was at that time the aeroplane of the privileged few. Fonck made his first appearance on a Spad in N. 103.

Fonck at that time had nearly six hundred hours of flying in the army on a Caudron; four citations, the Military Medal and one British decoration. Two enemy aeroplanes brought down was his official score. From a plain soldier he had been successively promoted to corporal, sergeant, adjutant, and chief adjutant. He was then twenty-three years old.

Fonck arrived at the N. 103 at the very beginning of the month of May. The 5th of May he brought down his third aeroplane, his first victim on a fighting plane.

Three days after his victory, on May 8th, he had the joy of being decorated with the British Military Medal in the following order:

> H. M. The King of England has been graciously pleased

to confer the following decorations on the soldiers of the French aviation whose names follow, who have distinguished themselves by their bravery during the campaign:

Military Medal: Adjutant pilot Fonck, René, Escadrille C. 47.

Six days after his first victory on a Spad Fonck brought down his second on the 11th of May.

Two days later came a new victory, the fifth, which earned for the young man the following *communiqué* and citation, dated June 7, 1917:

> Fonck (René), Adjutant-chief, pilot of Escadrille N. 103. Chasing pilot of the first order. The 13th of May he brought down at close range an enemy aeroplane. He followed it at close range to 200 meters and in spite of the violent fire from the machine guns below he persevered until he saw it crash on the ground, the 5th aeroplane brought down by this pilot.

From now on Fonck was counted among the "Aces." He had won this title with startling rapidity, three victories in eight days during his first two weeks in a fighting *escadrille*. His citations could not, as had been the case with Dorme, nine months before, keep up with his victories. The seventh citation, that for having brought down his fifth aeroplane, was dated June 7th, the sixth for his fourth victory was dated June 8th, and the fifth for his third Boche was dated June 14th!

After his victory of May 5th, when he had been only a few days with N. 103, Fonck, a debutant on the Spad, was hailed as a pilot of the chase of the first order! He fully justified this praise and enthusiasm of his officers.

June 12, 1917, he brought down within our lines his sixth enemy aeroplane. On the 9th of August, while on a patrol over the enemy lines, he perceived two French aeroplanes of a bombardment *escadrille* engaged in a desperate combat with three enemy machines. It was an unequal fight. Fonck dived into the

LIEUTENANT RENÉ FONCK
The world's most polished air duellist, who has shot down more than 59 enemy aviators, including six in one day.

fight and took on the Boche nearest him. In a few seconds this one fell in flames, and a second, badly out of control, got away for a landing within the German lines.

Now began the period of his grandest exploits. On August 19, 1917, while in enemy territory, Fonck suddenly found his aeroplane surrounded by four of the enemy. He accepted combat. Two minutes later an enemy fell into space. The survivors reformed themselves for another attack.

Fonck regained his superior altitude and again descended upon them. They did not wait his arrival. They knew their master!

The next day, August 20th, Fonck shot down his ninth aeroplane. The following day, August 21st, his tenth; on August 22nd, his eleventh! Three in three consecutive days.

These rapid victories almost discouraged the citation dispenser. Fonck was proposed for the Legion of Honour, and on October 21st he was named *Chevalier*. At that time he had won his eighteenth official victory.

> Fighting pilot of great value, uniting with illustrious bravery exceptional qualities of skill and coolness. Entering the fighting *escadrille* after 500 hours flying in the army corps he has become in a short time one of the best fighting pilots in the French Army. Brought down his 8th, 9th, and 10th enemy aeroplanes on August 20th and 21st, 1917. Already cited seven times and holds the Military Medal.

Five aeroplanes shot down in one month, and four of these in four days! Such a record made Fonck the equal of the greatest champion.

On September 14th Fonck encountered, at 20,000 feet, an enemy flying over Langemarck and quickly returned home with his twelfth official victory. He brought with him irrefutable proof of his success in the form of his antagonist's barograph. The German aviators carry in their machines on all important missions a barograph which registers the height attained during the whole course of their flight. The Boche Ace who had been shot down by Fonck carried an instrument, and its reading by the airmen of Fonck's *escadrille* showed them the whole story of its owner's performances on that morning.

Two small flights of two or three thousand feet were registered at the beginning of the chart, and then came a long bold sweep of the pen which ascended in a steady line from the ground up to 20,000 feet. Here the unlucky airman met René Fonck. A perpendicular down stroke of the ink indicated all too clearly what happened to the aeroplane and its occupant. Before the ground was reached the machine was falling with such speed that the barograph could not keep pace with it and the black line dwindled out some 5000 feet before the crash came. Through some miracle the delicate instrument was not in the least injured by the impact with the ground.

September was for the French pilots a month of mourning. Guynemer disappeared above Poelchapelle on the morning of September 11th. Every pilot at the front vowed to avenge his loss.

On September 15th, Fonck shot down an aeroplane over Zonnebecke. On the 22nd his fourteenth victim fell into the forest of Heuthulst; on the 27th another fell before his bullets in the region of Zonnebecke, but it was not verified. And finally, on September 30th, he found himself face to face with the German pilot, Wissemann, who had written to his family in Cologne that he was the conqueror of Guynemer and after such a victory he need fear no one. He wrote:

> I have now nothing more to fear. I have triumphed over the most terrible of all our enemies. I have brought down Guynemer.

The encounter between Fonck and Wissemann occurred at a very high level. Fonck was at 24,000 feet, leading a French patrol of eight machines, and his companions were several thousand feet below him.

Suddenly Fonck discovered at about his own height a superb two-seater Rumpler. He hurled himself in for the attack. His adversary, contrary to Fonck's expectations, did not take to his heels but accepted the combat. With great courage he stood his ground, only showing his nervousness by opening fire against the Spad when at a very great distance.

This was courage minus judgment. The German overlooked the enormous handicap his heavy Rumpler was under at this high altitude as compared to the lighter Spad. The Spad manoeuvred about him with ease, keeping constantly out of range of the Rumpler's guns until the looked-for opportunity offered itself to the adroit Fonck. With one quick swoop the Frenchman was behind and under his adversary. One burst of only six bullets—and the Boche machine turned over and dropped like a stone.

The passenger was hurled far out of his cockpit as the Rumpler turned over, and his falling body passed within thirty yards of Fonck's machine. More strange still, the falling Rumpler itself fell straight through the midst of Fonck's patrol below and so near one of them that its wings actually grazed it in passing. A few more thousand feet, and its wings folded up from the strain and the wreckage plunged on to the ground.

Fonck soon landed near the *débris*. The pilot was found nearby, a bullet through his head. He was a captain with no papers on his body but with bright new stars on his shoulders indicating that he was but recently promoted.

The passenger, also a captain, was found some yards away. He had three bullets through his body.

A short time later a German *communiqué* stated that Captain Wissemann, recently promoted to a captaincy after his victory over Guynemer, had disappeared September 30th. Since the aeroplane shot down by Fonck was the only machine brought down on September 30th in French lines, there was little question as to the identity of the victim.

It was Fonck's fifteenth victory.

During the following month of October Fonck flew but seldom, owing to the bad weather conditions. His flight diary shows altogether but thirteen and a half hours' flying for the entire month. But these few hours were sufficient to enable him to shoot down ten enemy aeroplanes, of which but four were officially credited to him, the balance falling beyond the vision of witnesses.

On October 17th he shot down two in one flight, one of which fell within the French lines. These constituted his sixteenth and seventeenth official victories. The next day another fell into the forest in flames.

His next citation is dated October 25th.

Incomparable pilot. Continues the series of his wonderful exploits. On September 30th and October 17th, 1917, he shot down his 15th, 16th and 17th adversaries.

On October 21st Fonck shot down his eighteenth official aeroplane in flames in the vicinity of Paschendaele. On the 27th, while on one patrol, he brought down three more, two of which were in flames, but only one of which fell near enough the French lines at Westrosebeke to be recognized. Following this nineteenth official victory René Fonck received his thirteenth citation, dated November 8th.

Fighting pilot whose magnificent fighting qualities are enhanced each day. On October 21st and 27th, 1917, he shot down his 18th and 19th enemy aeroplanes.

Fonck was commissioned Second Lieutenant after his nineteenth victory. His twentieth fell on January 19, 1918, and with it another not officially credited, both in the region of Beaumont.

But to continue the enumeration of Fonck's fifty-nine official victories (and perhaps an additional unwitnessed half a hundred for those actually destroyed by this marvellous duellist of the air) would be but a repetition. Already he has surpassed Georges Guynemer's total of fifty-three aeroplanes shot down. René Fonck has attained the highest score of any French Ace, higher than any British Ace, save Major William A. Bishop, now retired with a total of seventy-two, and higher than any German

Ace with the exception of Captain von Richthofen, killed after having conquered eighty antagonists.

René Fonck is the King of the Air, the highest scored fighting pilot now in active service, and the greatest master of the art that the world has ever seen.

Practically all the honours and decorations that France, Belgium, and Great Britain can confer upon a French aviator are now his. Countless times has he flown to the assistance of a British or Belgian comrade in the thick of a desperate fight and rescued him from almost certain defeat. There seems to be in Fonck a supernatural ability to foresee and forestall the movements and even the thoughts of an antagonist in aerial combat that renders this brilliant airman invulnerable.

He has never been wounded. He has never narrowly escaped death. He has never owed his safety to one of those miracles which so frequently intervene to prolong the fighting days of the men in his profession. His career in short proves that it is humanly possible to so perfect oneself even in this new field of perilous adventure that all opponents are at a disadvantage and are doomed to defeat when they accept combat.

On May 8th this debonair hunter, then a First Lieutenant, flew to his customary position of 20,000 feet above the German lines near Montdidier and within two hours shot down *six German aeroplanes*.

In all, Fonck fired fifty-six shots—an average of less than ten bullets to a machine! The first encounter lasted less than five minutes, at the end of which period the young David withdrew and watched three enemy aircraft descending wing-over-wing to the ground. The first two had been destroyed in less than ten seconds, and the third fell after three or four minutes of manoeuvring for position.

Here ended the first engagement.

After returning to his aerodrome for an hour, Fonck again went aloft over the same country, descended upon a German machine which was engaged in regulating artillery fire for his gunners, and then took on a group of four single-seater Pfalz fighters who were convoying another squadron of five two-seater Albatross towards the French lines.

Fonck selected the rear Pfalz patrol and at the first attack tumbled it to the ground. Evading the fire of the other Huns, he watched for his second opportunity. It came during an attack of the whole group upon him. As they passed him he whirled under the tail of the last one, and in a single burst from his machine gun the enemy dropped.

The German fighters had had enough and quickly disappeared homeward where Fonck was content to let them go. He never attempts too much. Six in one day was quite enough to satisfy this cool-headed Frenchman. It had been duplicated but once—then by the Englishman, Trollope, about two months previously.

Interrogated one day by his friends as to his marvellous exploits in air, Fonck revealed himself and his conclusions on the subject of air fighting in a remarkably clear way.

"Yes," he said, "I have come up quickly. And only four were homologated out of the thirteen I got in October. I have actually destroyed thirty-two up to today, but only nineteen of them are officially credited to me.

"I always fly very high. And that is very trying on one. For that reason I fly little.

"Yes, it is true as they say that I have never been touched. Moreover my aeroplane has never been hit—not one single bullet!"

One must compare Fonck's fighting exploits to those of other great Aces to entirely grasp the significance of this startling statement. After bringing down thirty-two enemy machines in single combat, after flying for upwards of a thousand hours over German lines and engaging in scores of combats which resulted in no victory for either side, this adroit pilot had never received a single bullet *even in the broad wings of his aeroplane.*

Guynemer returned to camp proud of the many wounds his aeroplane declared. His clothing, even his flying helmet, was frequently ripped by enemy bullets. Eight times he was shot down—seven times he miraculously escaped death from the fall.

Dorme, the most finished tactician and best pilot of his day, was nicknamed "the Unpuncturable" by his comrades because he had received but two bullet holes in his machine after bringing down ten enemy airmen. Pinsard, Heurteaux, Nungesser, Lufbery, Deullin,—all the air fighters who survived long enough to amass an imposing score of victories,—all returned upon occasions with their aeroplanes riddled with shot and sometimes suffering from severe wounds themselves.

But the present French Ace of Aces up to April 3, 1918, had never once permitted a bullet of the enemy to come near to him. He had surpassed all records in the quickness with which he took rank among the champions; he never avoided a combat, he never abandoned a field of battle, he never was dismayed by an overwhelming strength of the enemy; yet through his superlative caution, coolness, and judgment in combat he evaded all peril to himself and came home with another victory or two on his tablet.

A character and personality such as Fonck's is deserving of the very closest scrutiny and emulation. His methods which have brought him such stupendous successes should be imitated by every pilot who covets a long fighting career. These methods have proved their superiority over those of any of his opponents, as is duly established by the list of his victories. It is true that Fonck has fought many drawn battles, two or three of which were with the mighty von Richthofen himself, where neither contestant could break through his antagonist's guard. But this very feat of self-defence itself constitutes a trick worth the knowing.

Guynemer disdained the art of self-defence. His method was to hurl himself through the guard of the enemy, risking the bullets which a benignant good fortune diverted from his path. Through sheer audacity and determination Guynemer won victories which even his most devoted friends considered more miraculous than merited.

"Guynemer!" said René Fonck, "I have been astonished for a long time that he has not been killed. An excellent shot he was to be sure. A great fighting pilot—yes. But he drove himself with a mad and blind determination into an attack. He went straight at the enemy with a drawn sword, like the champions of old, Lasalle of the First Empire, Murat, the Maréchal Ney! Without a moment's reflection he would dive straight down a stream of bullets to begin firing himself when he got his enemy at the very end of his gun. He plunged blindly into a group—he plunged into everything.

"His wonderful superiority in shooting, his very blindness to danger often made him successful, but you must remember he was brought down more often than any other Ace. Eight times he was shot down and I cannot count the number of shattered struts, the control wires cut by bullets, the fuselage holes, the rudder bar in sections, the holes in his windshield, in his motor, and through even his flying clothes. His was a method intrepid, superb—but how foolish!"

Pressed further on this point of "method", Fonck continued:

"Why risk this useless audacity when one knows that a combat always prolongs itself through various kinds of manoeuvres during any one of which an opportunity can be seized for a safe attack! The enemy eventually becomes fatigued; sooner or later he loses his nerve—and then he is at one's mercy."

"The great air fighter was Dorme," continued the great Ace with much modesty. "Guynemer himself admired Dorme; and Commander Brocard considered Dorme unequalled. Then we have Deullin; and Madon; and there are others who are coming to the front now from among my young ones of N. 103."

But Fonck's leadership of his beloved N. 103 was ended with the German offensive of March, 1918, and the matchless young champion was called into the fighting unit of the Cigognes which comprises the choicest of the French Knights of the Air. The losses of Guynemer, Dorme, De la Tour, and Auger, the absence of Heurteaux and Pinsard, mending from their wounds, and the retirement of Brocard into the Department of Aviation—these vacancies had sadly decimated the gallant *escadrille* of the Cigognes. Fonck's science and prowess would wondrously strengthen this crippled unit. Parsons and Baylies, the Americans, were likewise added to the Spad 3. With renewed vitality this famous fighting squadron met the Huns' advance upon Soissons. Fonck's priceless aid may be indicated in the score he personally rolled up during the ensuing three months. He shot down officially twenty-four aeroplanes of the enemy.

Fonck's opinion upon the most efficient fighting formation of aeroplane units is well worth considering.

"Early in the war," he says, "individual scouting for enemy aeroplanes was successfully practiced by Pegoud, by Garros, Gilbert, and Navarre. Even in the day of Nungesser and Guynemer this form of hunting met with some success.

"But when the Germans inaugurated group-flying they taught us something. Incidentally they made us pay dear for the lesson. For we had been following an *effete* method of free-lance combat.

"I am by no means in favour of flying over in big groups like those of the von Richthofen squadrons. I prefer to fly in groups of three—a leader and a man behind each wing. I generally fly in this way with two comrades. I like to have other groups of three sufficiently distant so that they will not hinder the manoeuvres of another group yet sufficiently near at hand so that they can understand one another's signals and give help at crucial moments.

"Too big a number may easily prove a peril, especially against a clever and daring enemy capable of practicing the only tactics suitable to the occasion, which is to throw himself into the middle of the mob, paralyzing thus his adversaries who can neither manoeuvre nor fire from fear of injuring each other, whilst he on the contrary retains every facility of action.

"The Boches had one rather bitter experience of this; it was from one of their patrols of seven aeroplanes that I brought down my last three!"

All of which sounds exceedingly simple in the telling, but one can only wonder at the incredible perfection that this youth of twenty-three has attained that permits such mastery over his expert enemies.

It is true that most of Fonck's combats are against five or more enemies, for the German method is to fly only in group formation. While delivering the *coup-de-grâce* to one he must prevent a surprise attack from the others. How he actually succeeds in this could perhaps never be satisfactorily explained by him, yet that he does succeed is beyond question. No other man, dead or living, has ever equalled this marvellous pilot in air duelling.

And this is Fonck's statement of certain necessary maxims that are prerequisites for a successful air fighter.

> One must be in constant training—always fit—always sure of oneself—always in perfect health. Muscles must be in good condition, nerves in perfect equilibrium, all the organs functioning naturally.
>
> Alcohol becomes an enemy—even wine. All abuses must be avoided. It is indispensable that one goes to a combat without fatigue, without any disquietude either moral or physical or mental.
>
> It must be remembered that combats often take place at altitudes of twenty to twenty-five thousand feet. High altitudes are trying on one's organism. This indeed is, at bottom, the reason that keeps me from flying too continuously. And I never fly except when in perfect condition. I am careful to abstain when I am not exactly fit. Constantly I watch myself.
>
> It is as necessary to train as severely for air combats as for any other athletic contest, so difficult is the prize of victory. Yet if one finds oneself in prune condition, all the rest is play.

And these precepts come not from a Sunday School teacher but from a youth who has demonstrated his theory with as thorough a test as can be imagined.

All the rest" may be play, yet there is in that little play of René Fonck, the French Ace of Aces, a secret of quickness and anticipation that is indeed super-human.

CHAPTER 9

Other French Aces the Spectacular Career of Armand Pinsard

Armand Pinsard, born May 29, 1887, after an eventful youth entered the army as a cavalry officer and by a series of brilliant exploits in the Morocco Campaign of 1905 won at the age of eighteen the Moroccan Medal—his first decoration.

From Morocco Pinsard returned to France, where by chance he met Guggenheim, the aviator who gave the young cavalryman his first flight through the air over the Etamps aerodrome. So enthralled was Pinsard that from the moment of his descent to earth he had but one object in life. And to this end he devoted a determination that cannot be denied. He wished to become a pilot. He left no stone unturned to secure his transfer into aviation.

In May, 1912, his request was granted. He was sent to Chateau Fort where he quickly mastered the dangerous art of flying, and to his great credit it may be said that he accomplished his training and secured his brevet without once breaking his machine.

His first step filled his teachers with consternation. Pinsard stepped into his machine, an old-fashioned Borel, and despite the protests of the instructor he opened the throttle and sped away. Oh, joy! He had his opportunity at last!

He pulled back the control, and his magic mount quickly climbed away from earth. Another pull, and she climbed still more steeply up. The neophyte was rejoicing on his seat when—*Sapristi!*—it became necessary to turn to avoid collision with the trees. And the pupil had not the slightest idea how to contrive a turn.

He moved every control in sight and immediately saw the trees before him passing away under his wing. Without knowing how he had accomplished it he dropped to the ground in a perfect landing only a few feet away from his starting point.

After this *début* he learned so quickly that he soon obtained his license from the Aero Club, and later his military brevet.

Once attached to the military centre at Saint-Cyr the young pilot was forced to abandon his old Borel and learn to fly on the more speedy Morane. His success was demonstrated in the Grand Manoeuvres of 1913, where his daring flights won for him the Military Medal.

1914 arrived and found Pinsard still at Saint-Cyr in the Escadrille 23, then commanded by Captain Vergnette.

On the night of August second we find him with Pegoud, Vedrines, and several other famous before-the-war airmen who had been hastily summoned by the authorities to their country's defence—all standing on the flying field at Buc, anxiously awaiting the arrival of the expected Zeppelin raiders over Paris.

Two days later Pinsard was sent with all speed to the front in a new machine for reconnaissance. Garros went with him in his own machine with which they both returned to Paris. Then both impatiently awaited their call to active service at the front.

The M. S. 23 was forming anew at Buc. Famous airmen—the most famous then in France—were assembled to form this unit. Eugene Gilbert, Marc Pourpe, and his mechanic Raoul Lufbery, the American, and other well-known fliers were summoned to Buc. Pinsard was at this time a sergeant major.

Pinsard was full of enthusiasm and energy. His *escadrille* was stationed at Breteuil under the orders of General Castelnau, and there early in September, Pinsard gained his first citation and was promoted to an adjutancy in recognition of his heroic and perilous flights over enemy positions.

In October Pinsard participated in a bombardment expedition against the German Headquarters at Thielt, at which place the Kaiser was then visiting. For this exploit Pinsard received promotion to a second lieutenancy. The following month he was the hero of an extraordinary adventure.

He left one morning for a reconnaissance, carrying along as his passenger Captain Chaulin. Through engine failure his machine was compelled to come to the ground several miles back of the German lines. Having little time left to choose a safe landing ground Lieutenant Pinsard circled down to the nearest clear space, where he made a quiet landing. By an exceptional chance no German soldiers were in sight.

For two hours the two Frenchmen worked frantically over the stubborn engine in conspicuous view of the whole surrounding country, but not a soul came to interrupt their industry. Captain Chaulin stood with lighted tinder in his hand ready to set fire to the machine while Pinsard made a last dejected survey of his engine.

Just as the Captain announced the coming of a band of *Uhlans*, Pinsard found the cause of the *panne* and requested two more minutes to set it right. He made his repairs and started the motor with a swing of the propeller at the same moment that the German horsemen burst upon them. Chaulin was already in his seat. Pinsard leaped into his and opened wide the throttle. Their warm clothing, their tools, and even their arms were abandoned in their haste.

With magnificent coolness Pinsard rushed his machine full into the faces of the oncoming horses. Could he possibly lift her over their heads? Would they scatter and give him room? All now depended upon that, barring the possibility of death from a bullet.

The horses became frightened and unruly at the moment their riders stopped them to take aim. The aeroplane, with a healthy roar, passed between them and over them, and waving a free hand disdainfully at his enemies, Pinsard climbed steadily away and soon passed from their sight into the French lines. But although they made their homeward trip in their shut sleeves both officers confessed themselves sufficiently warm.

It was Pinsard who volunteered for the first "special mission" carried out by French airmen. A spy was to be carried into the German lines by aeroplane and deposited there. Far from a pleasant task under any circumstances, capture in this case meant execution. His success set a mark for his fellows and brought him his second citation.

Then on February 8, 1915, came the catastrophe. Fate, considering she had done enough for this venturesome youth, abandoned him. While well back of the enemy lines on another tour of observation another *panne* of the motor dropped Pinsard's aeroplane within the German territory. And this time there was no smooth spot within reach nor even a rough spot remote from his vindictive enemies.

Selecting the most favourable spot within sight Pinsard landed amid stumps, logs, and rocks. The last melancholy pleasure he recalled was the impression that fire itself would not have left less wreckage of his aeroplane for the Huns. As for himself, he came to consciousness within a German hospital. His passenger, Lieutenant de Chauffand, had likewise escaped death and reposed in a bed beside him.

For a month the gallant Pinsard occupied a hospital bed in Cologne while his comrades in France mourned him as lost. Every wakeful moment he occupied with plans for escape. As soon as he was able to get about he was sent to a prison camp nearby, from which he immediately attempted an escape. He was recaptured, sent to another detention camp, and put in a cell for thirty days with only bread and water for food.

Pinsard was a turbulent prisoner. Half a dozen prison camps in Germany will testify to that, for six different times he was caught in escaping, and each time he was punished by an ever increasing term in filthy underground dungeons at a new prison. But never was his spirit broken. His one idea was to escape and rejoin his comrades, and one good day to avenge himself for the hurts he had received.

On one occasion the resourceful prisoner jumped from the window of a moving train which was conveying him to a new internment camp. He succeeded in creeping towards the frontier of Holland for five nights when he was again recaptured. This time he was sentenced to thirty-five days in a dungeon.

This was a terrible punishment. The prisoner was confined within a dark underground cell without either air or light. His bed was a single plank attached to the wall and during the day padlocked on edge so that it could not be used. It was necessary then to remain standing through the day unless, overcome with fatigue, the exhausted prisoner preferred to lie down in the filth of the floor which was alive with rats and vermin.

His sole visitor was his jailer who came night and morning with bread and water and a tin of thin soup—his only food for thirty-five days. The yellow gleam of his stinking candle was the only light which penetrated into this frightful cell. One wonders how a human brain, a human physique accustomed to the most active exercise, could endure such a long and depressing punishment. The lack of nourishment, the horrible sleeplessness amid the vermin, the torture of being perpetually alone in the thick blackness, having no notion of the hour or even the day—it seems amazing that a man with the nervous energy of Pinsard did not go mad.

Pinsard admitted that once the impulse to beat out his brains against the wall of his cell completely mastered him, and he was about to execute his plan when at that very instant his jailer came to him with letters from France and permitted him to read them by the flame of his candle! Surely Fate was still on the watch!

The letters gave him new courage; energy and desire to live enveloped and sustained the prisoner when he remembered that friends in France thought of him and loved him.

When Pinsard was told his durance vile had ceased, and that his thirty-five days of martyrdom had passed he lacked the physical strength to climb up from his cell to the pure air he had so long desired. He was carried out to the common prison by the

Huns and deposited among the other prisoners who shed tears upon perceiving his condition.

These friends had been saving their own food for Pinsard against the day of his release when, as they well knew, he would be in sore need of nourishment. Thanks to the store which had been secreted for him, and his remarkable spirit and constitution, Pinsard rapidly recovered his strength and began his plans for another escape. And this time he was destined to succeed. Since February Pinsard had familiarized himself with the interiors of the prisons on the Island of Stralsund-Danholin, then the Bad-Stuer prison, in Mecklenburg, then at the Halle-sur-Salle, and finally in February, 1916, at the Ingolstadt Prison in Bavaria, the Fort of Prinz Karl from which he at last succeeded in escaping in company with Captain Ménard, another French prisoner.

Neither could speak German. Collecting the little food which they had saved from their meagre store against this emergency, which was doubled by another quantity given them by their loyal comrades in misery, the two Frenchmen evaded the prison guards one dark night and directed their cautious footsteps towards the border of Switzerland, two hundred miles away.

Within an hour of their escape they heard the prison dogs baying in their pursuit. But Pinsard had been caught before in this manner and was prepared for them. With garlic and pepper which he had taken pains to provide he rubbed the soles of his shoes and those of his companion. The dogs arrived at the spot where this operation was completed, and with a few howls of disgust, which came to the two fugitives less than a mile away, the chase was abandoned.

Walking by night, sleeping by turns through the long days, Pinsard and Menard crossed the forests, swamps, and fields by compass, always avoiding the villages and houses. In fifteen days they reached what they supposed was the border, when to their dismay they discovered they had gone astray and had arrived at the edge of the wide Lake Constance. Another twenty miles must be covered to take them around the water. And they had had no food for forty-eight hours, Ménard's feet were blistered and bleeding, and both men were nearly fainting from exhaustion.

Heroically persevering, they at last dragged themselves up to the very line of German sentries which were patrolling across their road to freedom. Pinsard and his companion armed themselves with their knives. As the two sentinels reached the opposite ends of their beat the fugitives slipped cautiously through the centre. What a moment of hope and anxiety for the brave Pinsard!

In a delirium of joy at finding himself on neutral soil Pinsard first grasped Ménard by the hand and then ran with him at desperate speed across the intervening space to the Swiss woods beyond.

They had not been seen. At break of day they arrived at a railroad and following its course soon came to a Swiss village. With clothing in rags, a fifteen days' growth of beard upon their emaciated faces, and strength so feeble that they had to cling to each other for support, their appearance within the station created something of a sensation.

Soon they were seated at a table devouring an omelette. A train arrived outside. Learning it was *en route* for Geneva, Pinsard called for a pan, and filling it with food, he dragged Ménard aboard the train. That night, arriving without incident at Geneva, the two refugees were able to purchase clothing and shoes. The next morning they passed across the border by automobile. At last they were in France!

Thirty days' leave was given the intrepid Pinsard to recover his strength. At the end of this leave he appeared before his officers and requested to be taken back into his old *escadrille*. He desired but the opportunity to avenge his wrongs and to bring down Boches from on high.

But during his long imprisonment aeroplanes and air tactics had changed to a remarkable degree. It would first be necessary to return to training school and there learn the new features of his old art.

This was soon accomplished. Pinsard stepped into the new

fast Nieuport fighting aeroplane, and climbing aloft with all his old audacity, he put the tricky little scout through all its manoeuvres just as though he had never ceased from practicing.

Pinsard was welcomed rapturously by all his old comrades who remained in this perilous service, and was immediately given a lieutenancy in the most distinguished fighting *escadrille* of France—the Cigognes.

And worthily has he acquitted himself in his new field. Fighting furiously upon every possible occasion and devoting his utmost energy to the pursuit and destruction of the Huns who owed him so much, Pinsard shot down his fifth enemy machine on March 7, 1917, and took his place among the Aces. At the end of May he had shot down his fifteenth official victim and twice had narrowly escaped death in combat himself. The first occasion was when some dozen miles back of the enemy's lines his machine was struck by shrapnel which injured it so badly Pinsard barely crossed to his own lines before it collapsed. Again on May 30th he returned from a combat with a slicing cut across his temple occasioned by the bullet of an aeroplane antagonist.

Pinsard was given command of his own *escadrille* at the end of 1917 and accompanying this promotion came his election to the Legion of Honour of France. Already he held the *Croix de Guerre* with fifteen palms, one palm for each citation for distinguished conduct, the Military Medal and Moroccan Medal which he had won before this war, and finally the Military Medal from Italy.

On June 12, 1917, a stupid little accident in landing nearly terminated the extraordinary career of this airman, and he was compelled to spend several months in complete rest. But the late spring of 1918 found him again in the air with his gallant *escadrille* and again throwing his entire energies into the conflict against enemies he has so much cause to hate. Late in June he shot down his nineteenth Boche aeroplane to help balance the score he has against them. In July he downed his twentieth.

Long may this valiant soldier of France live to increase his score. Despite his fourteen months' imprisonment, Armand Pinsard, beginning again at the bottom of the ladder in August, 1917, now stands seventh in the glorious list of the living French Aces.

Charles Nungesser

Charles Nungesser of Escadrille N. 65, now the second Ace in France, first entered the war in the French Hussars. He gained there at the end of two weeks the Military Medal. Before the war Nungesser was a boxer of some repute.

Passing into aviation Nungesser took part in fifty-three bombardments both by day and by night, on enemy positions. Then he took up hunting enemy aeroplanes and began his remarkable career of successes interrupted by frequent injuries from wounds received in combat.

While trying out a new machine at the end of 1915 Nungesser had a fall which broke one leg and his shoulder, and suffered injuries so serious that a less hardy constitution would have succumbed. Refusing a discharge, however, he left the hospital and hobbled about his aerodrome with a cane and at first opportunity again flew his machine against the enemy attacking Verdun.

He had arrived at the aerodrome the first of April. The next day he brought down an observation balloon. The day following he shot down an aeroplane and still another the next day. On every flight he engaged in combats and rarely failed to inflict some damage to the enemy machines.

On May 19th his name first appeared in a *communiqué*. On June 22nd he had won his eighth official victory, and on July 22nd he had his tenth. It was then a race between Nungesser and Guynemer who on the same date had his eleventh official victory. On September 26th Nungesser shot down two aeroplanes and one captive balloon, bringing his score up to seventeen, three of which had been balloons.

Then another wound sent the heroic airman back to his bed. Seventeen times this hero has been wounded in combats! Today he is wearing the badge of the Legion of Honour and has a total of 45 enemy aeroplanes shot down.

René Dorme, the Beloved

Upon the disappearance of Lieutenant Donne, the Cigogne, on the morning of May 25, 1917, a wave of grief and sadness swept through the aerodromes of France that was unexcelled even by the loss of Guynemer, Dorme's captain and admirer, who disappeared four months later under singularly similar circumstances.

Hardly an airman in France but knew and loved Dorme. A marvellous shot, an unequalled student of tactics, a relentless and furious fighter, Dorme possessed the sunniest of natures and a fineness of character that attracted and charmed everyone he met. He was known as "Père Dorme." Even Guynemer himself described him as the greatest air fighter in France.

Born of the humblest parents on January 30, 1894, at Aix-Abaucourt near Verdun, where his father was a station master, René Dorme received but little education before he entered upon his military career at the age of eighteen and was sent to Africa with the 7th Artillery.

His regiment was recalled to France at the outbreak of war, and Dorme in February, 1915, passed into the Air Service—the one desire of his heart. Stationed first with the air defenders of Paris, Dorme flew a two-seater Caudron and saw but little of the front. Finally on April 3, 1916, Dorme, while on a short expedition near the lines, took on a single-handed attack against six enemy aeroplanes, and one of them he shot down with significant ease. His victory brought him an invitation to join the Cigognes, whose commanding officer, Captain Brocard, was on the lookout for such promising material.

Never was confidence better placed. As soon as Dorme possessed the opportunity to hunt the Boches in a fast Nieuport, his successes piled up. His skill appeared marvellous even to his comrades of Escadrille N. 3 who were the *élite* of the fighting airmen of France.

Sober, thoughtful, and silent, Père Dorme soon found him-

LIEUTENANT CHARLES NUNGESSER.
Famous French Ace, seventeen times wounded, with a record of 38

self the most popular member of his squadron. His comrades discovered in short order that Dorme, who flew tirelessly and endlessly, was a past master in his art. Not a day passed without a combat, and few combats occurred without leaving Dorme master of the field. How many victories he won on his many deep raids into German territory no one person ever knew. This modest boy seemed to feel reluctant to tell of his achievements before such a distinguished group of comrades.

Finally, after Donne's tenth official victory, it was discovered that this consummate pilot had handled every one of his numberless encounters with enemy planes with such masterly skill that but two bullet holes had ever been permitted to puncture the wings of his machine. He had always so adroitly manoeuvred his own machine while attacking the enemy groups that none of them could bring him into the range of their guns. Yet at his own good time Dorme selected a victim and with a short burst from his gun ended his career. "The Unpuncturable Dorme" was a nickname that clung to him until his disappearance.

Not one of the French Aces was reputed to win so many uncredited victories as Dorme. When this point was suggested to the silent young hero one day he smilingly replied:

"Ask the Boches. They know!"

In September, 1916, Dorme brought down seven Boche machines. Early the following year he passed all his comrades save Guynemer in his official score, while this number was more than doubled in reality, as his comrades in the Cigognes knew. But Dorme continued indifferent to popular recognition of his prowess. With almost girlish modesty he turned the subject away from his own achievements. On one occasion, when De la Tour asked him if he had not seen his last victim descending in flames, Dorme replied, "I think so; but I am certain that you destroyed yours." De la Tour looked at him a moment and said:

"Then I destroyed him with a glance, for I didn't fire a shot." To which the guilty Père Dorme replied with a shout of laughter.

On the morning of May 25, 1917, Dorme went up with his

comrade Deullin, at six-thirty o'clock. As usual Dorme led the way deep into the lines of the Boches, Deullin following in his wake.

The hunting seemed especially good this morning. Deullin saw his companion shoot down one enemy aeroplane, then he himself dove into the attack on a group of four advancing enemies. He fought them furiously and pursued them as they fled without paying any further attention to the whereabouts of Dorme. Finally he gave up the chase and turned his machine homewards. Where was Dorme?

Deullin searched the heavens far and near, but no sign of a Spad could be seen. His tank was almost empty, and he could no longer stay up. Dorme must have returned without him.

As Deullin flew towards the French lines he saw an aeroplane burning far below him. He descended and thought it might be a Spad. The very flames and smoke from the burning aeroplane seemed to be bidding him farewell. But this was absurd! Dorme had never been injured. Every night his comrades had gathered around his aeroplane and ironically searched for bullet holes which they never found. Dorme would never permit a shot to surprise him.

Nevertheless Deullin flew home with despair in his heart. He was returning—alone!

All day long his comrades hung over the telephone. Somebody would surely notify them before long to send a motor for their absent comrade. Dorme must have landed with a stalled engine in some distant place. But darkness settled—and still no message!

That night the gay Cigognes counted hours of agony. False hopes and baseless rumours were run down one by one. A Spad had been seen landing in the French trenches! After an hour's frantic inquiry it was found to be true—this rumour—but it was not the Spad of Père Dorme.

During some days they kept on hoping. Every day they made minute searches of Dorme's last fighting ground, ready to land at the wreckage if found and satisfy themselves of his fate. But nothing was found—absolutely nothing.

Dorme may have been forced to land, in which case he would of course set fire to his aeroplane and hide, waiting for an opportunity for escape to his own lines. So nothing must be said that would get to the ears of the enemy and cause them to be on the lookout for Dorme. Thus his comrades argued as they hoped against hope for tidings of their quiet, smiling comrade. Then at last came tidings.

One sultry afternoon, two weeks after his disappearance, the customary air message was dropped into the flying field of the Cigognes by an aeroplane of the enemy. It announced that Pilot Dorme had been killed in a combat. But no date—no particulars—no proofs in the shape of the personal belongings that usually accompanied such messages. How had they heard—these enemies—that Dorme was missing? Dorme killed in combat? Never! The Hun had not yet been trained that could conquer the incomparable Père Dorme, the Unpuncturable Dorme in combat! But René Dorme has never returned!

Lieutenant Georges Madon

Sub-Lieutenant Georges Madon is twenty-five years old; if we cannot count him among the youngest of the French pilots he is nevertheless a very skilful one and such an insatiable fighter that to relate all his exploits would make a very long story.

He was born at Bizert, and passed his youth sometimes at the seashore, sometimes in town, but always living out of doors. His devotion to sports made him a man of exceptional physical strength. Madon is short but with erect carriage; his firm step and strong face give one even at first sight the impression of a determined, combative character. Beneath this is a charming nature, a heart of gold, and a loyal sympathetic comradeship. All his youth Madon loved violent exercise. He seemed to feel an innate necessity of giving vent to his strength in contests and struggles. It was by this devotion to sports that he developed those powers of endurance, of taking in a situation at a glance, of coolness, which make him at the present moment one of the greatest of the Allies' pilots.

Directly his studies at the college of Tunis were finished Madon felt himself irresistibly drawn towards aviation. At last his dream was realized, and he began his training on a Blériot at the school of Etampes. On June 7, 1911, he brilliantly won his brevet of the Aero Club after a short apprenticeship and without a single breakage.

On March 12, 1912, he enlisted in military aviation and was first attached to the centre at Avord and afterwards at Belfort. Thus Madon was one of that splendid band of pioneers who made possible, many paying with their lives, the full conquest of the air by man.

In peace time Madon distinguished himself by his fearlessness and skill. A faultless pilot, he was celebrated throughout the circles of military aviation for the stunts he performed on his Blériot. The two years before the war he spent in doing everything possible to perfect his flying and make of himself a true bird-man. He kept up his athletic training, still played football, boxed, and engaged in all his old sports as vigorously as ever.

When the war broke out Madon was ready! Detailed to the Bl. 30 in the Soissons sector he set to work bravely on his mediocre machine. The Blériot had not the qualities of a fighting machine. Slow, difficult to get high in the air, it had but one advantage—its tractability; it was moreover equipped with a wheezy motor that threatened to break down at any moment. To fly over the Boche territory under these conditions was not exactly pleasant. Nevertheless wonders were accomplished by the Escadrille Blériot 30, and the inferiority of their machines was more than offset by the quality of the pilots. Regulating artillery fire, reconnaissance, night bombardments, which Madon was one of the first to attempt, occupied the young veteran's life for some months. And that this life had its dangers we shall see from an adventure that came to him on October 30, 1914.

In the course of a reconnaissance at 7000 feet in the region of Chemin-des-Dames a 77-millimetre shell in full flight struck his engine and demolished it. The wind blew rather strongly from the French lines, and the unsteady machine refused to dive. The French territory seemed inaccessible, the more so as machine guns, *canons* and rifles of the enemy were directed upon him. The agonizing descent continued. At about 600 feet Madon saw that he and his passenger were almost directly over the first line trenches of the Boches. He plainly saw the trench soldiers aim carefully at them as though at a target. In an excess of rage he fairly forced his machine to dive and he dropped directly toward the group which immediately dispersed in terror.

Drawing up his machine on the edge of the parapet he flew along the ground until he was stopped by the barbed wire. Then under a rain of bullets he and his companion made for the French trenches where the two were received with open arms. The enemy tried its best during the entire afternoon to demolish the old bus with their 105's, but they were not successful and during the night the two went out with some trench soldiers to look for souvenirs from their machine. The next morning an enemy machine appeared to regulate artillery fire on the stranded aeroplane; at the first salvo the unfortunate Blériot flew into splinters. Soon after this Madon was promoted to sergeant.

On March 12, 1915, the Blériot Escadrille was changed to a Farman. Madon went to Bourget and in two flights he had mastered the new machine. On April 3, 1915, he left the training school with his mechanic, Corporal Châtelain, on an 80-H. P. Farman aeroplane to rejoin Escadrille 44 at Toul. Leaving Bar-le-Duc he was caught in a fog and lost his way. When he got his bearings he was so far out of his route and the weather was so thick he had to renounce his original project. On the fifth, in spite of a dense fog, he tried to reach Belfort. It was during this flight that he lost his way completely and landed on Swiss territory at Porrentruy.

The aeroplane was instantly surrounded by a crowd of French Swiss who welcomed the French aviators. The aviators were not a little surprised to find that they were not on French soil, and their first care was to get away at the greatest speed possible. They were unfortunately stopped by a German Swiss-company.

They were interned at Saint-Gall, and were closely watched; whether in their own room or at the canteen or on their walks they were always accompanied by at least one non-commissioned officer or the police. Moreover all the borders were guarded. Of course their keepers were chosen from the regiments of the German Swiss, which means that the prisoners were very carefully watched. An escape under such circumstances seemed difficult, but Madon was not one to be discouraged by the difficulties. He, on the contrary, was merely stimulated by the measures taken to prevent his escape and patiently waited a favourable moment to evade them.

The two prisoners were always making plans and in spite of attempts to lower their morale, they kept their courage and strength up to the mark. They first made use of the privilege of taking walks as a means for exercise; then they began to look on it as a means of escape should the opportunity ever come.

Twenty-two days after their arrival at Saint-Gall they were transferred to Berne on the very evening before they were to put their plan of escape into execution. At Berne they recommenced their preparations, but they were soon taken to Hospenthal on the Saint Gothard, where they found Sergeant Pilot Martin and his mechanic who had been forced likewise to land on Swiss soil when returning from a bombing expedition.

Madon again prepared his escape and for the purpose procured some civilian clothes.

On the night of September 17, 1915, he and Châtelain took their departure. Their room was on the first floor. A sentinel stood in the hall by the door which was locked with a key from the outside; another sentry stood beneath the window. Outwitting this guard, the two let themselves down by a rope from their window, and left the country by the Furka Pass in the direction of Italy. They succeeded in surmounting the Saint Gothard fortifications which were guarded by a battalion of Italian Swiss, but they were unfortunately arrested some days after at Gletch by a sleeping sentinel whom Madon stumbled over in the darkness.

Taken back to Andermatt, about two miles from Hospenthal, they found there Martin and his mechanic and afterwards Lieutenant Eugene Gilbert, who came to complete the colony of interned French aviators.

Transferred to Zurich, Madon and Châtelain, in the course of their walks, made the acquaintance of a Frenchman discharged from the army on account of his wounds in the war. He took it upon himself to arrange their escape. When they went out for a walk they would slip a letter into his hand or would send him a message by Madon's dog. In this way they carried on a surreptitious correspondence with him and arranged their expedition in all its details.

On December 27, 1915, as they were out taking a promenade they succeeded in getting the officer who was with them to accompany them to an out-of-the-way place. There they chloroformed him, gagged and bound him, and put him into an automobile which was waiting to hurry them to Lausanne. A power boat awaited them there. Into this they stepped, still supporting their guard. A curious customs officer raised a slight alarm, but they were able to satisfy him by a ruse, then away they went to Evian, France, and liberty! With what joy the two fugitives, after nine months of captivity, found themselves once more on French soil!

Madon and Châtelain at once went back to their flying station where to celebrate their return they were given—Madon sixty days of close confinement, and Châtelain sixty days in open prison. A strange welcome to those who had braved so many dangers and surmounted so many difficulties to return to fight again!

In explanation of this unjust court martial it may now be said that there were some malicious and unjust rumours about Madon's reasons for landing on Swiss territory. The authors of these charges took care to remain anonymous and Madon by his explanations and conduct eventually showed they were the result of misunderstanding and jealousy, with no foundation whatever. He was soon released.

Early in January, 1916, Madon left for the Verdun front with Escadrille M. F. 218. He arrived in time for the great attack of the hordes of the Kaiser who now rushed madly to the assault of this heroic citadel. During four months he did his utmost without counting the cost. Regulating the long-range artillery fire, reconnaissances, night bombing, he even did his part in air fighting on a Farman, which was no match for a fighting machine.

At last he realized his dearest hopes and was detailed for fighting aviation on May 18th. He left for training at Pau and September 1st Madon was put into Escadrille N. 38.

From this time on his career has been a succession of victories won with remarkable skill and daring. One cannot give a better idea of Madon than simply to set down his plain unembellished record.

On October 30, 1917, he had totalled sixteen official victories and twenty unofficial. These thirty-six victories obtained in one year speak for the man; but merely giving the number does not adequately convey to the mind of the layman the rare courage, skill, and judgement which were required to achieve this total.

Besides these, one should remember also that his twenty unofficial victories were in the majority of instances not verified because they were brought down too far within the enemy's lines. But we have Madon's own testimony, which for anyone who knows him is sufficient, and besides he often brought back eloquent proofs of his conquests. Three times he came back with his propeller covered with blood and brains, and one day in May, after having charged an enemy two-seater, he came back with the observer's glasses caught in one of his wires. These details will show how close to the enemy aeroplanes Madon fought.

He is a wonderful marksman as well as a skilled pilot, In May he attacked alone a patrol of seven Albatrosses, of which he brought down three. Then he fought a second patrol of nine and brought down two. The Ace had now aroused such terror in the enemy fighting *escadrilles* it was said they took to their wings at full speed at the mere sight of a Spad, fearing it might be Madon.

On July 2, 1917, Madon attacked a two-seater at 20,000 feet, but carried away by his zeal he miscalculated the distance and collided with his adversary. His right wing was almost entirely stripped of its canvas, and his elevator was broken. From 6000 feet a tail-spin is a terrifying thing, when one is powerless to stop it. He saw death imminent when by a miracle the aeroplane of its own accord came out of the spin, and the descent became slower. But the almost total lack of canvas on the right wing forced the machine to veer, and Madon saw with horror that the wreck on which he was travelling was taking him straight back to the enemy. By a supreme effort he brought the machine almost into the right direction; he could not however prevent its diving, for his elevators were useless; thus he arrived headfirst on the ground at a mad speed.

Fortunately the bodies of aeroplanes and of men can stand a lot. Madon received only a broken finger and a thorough shaking up. Meanwhile the Boche aeroplane fell beside him with its tail cut off. Unfortunately it was not counted, not having been seen from the French lines.

Such an accident would have cooled the ardour of a less enthusiastic spirit. It was nothing to Madon, and his few terrible moments only served as a stimulant, for between that flight and November 1, 1917 he brought down ten more Boches with his customary coolness.

The career of this Ace was full of incidents. Witness the following misadventure which happened to him March 17, 1917:

Attacking bravely two Boches behind their own lines he put the first to flight. The second was seriously injured, and Madon followed him to within 2000 feet of his landing place. When he wished to regain the altitude his motor would not pick up on account of the low temperature, and he was obliged to make a landing a few yards within the Boche lines. He remained for nearly ten minutes to warm up his motor, which began to work at precisely the right moment. It was only just in time; a crowd of Boche soldiers came running toward him, shouting and gesticulating. Madon turned on his gas and pushed resolutely through, taking care to make use of his machine gun to disable a few Boches and to assist his own escape to our lines.

He had had a similar experience at Verdun the first of the year, but there his motor had picked up the moment his wheels touched the ground.

One must recognize that such incidents are sufficiently eloquent and permit one to see clearly the remarkable quality of Madon's work. They are only a few examples, chosen because they are typical, but they serve to show the skill, the coolness, and the zeal of this great Ace in combat.

Between times when the weather was not favourable for hunting Boches, Madon amused himself with firing his machine gun into the enemy's trenches. At such times he gave the trench soldiers a real exhibition, placing himself almost on the enemy's ground to fire and letting them see the difference between his work and that of the Albatross drivers, who usually fired from a distance of 1200 to 1500 yards. The first of January, 1917, in the course of a reconnaissance, he came down to 400 yards, poured his machine gun into a train, and by the accuracy of his aim and the destruction it caused, he forced the train to stop.

We have already spoken of Madon's lack of luck in the official verification of his victims; we will substantiate this by recalling this little incident. On April 6, 1917, there was a great attack on enemy observation balloons at the front. Madon left to escort the French fighting planes but finding a favourable opportunity at hand, he himself attacked a balloon and set it on fire. By an incomprehensible error this success was not attributed to him but to someone else.

Madon has naturally been rewarded for his exceptional services, though not always as lavishly as one might have wished. One can judge something of them by reading his citations which already make a creditable sized volume. He has been promoted successively to sergeant, to adjutant, and sub-lLieutenant; his breast is ornamented with the Cross of the Legion of Honour, the Military Medal, the *Croix de Guerre* with ten *palms*, a star, the

Italian Order for Valour, and the Roumanian Order for Valour.

Further commentaries would appear superfluous. But too much cannot be said of this great Ace, of his skill, his courage, and moral value, who up to July 1, 1918, had to his official score thirty-four enemy aeroplanes brought down, thus standing below only Fonck and Nungesser among all the living French Aces.

Lieutenant Viallet

The French pilot, Viallet, now an Ace with eight victories, had an encounter with the great German Ace, Captain Boelke, over the Verdun battlefield on April 28, 1916, which lingered long in his memory. In fact, he later described the event as one giving him the strongest emotion of his existence.

Viallet had been directed to protect the progress over the lines of a photographic reconnaissance, and he set off in his two-seater bi-motor Caudron early one morning, a similar defensive craft guarding the other side of their charge.

The three machines proceeded over the trenches, and the business of the day began. Suddenly the second Caudron, which was at a considerable height over Viallet, began a rapid dive towards home, passing in the rear of the Ace. He quickly turned about and discovered two enemy Fokkers on his comrade's tail, and immediately rushed in to the rescue.

As the two Fokkers turned to receive his attack he suddenly became aware of a third enemy which was hurling himself down from a great height. From the marking on the planes he discovered the newcomer to be the champion of the Boches, Boelke!

Viallet's heavy two-seater machine was slow to manoeuvre and no match for the Fokker in speed. Boelke arrived at top speed and at fifty yards began to open up with his two machine guns. At the same instant Viallet executed a *renversement*, causing Boelke to pass overhead and for a moment to come within range of the rear gun on Viallet's Caudron—a moment which the gunner seated behind Viallet did not fail to employ to the fullest advantage.

But Boelke likewise reversed his course sharply, and at the next swoop Viallet felt the broadside from the enemy machine take effect on his own. A dozen bullets struck his right-hand motor—the one on the left was in flames! To make the matter worse, the rudder control on the left was severed!

From his elevation of 11,000 feet Viallet realized he was in for a flaming spectacular tail-spin to the ground with an occasional slide on his tail, or on one or the other wing to relieve the monotony. He glanced back at his gunner and made a grimace of despair.

The last slide began. It could end only in the crash!

At 2000 feet above Verdun the machine miraculously yielded to the pilot's efforts and re-established its obedience to both the elevators and ailerons. Viallet circled ponderously into the wind as the aeroplane settled and by a combination of skill and great good fortune he managed to come smoothly to ground upon a level space behind the fort of Chaulnes. Viallet had been shot down but not destroyed by the German champion.

He and his passenger had just time to remove the two machine guns from his aeroplane when the shells of the enemy began to drop about the doomed Caudron.

The next day the German *communiqués* announced that Boelke had destroyed his fourteenth adversary! Viallet shook his head gloomily in denial of this claim, remembering vividly the while however the indelible impression he had received of the darting Fokker with four black crosses on top and bottom—the individual mark of Captain Boelke.

It was for Viallet his thirteenth combat! He admitted later that he was glad to pass the fatal number. When questioned about the combat he said:

"Boelke should have had me. He committed one fault. If he had followed me instead of attacking me face to face I would have been a dead one."

Gabriel Guérin

Sub-Lieutenant Gabriel Guérin was born at Havre on July

25, 1892. He is a sportsman in every sense of the word, and his example shows how wise the French Secretary of Aviation has been in wishing to recruit his pilots from among those who have already distinguished themselves on the sporting fields.

When the war broke out Guérin was a private in the 28th Infantry. Up to June 16, 1916, he continued to prove his heroic qualities in the trenches and was the object of two citations. Two citations for a *poilu* mean really remarkable deeds.

But his work did not satisfy him. He felt that he could be of more use in the air. Accordingly in August, 1916, he received his transfer into the fourth arm, and in October obtained his brevet on a bombing plane. His qualities, recognized by the officers and envied by his comrades, especially fitted him for the chase, and during the winter he took a new course of training.

On April 25, 1917, after what seemed to him a very long time in the training camp, he was attached to the famous Spa. 15. Here he found the celebrated Ace Jailler. Jailler's one delight was to pick out those among the newcomers in whom he saw the material for future Aces and these he trained himself under his own direction. He recognized the desired qualities in Guérin and at once took up his training. This was neither long nor difficult.

On May 24th the newcomer won his first victory, scarcely a month after his arrival. He was rewarded with the following citation:

> Guérin (Gabriel), Corporal of Escadrille N. 15 (formerly in the branch of the infantry), young pilot, animated by the best spirit, giving under all circumstances an example of the greatest fighting qualities.
> After many severe combats since his entering the service, he has succeeded on May 25, 1917, in bringing down an enemy aeroplane.

The following day he sent to the ground a demolished aeroplane which was not credited. But on June 3rd he had his second and the 15th his third official citation:

Pilot who by his zeal and his thoughtful determination attests himself each day an aviator of the chase of great value, has brought down his second and third enemy aeroplanes.

A few days later came this new citation:

Young pilot of great skill, of absolute devotion, superb in his coolness and reasoned energy. June 15, 1917, having been but one month in the *escadrille*, brought down his third enemy machine.

This was a slight exaggeration as Guérin had been with his unit since April 25.

July 10th, fighting alone against two two-seaters escorted by three one-seaters the future Ace succeeded in putting to flight the whole group but could not bring any down. All he could do was to prevent the Boches from accomplishing their mission. But on July 23rd it was a different story. There he was entirely successful. This earned for him the Military Medal:

Does not cease to give the most glorious example of courage, force, coolness and devotion. July 23, 1917, brought down his fourth enemy aeroplane. Already five times cited in orders.

Four days later a new victory which from lack of a sufficient number of witnesses could not be credited. The fifth official was brought down August 20, 1917, at only 400 yards above the enemy lines, and crashed to the southeast of Consenvoye:

Pilot of the chase without a peer, he has spent himself without reserve during the attacks on Verdun. August 20, 1917, has brought down his fifth official aeroplane.

August 20th yielded a probable but not recognized success. Again on September 7th near Septsarges, Guérin now Adjutant was equally unlucky.

But on September 10th he sent down to the south of the Caures Woods his sixth. And the glorious series continues: the seventh fell on November 1st in the region of Chevrigny; the eighth, a two-seater Rumpler, came down in flames November 11th; the ninth was also in flames in the region of Vaudesson on December 2nd. This is his first victory as *Sub-Lieutenant* Guérin. The tenth, a two-seater, was brought down within French lines at Louvercy, on December 22nd, in collaboration with Adjutant Garaud and Maréchal des Logis Hanriot; the eleventh followed the next day and crashed near Beine,—this in collaboration with Brigadier Artigau. The two comrades had another probable victory during the same fight.

> Pilot of the chase without a peer. Officer of the greatest moral value. Joins to his qualities of courage and self-sacrifice an incomparable skill in manoeuvring. Is the soul of his *escadrille*. December 22, 1917, brought down an aeroplane within our lines, and the next morning again brought down an aeroplane that was shattered in the air and crashed into the enemy trenches, 10th and 11th victories.

Guérin was very unlucky with his verifications and had at least double the number of successes that were ever credited to him, but his work continued without interruption. In July he brought down his twenty-second official aeroplane, thus making him fourth in the list of French Aces.

Captain Heurteaux

Captain Heurteaux, who succeeded Commander Brocard as Chief of the famous Escadrille N. 3, was the youngest and one of the most remarkable of its officers. Born at Nantes he came out of Saint-Cyr August 2, 1914, and began the war as Sub-Lieutenant of the Hussars. During the first three months of war while in the cavalry he obtained three citations.

Two of these follow:

> August 23, Sub-Lieutenant Heurteaux, in charge of a reconnaissance arrived at the moment of a violent attack of the Germans against our infantry. A lieutenant at the head

of a squad of hussars had just been wounded. Lieutenant Heurteaux assumed command of the squad and as our infantry weakened, leaving in danger a battery of artillery, he posted his fighting squad on foot in the abandoned trenches and kept them there until the withdrawal of the artillery battery, sustaining the combat up to 150 yards from the German infantry.

This citation to the regiment only, in spite of the splendour of the exploit which has assured the safety of a battery, was followed by another of September 26th:

Sub-Lieutenant Heurteaux, . . . has given proof of his bravery and energy in destroying on September 22nd at Augest-en-Santerre a patrol of German Hussars composed of a non-commissioned officer and five cavalrymen of whom three were killed and one taken prisoner.

Some months later when there was a call for volunteers for aviation Heurteaux offered himself and was accepted. He started as observer in the *escadrille* of Garros with whom he took part in many operations, notably in bombing Ostend and dropping tracts on Brussels. Then he became pilot and continued to merit the praise of all.

What impresses one in Heurteaux is his juvenile air, his open, honest face, and the directness of his look which can be both sweet and forceful. Those who see him at his work admire above all else his capacity for labour, for attention to details, and for method in his combats. He and Guynemer would get up at the first ray of dawn to wait for the Boche to appear, and both spent two hours each day examining their equipment. Add to this a proverbial modesty and simplicity and one gets something of the likeness of Heurteaux.

When Heurteaux wrote to his family he told less about his exploits than the *communiqué* told. But his chiefs and his comrades never hesitated to say what they thought of him. Thus Commander Brocard is always speaking of his "extraordinary skill and incomparable bravery." As soon as Heurteaux had ar-

LIEUTENANT RENÉ DORME

Called the "the Unpuncturable Dorme" who disappeared May 25, 1917, with a record of 23

CAPTAIN ALBERT HEURTEAUX

The first French Ace to bring down an enemy plane with a single bullet. Wounded with a record of 21

rived at the *escadrille* the commander of the Storks had divined him. When Brocard left his unit for administrative life he did not hesitate to intrust the command of his beloved N. 3 to him whom he considered from every point of view the one most capable of assuring its continued successes to Heurteaux—who was then but a lieutenant.

Before going over the career of this great Ace, at that time the third of the French wearers of palms, let us outline a few of his deeds which serve to illustrate his great qualities.

He was the first to bring down an enemy aeroplane with a single bullet. A record that only Guynemer has equalled.

One day being surprised by an *escadrille* which he thinks was that of the German Ace, Boelke, thanks to his resources as a flyer he succeeded in effecting a truly miraculous escape.

Heurteaux exhibited a typical detail of the French spirit of raillery. At times when the enemy pilots were passing very near to him he was accustomed to wave them a greeting with his hand. This infuriated them, and they replied with a shake of the fist.

Heurteaux became the terror of the enemy. The pilot and the gunner of a two-seater were brought down in our lines one day and taken before the general to be interrogated. He said to them:

"Do you know that that was Heurteaux who brought you down?"

The pilot answered, "Yes, I know it. *And I am very proud of it!*"

It was on May 4, 1916, that Heurteaux brought down his first victim.

His second success brought him the following citation and with it the Legion of Honour:

Served at the front since the beginning of the campaign. As a cavalry officer he proved his qualities of coolness, audacity and devotion which brought him two citations. In aviation since December 1, 1914, he distinguished himself first as observer, as bombarder, and in reconnaissance, then as fighting pilot. He has brought down two German aeroplanes on May 4, and July 9, 1916.

But it was not until July 9 that he began his prodigious series.

Heurteaux and Dorme then began their race for Boche machines and they kept neck and neck until the month of May, 1917, on the third day of which month Heurteaux brought down his twenty-first victim and was severely wounded on the following day. After recovering from his wounds which kept him several months in the hospital, Heurteaux was sent in the spring of 1918 on a government aviation mission to the United States. Throughout his three months' stay in the United States Captain Heurteaux was able to move about only with the aid of a cane.

Heurteaux was celebrated among his comrades and hated by his enemies for the contemptuous manners he displayed towards his adversaries in a combat. He insisted that his gestures of contempt tended to put the Boches in a temper, and that in this state of mind they frequently became easy victims. On one occasion, however, Heurteaux's comrades had the laugh on him. During a combat he passed very close to an enemy airman. Leaning over the edge of his cockpit Heurteaux placed the tip of his thumb to the end of his nose and wiggled his fingers derisively in his antagonist's face. Before he had fairly completed his tactful manoeuvre and while his thumb was still at his nose, a bullet from the enemy's gun passed through his hand. Smarting with pain Heurteaux was forced to retreat in much discomfiture to his aerodrome.

When Heurteaux was in New York, I questioned him as to the location of the wounds which still troubled him. For answer he indicated the fingers of his right hand, then with the same hand he touched his left shoulder, left arm, left side, left knee and left foot and smiled proudly without speaking.

This young hero had but one ambition—to get back to his Cigognes and begin increasing his score. He returned to France in June, 1918, and at an early date we may expect his reappearance at the front.

Adolph Pegoud

Adolph Pegoud, the first French pilot to loop the loop and the first to drop from an aeroplane by parachute, entered the war after having seen some aviation service in the Morocco campaign.

Born in 1889 at Montferrat, Pegoud was one of a handful of French aviators who was celebrated the world over before the war began. At its outbreak it was natural to find him engaged with his machine in reconnaissances over the German lines and later to see him departing on long-distance raids into the enemy's lines with heavy bombs attached to his machine.

His list of such raids totalled more than any of his comrades at the time of his death, and his method of dropping his explosives at such low heights that a hit was certain made him a model which all his fellow pilots sought to imitate.

On July 11, 1915, Pegoud brought down his sixth enemy machine and received the Military Medal. On the last day of August, 1915, he attacked a two-seater German machine piloted by Corporal Kandulski who carried Lieutenant von Bilitz as gunner. In the combat which ensued Pegoud was struck by a bullet which cut an artery, and he struck the ground in a fainting condition just within the French lines, near Belfort. He died before he was removed from the wreck of his machine.

During the military funeral which was given this famous airman, enemy machines circled overhead and dropped flowers upon the procession. Among them were several notes of condolence written in all sincerity by his old friends in the camp of the enemy.

The following day the Legion of Honour was conferred upon this gallant pilot of France.

CHAPTER 10

Balloon Observers

We hear very little of the courage of the balloon observers, but many wonderful pages could be written of their heroic deeds! The public has small understanding of the dangers they face and the skill and presence of mind necessary in their moments of peril. The observation balloon is the eye of the artillery which every Boche is interested in destroying. With machine gun and musket the balloonist leans over the edge of his basket until the very last moment and then throws himself out into space, relying upon the support of a parachute which may betray his confidence.

Imagine the state of mind of an observer who thus hurls himself into the air. He has nothing below him to sustain his weight; he must trust utterly to the giant parasol which lowers him to the ground, and to the last moment he cannot be sure that he will not meet with some catastrophe. Let us admire the superb pluck of these soldiers who leap from great heights entirely ignorant of the fate in store for them!

Besides the hostility of the enemy they constantly risk that of the elements. Thus on May 5, 1915, a violent tempest raged over the greater part of the front. A great number of the French balloon squads found no time to draw their balloons down to earth. Many of them broke their cables and rose into space: twenty-four were carried away and of these twenty-one went over to the other side of the lines. One basket was separated from its balloon. It was thus that Lieutenant Bassetti was killed. Four of the escaped balloons carried two men. Twenty-eight balloonists on this occasion were victims of the elements. All destroyed whatever papers they possessed that could be of any use to the enemy. Not until this task was accomplished did they think of their personal security. Sixteen parachutes opened as they should. Eleven balloonists were able to descend to the ground without accident. The others were victims of misfortunes that caused either death or serious injuries. The greater part of these accidents were due to the parachutes catching in the cordage of the balloons.

Two observers who succeeded in reaching the ground were dragged along by the parachute and killed. Another, during his descent, was blown by an adverse wind over into the enemy lines. One whose parachute was whirled away was carried all the way into Belgium where he finally landed without accident. Another, whose balloon tore from its moorings, landed safe and sound. Seven men on five balloons were carried away. Five of these heroes met death: Sub-Lieutenant José Garcia-Calderon, volunteer, Sub-Lieutenant Bassetti, Sergeants Solats and Spiess, and Adjutant Contentin.

Garcia-Calderon did not leave his ship to come down until he had thrown overboard his dispatch pouch containing his papers and 'his notes on the observations he had made, but he was killed as he reached the ground.

Spiess, the son of the inventor of the rigid dirigible, recently deceased, was one of those who had no trouble in reaching the ground. Unfortunately at the moment of landing he was dragged through shell holes, barbed wire entanglements and pickets, and sustained a fractured skull.

Contentin had his basket tipped upside down as he was descending. He was thrown out and crashed on the ground. His parachute had caught in the cordage and was broken.

This tragic adventure shows something of what balloon observers have to fear. Now note what courage has been displayed by these men whose names are rarely mentioned in *communiqués* and whose heroism has often to remain anonymous.

On August 29, 1916, two balloons were destroyed by lightning; their observers leaped out with their parachutes and landed in our territory.

Adjutant D., carried over into the German lines during a severe storm, succeeded before jumping overboard with his parachute in destroying his apparatus and all his maps and papers so that they should not fall into the enemy hands. In the landing he was seriously wounded.

Two French soldiers, D. and M., were taking observations on one occasion when they were struck by a 130 shell and sent down from 2000 feet. During this terrible fall they marked a German battery and without a thought for their own safety, they continued to telephone information to the artillery for which they were operating even as they were falling.

Sub-Lieutenant G., having met with an accident, jumped out with his parachute, carrying all his papers. When he reached the ground he was dragged more than 1500 yards. Covered with wounds he had only one thought—to return enough fragments of himself to his superior to be still of some use to his country.

In October, 1915, Sub-Lieutenant G., watching the destruction of a neighbouring balloon by an enemy aeroplane, refused to allow himself to be drawn back to earth. Attacked in his turn he replied with shots from his rifle and forced his enemy to fly off. He then went on with his observations. Another time, on March 9, 1917, his balloon caught fire. He gathered up all his documents and dropped with his parachute into space.

Sergeant L. is used to thrills. On March 19, 1916, when the ropes of his balloon broke under the violence of the wind, he threw himself down from 900 meters and was drawn along the ground more than 1200 yards. Three days later his balloon was set on fire by lightning. He jumped from 220 yards, injuring his hands and face. The next day he was back again at work!

One recalls the case of Sub-Lieutenant L. On March 16, 1916, his balloon broke loose and started for the enemy's lines. He carefully destroyed his notes and papers and jumped down from 3200 feet. He landed safely 300 yards from the front lines.

Read this citation:

Ensign Regnard, balloon observer of artillery, has been remaining in the air between 10 and 12 hours consecutively, day and night, in spite of the fierce bombardment and bitter cold. First attacked by the German aeroplanes, and then exposed to the enemy's artillery fire, on February 5th, March 10th and 26th, 1915, he refused to allow his balloon to be drawn down until he had accomplished his mission.

What shall we say of this heroic devotion to duty?

On March 20, 1916, Sub-Lieutenant T. was making observations. His balloon was caught by a strong wind which injured it and tipped over the basket. The men below began pulling him down, but the cable stuck, and it looked as though the rope would snap at any moment. What made this situation especially tragic was that the group who were trying to pull him down on this perilous journey had been placed under fire by an enemy battery. Thereupon, during all his dangerous descent, he took on himself the duty of regulating by telephone a counter firing that permitted the annihilation of the enemy battery.

Let us continue the compilation of our golden book of the balloon observers. October 16th, the cable of Sub-Lieutenant A's balloon was cut by artillery fire. The observer jumped out and landed safely on the ground near the lines.

In July, 1916, Sergeant B. was attacked when he was up 1200 yards by an enemy aeroplane. What did he do? Simply asked them to give him more rope that he might go higher to continue his observing, although his balloon had been pierced by twenty bullets, and the neighbouring balloon had fallen in flames beside him.

Sub-Lieutenant B. had already made two descents by parachute when, during the great storm of May 5, 1916, he destroyed his papers, jumped to the ground, and in spite of being dragged 800 yards over shell holes, landed safe and sound. March 9, 1917, his balloon having caught fire, he again attempted and succeeded in a descent.

Sergeant B., on August 29, 1916, saw his balloon set on fire by lightning. He jumped with his parachute and seriously injured himself in landing. He was for a long time unconscious and when he recovered his senses his first thought was to give the information about the enemy batteries that he had obtained a few moments before the catastrophe.

Sometimes the descents terminated in serious mishaps. On March 16, 1917, Sergeant B. found his balloon in flames. He waited until the basket itself should catch on fire before jumping. The parachute had more than a third of its surface burned, but he hoped it would carry him to the ground. Since his velocity kept increasing with his fall, he soon crashed like a stone upon the earth he had been safeguarding. But happily his injuries did not prove fatal.

Here is an act of remarkable courage. On March 23, 1917, Sub-Lieutenant M. was attacked by an aeroplane which pierced his balloon with bullet holes. He was pulled down over Verdun and reached ground unharmed. He had his balloon repaired and returned at once to continue his watch. In the same way on March 28, Lieutenant S., whose balloon was set on fire by an enemy aeroplane, descended with his parachute and instantly went up again in another balloon.

There have been observers who returned successfully the enemy's fire, like Sub-Lieutenant P. who, attacked at short range by an aeroplane which was sending incendiary bombs at him, replied with such precision of aim that he caused the attack to cease instantly and obliged the Boche airman to withdraw.

It is not only the observers who have the right to our admiration. Those on the earth often have an opportunity of showing their courage as well.

On August 29, 1916, the military telephone operator Domaget, who continued to operate his telephone at the foot of a balloon in spite of the electrical discharges, was killed with the receiver in his hand.

These are some extracts from the chronicles of the balloon observers. We could cite many others, such as those of Sub-Lieutenant Tourtay, considered the Ace of balloonists. He has been awarded the Military Medal, made *Chevalier* of the Legion of Honour, and has five palms on his cross. From the beginning of the campaign he has carried on his difficult and dangerous work.

Let us salute all these brave men. They carry on their work in the midst of the greatest dangers, a work whose value we may surmise from the persistency of the enemy's attempts to prevent it. And they are never mentioned!

What should we do without these eyes in the sky, and what would become of our artillery without the balloons to guide them? That is why, when each time the activity on a certain front begins to be feverish, the first act in the drama is to destroy the enemy's eyes and to assure to our own the most complete visibility. There is the aerial guard surrounding them; there are the *canons* below. Unlucky for the Boche who attempts to pass!

On our part we show little mercy to enemy balloons, and our fighters give battle to them until they are either set on fire or, recognizing their defeat, they have themselves drawn back to earth. Attacking observation balloons stands with the short-range combat as perhaps the most perilous mission demanded of fighting aviators.

These captive balloons or *drachens* rarely attain a height greater than 3000 feet above ground: that is to say, they are found in the most dangerous possible zone for the attacking aeroplane, since it is within the range of both anti-aircraft shells and bullets.

The *drachens* are often placed near special anti-aircraft batteries, and when they are attacked by aeroplanes, a heavy fire generally welcomes the scout who attempts to bring them down—a bombardment so much the more dangerous because the shots are fired at close range by gunners specially trained in marksmanship and fast firing.

When the hunter of *drachens* sets out to accomplish his mission he has had his equipment and motor most minutely prepared and inspected, and all the details of his attack are arranged long in advance.

The majority of our Allied Aces have one or two *drachens* to their credit, but in the same way that Fonck is the "Ace of Aces" of the French fighting aviators so is Adjutant Bloch the French "Ace of Aces" of the *drachen* fighters. He counts six enemy balloons on his score card. Adjutant Coppens, the Belgian, has twenty-seven. Gonterman, the German, claimed thirty when he was killed on November 3, 1917.

The chase of the *drachens* demands the qualities of coolness, of skill, and of extraordinary courage, joined to an utter disdain of danger. Bloch, the French Ace, possesses all these qualities in the highest degree, and he adds to them what constitutes his greatest charm for his friends, an unrivalled modesty, almost excessive in fact, for it is very difficult to obtain from him an account, however short, of his exploits. Like all men of action he speaks not at all of what he is going to do and very seldom of what he has done.

Decorated with the Military Medal, with the *Croix de Guerre*, with his *palms* and the English Military Medal, Adjutant Bloch can indeed wear his decorations proudly, for they were earned valiantly in the fullest sense of the word.

Of the six *drachens* brought down he consented to recall only a few memories of his last victory.

"Of the balloon that I brought down that day I should like very much to speak to you," he said, "for really during that attack I experienced some rather strong emotions.

"That happened on the Somme. I had flown off on the search for *drachens* when I perceived one of them being lowered to the ground, and as it settled, the Boche balloonists seemed to be very busy. Should I try to destroy the balloon? Would it be a piece of foolishness? For to destroy my adversary it would be necessary for me to descend to within ten yards of the ground right in the enemy's territory. I made my decision very quickly: I would make a try for it. Passing quickly from decision to motion I turned my aeroplane to the descent, and at a few yards from the balloon I set off my fuses which luckily struck my target and very quickly burned it up.

"But it was at this moment the emotions of which I have already spoken made themselves felt. Scarcely had I let go my rockets when I became the object of a violent fire of musketry; my machine was riddled in many places by the bullets; one of them went through my motor which soon gave less and less power. The speed of my machine decreased. I was still just above the ground, and having no power to raise it, my aeroplane refused to climb.

"I made as well as I could for our lines. I passed the German trenches at scarcely thirty yards above them, and at last, after a thousand agonies, I succeeded in making a landing among our friends the British. I then ascertained the extent of the injuries to my aeroplane: it was riddled with bullets; moreover a bursting shell had cut one of my wing struts, and lastly the fuselage looked like a sieve. It was full time I had come down; an unheard-of luck had attended me from the moment when I had destroyed my enemy *on the ground* up to the time when I had landed in the Allied lines. If the voyage had been much longer, my luck would have abandoned me.

"As you see, this little adventure was no joke from beginning to end, and in short it is, I believe, rather dangerous to destroy at so low altitude a well-guarded *drachen*. . . . It is a luxury that one may permit oneself for once; I think it would be folly to attempt it twice."

Chapter 11

The Bombers

Adjutant Baron, the French pilot, who said, "May the Gods prevent you from dying old!" was a most remarkable night bomber, and his long-distance attacks gained him many a citation in the *communiqué*. He was killed in a daylight bombing of the Mauser works at Oberndorf on October 15, 1916, the same expedition in which Norman Prince was mortally injured. Here is a typical story of Baron's methods of bombing, told by one of his comrades.

"Lorrach is to be our objective tonight.

"Sub-Lieutenant Lehman and his passenger, Lieutenant Perrot, also went along to do some execution with us, but alas! they did not return that night. They were compelled by a breakdown to make a landing in Hunland, but fortunately after having bombed their objective.

"It is midnight, Baron's favourite hour. Lieutenant Lehman departed first, not very well satisfied with the atmospheric conditions.

"An English military post had prepared for us some coffee with milk which Baron and I appreciated and did full justice to, while the mechanics tested the motor; then we went up.

"If ever there was a night little favourable to aviation this was that one. A heavy fog. At 500 meters we could not see a thing. We had a head wind and made no progress against it, but we were not driven out of our course. We went higher up to avoid the wind and to travel by the compass until we came within sight of Bale, whose street lights are very conspicuous and which is situated a little to the right of Lorrach.

"We flew along twenty minutes under these conditions. I strained my eyes to see the earth; my glasses clouded over, I took them off. The sharp moist air made me weep. I began to believe we would find difficulty in locating our target. I turned to Baron to indicate to him my impression, but I saw that he was uneasy, so I left him to think, for I know that when he is thoughtful he is making calculations. I continued to observe! He touched me on the shoulder soon and said to me:

"'My revolution counter is going lower; do you hear nothing suspicious about the "mill"?'

"The motor trembled a little, but I did not perceive that it was missing.

"'We might get on,' I said. 'But the motor is not making more than 650 revolutions, and we are not climbing a bit.'

"'There is nothing for it but to make some repairs; we will see if that helps,' my companion shouted.

"Baron tried to regulate the carburettor, and the motor seemed to pick up a little. At a distance we perceived where the lights of Bale now pierced the thick fog. We were at 3000 feet altitude, and we would have liked to go a little higher but were too heavily loaded. I had taken six shells of 75 pounds each and two rolls of cartridges besides.

"I did not see Lorrach, and I communicated this to my companion. 'They must have put out the lights, for one certainly should be able to see some lights from here,' I yelled.

"'All that is not cheering,' Baron said to me, and again he showed me the revolution counter which had commenced to fall again in a very disturbing fashion. This time the motor had some violent tremblings and then some stops that were far from reassuring.

"It was fatal: in this wretched fog the carburettor was filling with water! There were a few repetitions of this motor trouble, then suddenly the two air pipes belched forth flames. A sparkplug wire had broken, the gasoline flowed from the carburettor into the engine bed, caught fire, and now threatened the strut and the spar of the lower wing where they joined. I stood up in the cockpit and regarded the situation as not very good.

"'Baron, we must make a landing and I will try to repair it,' I shouted.

"Baron made no reply, but his face was set, and he turned the aeroplane homeward. He dived down a little to gain some speed, then came up again so as not to lose too much altitude. The tachometer indicated 400 revolutions and we were at 1200 feet. But seeing that my pilot was not manoeuvring to make a landing, I advised him that there was a fire on board, that so far no wood was burning, but that it would catch a blaze soon.

"'Very well, I will look for a landing place,' he said.

"During the descent I never took my eyes off the rear of the old bus. I took off my helmet to smother any flame that should break out. Baron made a spiral to the left which fanned the flame back to the motor. The intensity of the flame was diminishing, so I glanced over the ground above which we were making our evolutions with a little tightening of the heart, thinking it would not be interesting to make a somersault with such a load. I feared especially for my 75-pound bombs and I put the detonators in my furred pocket in order to render less violent the shock of landing.

"We might have gotten rid of our bombs, but since at this moment we did not know whether we were in France, in Switzerland, or Hunland, we both thought it would be wiser to attempt to make a landing, risking only the difficulty of jumping out with them rather than to risk making victims of friends or neutrals in dropping them without knowing where they would fall.

"We were still in the thick fog when something happened for which we had not dared hope. Coming in contact with some drier air the injectors cleared themselves, and the motor picked up to 600 revolutions. I breathed again.

"'Good luck,' Baron called to me, 'we shall be able to return home to Luxeuil with our bombs after all!'

"We were then just about half-way between Lorrach and Luxeuil. It occurred to me that if we could return to Luxeuil, we could go on to Lorrach. But we are taking a big chance of not being able to reach our objective at all. I impart my impressions to Baron, who decides.

"'Bad weather, bad motor; we will return tomorrow; it is taking too many chances,' he signals me. We continue on homewards.

"But now the difficulty is to find Luxeuil. This accursed fog keeps about us, and we fly for fifteen minutes without knowing where we are. At last, when we perceive the searchlights of the camp, the motor decides to bother us no more. It remains only to make a landing, which Baron accomplishes very gingerly.

"'We return from a long journey,' he said to me in descending.

"'I very much fear that the others will not return so easily,' I replied.

" Luckily I had my fez,' was his retort.

"It was his faithful mascot—this fez!"

A Midnight Expedition in the Fog

When half after eight sounded out gravely and solemnly from the nearby clock tower, the clarion in the middle of the village lifted its voice in a piercing shriek like a human voice, commanding the extinction of the candles. In the farms the lights went out one by one; little by little the singing ceased, and the night enveloped the great plain in its silence.

At the exit from the village the hangars spread out their circular canvas roofs symmetrically, their dark masses seeming to be crushed under a sky glittering with stars. The sentinel mounting guard whistled an air of his native heath. Far off the wan lights of the trenches kindled, flickered, and went out. It was the calm of night.

At the guard post the platoon was sleepily reading the newspapers when they were roused by the ringing of the telephone:

"Allo."

"Yes, this is the landing ground"...

"It is my platoon, Lieutenant"...

"Yes, eight bombs"...

"I understand. The mechanic Pradel is to prepare eight bombs. Leave thirty past nine. Very good."

"Hello.... Do not cut off."

"Yes, it is you, my Lieutenant? I will give you the observations at six o'clock. On the ground, nine meters twelve—west, my Lieutenant!"

The man with a nonchalant gesture hooked up the receiver, turned a minute crank, took again the mouthpiece for the sententious "Finished", and murmured:

"It is you, Victor? Good evening, Victor. It would be a whole lot better for you to go to bed than to be skylarking around at this hour of the night! Ring off, Central!"

After which he resumed his interrupted reading.

The electric conveyance at the extremity of the hangars purred regularly. One heard some brief commands and some men asking questions in a very loud tone, and soon the biplane was silhouetted like a great bird of prey by the glare of the brilliant searchlights.

"Wait. Take a little glycerine; it will be cold in a moment up there."

"Thank you, my Lieutenant."

The two men had donned their furred flying clothes and would soon be ready. There was nothing to distinguish the commander of the *escadrille* from his similarly equipped sergeant. They had the same clothes, the same helmets, the same boots, the same stubbornness, for one is Breton and the other is Béarnaise: soon, as they fly side by side towards Bocheland, the same hate will lead them on. They were old hands at this. For some months at nightfall they had left on a difficult machine to bomb the important railroad stations; this evening they burned to avenge a comrade fallen in the course of a day expedition.

"Pradel, have you cranked the engine?"

"Yes, my Lieutenant."

Lieutenant Le Coz and Sergeant M. gave a last glance at the map. The little electric lamp threw its crude light on the features of the two, and thus illumined their masklike countenances took on expressions of more energy.

"Are the balloons in the air this evening?"

"Yes, my Lieutenant, two. They will go up to 900; we shall be able to pass between the two and then follow the —."

"Of course."

"Have you the word?"

"Yes; dash—dot—dash."

"You are ready? Let us go there."

The mechanic wished them good luck, but the officer protested.

"It is not worthwhile; you know that we will always come back!"

The two men installed themselves. At the tips of the wings the red and green warning lights winked maliciously. The pilot tested his controls, the biplane with its red ailerons flapped its wings and moved its tail like a bird after a bath. The motors turned slightly, then stopped. The men took away the blocks, and the aeroplane rolled slowly along, parallel with the line of the searchlights. Then, increasing its speed, it leaped up, its shadow spread out, hovering over those who remained on the ground, and quickly disappeared. The canvas bird has plunged into the darkness; only the position lights that look like shooting stars and the sound of its motors still indicate its presence. They have left!

The nights of the summer days take a terrible revenge, and if the sky has been clear under the sunlight, the local fogs come with the moon; trailing first through the valleys their milky vapour, spreading out over the fields and forests, they soon form a thick veil, like an opaque curtain, between the earth and those who have set out in their frail skiff in defiance of the skies. The fog is the great enemy of the birds of night. Fairly high or very low, imperceptible or very heavy, it is always unfavourable to aviators. It hides the landmarks by shutting off the earth and makes the altimeter read incorrectly by varying the air pressure.

The fog extended very far within the enemy's territory. Not a star in the sky, not a ray of moonlight. On the ground not the slightest sign to indicate the route, not the trace of a village, not the discharge of a gun, not a light.... The pilot made the machine shake beneath the vibration of the motors, which were accelerating powerfully. The machine gunner put his head beside that of his comrade and listened.

"Which direction?"

The man pressed on a release, and a tiny searchlight threw its gleam on the compass.

"Straight ahead!"

Leaning over the side they endeavoured to identify the country. The lines did not appear. For a quarter of an hour they went on in the direction of X. The trenches should be there. Not a fuse. Not a shell burst. The men drew nearer together.

"Lieutenant, we are making a mistake in the direction."

The electric lamp is thrown on again; the compass shows its needle turning crazily from left to right.

"My compass is crazy."

"Mine too."

"What altitude?"

"Two hundred."

"How much gas?"

The luminous ray is turned on and the reservoir dial shows!

"Two hours more!"

The aeroplane dips on its wing. It is a change of direction, the motors run very well; at the tips of the wings the tiny lights, their only companions, shine sadly on the drooping planes. They are lost. Lost! Where is the north? Are they in France? Are they far from it? Is the landing ground still lighted? Will they be able to find it again? Will the motors hold out to the end? At times in passing over the woods and the rivers, the biplane turns somersaults. Will it be necessary to descend there in the blackness, attempt to touch that earth which they divine but do not see? Always just nothing. The minutes are long.

"Do you believe we are home again?" shouts the passenger.

"I do not know I" responds the pilot.

In the cockpit the machine gunner attempts to dislodge something. The instrument resists; it is the compass; now it yields under his efforts. Cautiously he suspends it between his knees; at last it is isolated from the motors and the beam of light covers it. The needle turns slowly, stops, and the man cries exultantly:

"Half turn! We are going north."

The fog on the earth dissipates and rises above them. The villages appear vaguely outlined. What is this one? A mystery. A long time they proceed thus in their new direction with the faint hope of recognizing something . . . but the night is black . . . the gas lowers rapidly . . . still five gallons—three quarters of an hour of flight.

"We have come to the end of the gas; we must try to land," shouts the pilot.

To land! Landing is certainly impossible. The darkness is impenetrable. It would mean reaching the ground at sixty miles an hour, in a forest, or on the housetops, and then if they should succeed in making it, will they not be prisoners? Prisoners or dead! However in a few moments the end will come. The cylinders of the motors will ask in vain for gas, and the twin motor will come down to the ground here, there, no matter where—that is sure. Then there came to each of them the thought of their own little province: one saw the granite cliffs of his Brittany, the sails spread full to the wind like a chest puffed out with happiness.

The other thought of Béarn with the blue torrents leaping down from the beautiful Pyrenees. They thought bitterly. All at once a redness appeared very far off, the lights of a great city. A railroad is marked by its line of light. Suddenly all goes out; the searchlights sweep out into the great vault, shaking frantically their long arms. Where is that city? In France, Germany, or the invaded country? They have been lost for two hours and a half. At eighty miles an hour they could have gone far astray.

In the usual way the pilot gave the word of command. No

fireworks in the air; moderate lights.

They are indeed in France. The two men interrogate each other further:

"Wait, we are over X. I see its main street."

"Perhaps. If so we shall find at the end towards the east the river, the railroad, the highway."

They went lower and found the points indicated; there was no possible doubt.

"Face the east," yelled the passenger in the pilot's ear.

The country is well known to them. Saved! If the gas is nearly exhausted, they know that they are near home. In the distance the lights of the landing ground now show an irreproachable line-up of six searchlights.

And soon, without a shock, the twin motor 1215, which all thought lost, landed at X. face to the wind.

There remained half a gallon of gasoline.

CHAPTER 12

Extraordinary Exploits in Air

The most frightful death that can be feared in war aviation is perhaps that of burning alive in mid flight far above the possibility of succour or escape. A shot in the fuel tank or a backfire of an overheated engine may ignite the petrol. The unfortunate pilot has but two courses open—to descend while his very motion fans the flames into redoubled fury, or to jump from his machine to certain death without the torture of burning.

Aeroplane parachutes are now perfected whereby a fair chance for escape is given to an unhappy pilot thus driven over the side of his doomed machine. A comparatively safe fuel tank has recently been devised which will quite adequately protect the petrol from ignition by bullets or shell. Thus necessity continues to be the mother of invention, and thus gigantic strides for the safety of aircraft are impelled by these uncivilized perils of warfare—to the eternal benefit of this fascinating sport.

German aeroplanes of late 1917 design are equipped with a device whereby a flaming fuel tank can be discarded by the pilot with one stroke of a lever. A small additional tank provides essence enough to take the aeroplane home.

Our first contingent of American-trained fliers to arrive at the front contained Ned Post, of New York and Harvard, whose daring flights at Governor's Island and Garden City have been witnessed by thousands of Americans.

On September 25, 1917, Lieutenant Post went aloft in a new type of aeroplane, the swiftest and fastest-climbing machine then known to aviation. He attained a height of twenty-two thousand feet in the frigid air before he discovered that he was numb with cold. It was the first trial of his new machine, and he had left the ground simply for the purpose of testing its capacities.

Volplaning steeply down towards his aerodrome, Post strained his new craft to the utmost with every variety of twist and turn that could possibly be experienced in the throes of actual aerial combat. Arriving at some two or three thousand feet above ground, the lieutenant moderated his contortions and looked carefully over his wires and supports to see that all had withstood the strain he had given them. To his horror he discovered that his fuel tank was ablaze, and that flames were spreading rapidly back along the length of the tail of his machine.

With his customary *sang-froid*, Post cut off his motor and eased his blazing aeroplane down to the nearest landing-place, unfastening his tools and throwing them out as he fell, and detaching as many of the instruments from the dashboard as could be loosened in such a perilous descent. As the aeroplane rubbed along the ground, Post dropped the control-stick, climbed out to the forward step, and before the roaring flames had time to swoop over him he jumped.

This cool escape from an apparently certain death, together with his forethought in saving his tools from destruction, was rewarded by a recent citation from his general, praising his skill and deportment as an airman, and recommending his coolness and judgment as an example to other aviators now training in France.

On September 10, 1915, a French reconnaissance biplane, piloted by Lieutenant Le Gall and occupied by Captain Sollier as observer, was circling disdainfully over the German guns at a low elevation and plainly within the sight of the admiring *poilus* from their trenches. Captain Sollier was correcting his map of the enemy's position and was jotting down in his notebook frequent items of interest as the enemy strongholds were revealed to his survey.

Le Gall, the pilot, amused himself with watching the futile

bursts of anti-aircraft shells as they dotted the air behind him. Far overhead sat a trio of scouting machines guarding them from attack by enemy airmen.

Suddenly a German shell burst directly beneath them. The explosion hurled the biplane violently upwards. The machine turned upside down, and as the two comrades looked at each other they saw a burst of flame gush from the ruptured fuel tank behind them.

The wind was blowing towards the French lines. As the aeroplane dropped, swooping this way and that, the hot flames alternately licked their faces, paused there for an instant, then swept away from them with the breeze, only to return to their torture with the following swoop. Their clothing was ablaze, and a landing-place was still hundreds of feet distant. They could not hope to reach it. The blazing machine must crash inside the German lines; the shock of landing might extinguish the flames, and in this case their papers would be left unconsumed in the hands of the enemy.

Captain Sollier, who sat nearest the blaze, reached forward and handed his pilot some of his maps and his notebook. Both began rapidly tearing the papers into tiny squares. No matter whether the fire consumed them or not, no information should be saved for the enemy!

The breeze carried the fluttering fragments across the trenches into the French lines, and as the white-faced *poilus* saw them falling they uncovered their heads and bowed low in their reverence for this last act of devotion to their beloved France.

Lieutenant Flock and Sergeant Rodde were flying above Mulhausen on March 18, 1916, in a slow-going observing machine, when suddenly out of a floating cloud above them darted a German Fokker which had been concealed from their view within the cloud. They turned and dived for safety, but the swifter fighting machine had them at its mercy. The German outmanoeuvred them on every turn, and, despite all their artifices, the Hun kept safely outside their zone of fire.

A running fight of many minutes ensued, and as the French lines drew closer, the French airmen were beginning to hope for a safe escape from the unequal combat, when suddenly their antagonist darted beneath them and, coming upright on his tail, poured a stream of lead into them from below. Their fuel tank was punctured, and immediately their aeroplane was ablaze. Without an instant's hesitation, Flock lowered his elevators and his blazing machine nosed down. Before the exulting Boche could recover his control the French biplane crashed into him, and the two machines, crushed into one blazing funeral pyre, sped swiftly downwards into the woods of Alsace.

On August 24, 1915, two airplanes left a French aerodrome at Chalons and passed over the German lines. One machine contained the veteran Adjutant Boyer and an officer observer; the other was piloted by Sergeant Bertin, who accompanied the adjutant as an escort and protector.

At a height of eleven thousand feet they were dodging the enemy shells, which were exploding on all sides of the two airplanes, when immediately in front of Adjutant Boyer's machine a black burst filled the air with flying missiles, and Bertin, from above, saw his companion's aeroplane falling out of control straight down into the Hailly woods.

He cut off his engine and dived after his friend, braving the increasing hailstorm of lead as he drew nearer the ground. No landing-place appeared among the trees below. The crippled aeroplane fell heavily into the treetops and lodged there. Repassing the spot at a low level, Bertin saw his two friends scrambling out of their wrecked machine, apparently uninjured. He saw the officer observer quickly descend to the ground, where he destroyed his maps and papers, and then set off at a run to hide from pursuit. At the same moment a mass of flames appeared in the treetops. Boyer had set fire to the wreckage before descending the tree.

German soldiers were running through the woods from several directions towards the wrecked aeroplane to make certain of the capture of the two Frenchmen.

Bertin, with instant decision, cut off his motor, and, quickly choosing the most favourable spot in the vicinity, dropped down through the trees and landed amid the bushes on the rough ground. He shouted to Boyer to come to him. Boyer answered, and came running through the forest with a score of German riflemen shooting at his heels.

Restarting the engine with one swing on the propeller, Boyer jumped into his friend's aeroplane amid a shower of bullets, and coolly turned and pointed the machine gun on his pursuers. Gradually the aeroplane accumulated speed, lurched through the rough brush until it rose from the ground, and, guided by the heroic Bertin, glided between the branches of the overhanging trees and soared nobly away into the free air. The two friends passed safely through the enemy's fire and ultimately regained their own lines, where both pilots were welcomed by their comrades with kisses and cheers. Each of these intrepid airmen subsequently received decorations and generous citations in official reports for this remarkable exploit.

An "incident" said to be unique in the annals of aviation, and adequately substantiated later by official reports, amazed the members of the French Escadrille N. 23, who witnessed it near Charmontois.

Two French single-seater machines from Escadrille N. 23 were patrolling over the French lines at a height of eighteen thousand feet very early in the morning of May 10, 1917. These fighting planes were piloted by Casale, an Ace of great reputation, and Legendre, a less conspicuous pilot of this famous escadrille.

Suddenly the Frenchmen perceived under their very noses, but some distance below them, a rare type of German aeroplane, containing pilot and observer, pursuing a leisurely path across the trenches into the French lines. The enemy machine was quite safely above rifle fire and appeared to be wholly unprotected. Not crediting their senses for a time, the two French scouts flew along above the Boche until he had passed so deep into French territory that he could not escape their attack, then they dropped closely behind him to get a look into this Hun mystery. It was not an ordinary occasion to find a Boche aeroplane, unattended, flying behind French lines.

Casale, who already had a list of seven enemy airplanes in his book, darted on to the stranger's tail and let go a dozen cartridges from his *mitrailleuse*. It was enough. At a height of thirteen thousand feet the German aeroplane wavered drunkenly for an instant, then fell over into a tail spin and dropped like a stone.

The two French pilots dropped swiftly after the falling Boche. They suspected the usual ruse which is practiced by an antagonist to gain a little time and position when unexpectedly attacked. Sliding swiftly down alongside the whirling enemy, they witnessed a remarkable proceeding.

The German observer had left his seat and was leaning back, striking savagely with his fists at the face of his pilot. The machine was descending, unpiloted and uncontrolled, faster and faster to a certain smash. Suddenly the pilot stood up in his cockpit, and, seizing his officer by the throat, lifted him up bodily and threw him headlong overboard into space. The rapid revolving of his machine aided him in the struggle and his antagonist offered slight resistance.

The pilot gazed after the falling figure of his companion a moment, then grasped his controls—and just in time! At less than a thousand feet above the trees he brought his aeroplane out of the spin and managed to pancake it adroitly into the treetops. The machine slid backwards through the branches, hurling the pilot forward as it fell. Landing as quickly as possible, Casale and his companion hastened to the wreckage. To their astonishment, they found the German pilot safe and sound. The officer observer was killed by the fall and was picked up some distance away. Upon investigation, it was discovered that he had been severely wounded in the first attack, several bullets having passed through his body.

Upon being questioned about the quarrel with his officer, the captured pilot told Casale that he was Corporal Haspel and his observer was Lieutenant Schultz. He stated that his engine had been struck by Casale's shots and the motor stopped. He discovered that his officer had been severely wounded, though he himself was unhurt. He turned and attempted to volplane back to the German lines, which could easily have been reached, he said, from his high elevation. But Lieutenant Schultz, his superior officer, insisted that they surrender without further risk of attack. Haspel refused to obey. The officer, severely wounded as he was, reached back and struck the pilot several times with his fist. The pilot felt the officer's fingers around his throat and the aeroplane fell into a spin. Then, in sudden anger, Haspel seized the lieutenant, and, aided by the rapid whirling of the downward spin, flung him from the cockpit. Before he could restore complete control of his machine it crashed into the trees and was lost. Then, so incredible was it that he could not yet believe it, he found himself thrown clear of the wreck of his aeroplane, and, picking himself up, discovered that he was without a scratch!

But Casale, looking at the still trembling corporal, said ironically to himself, "I wonder, now, if Lieutenant Schultz was choking him for trying to escape, or was it for trying to surrender?"

No answer was ever found to this riddle.

On the morning of September 24, 1916, a time when German bombing parties were nightly visiting the adjacent cities of France, Captain de Beauchamp, commanding the Morane Escadrille Number 23, together with one of his pilots, Lieutenant Daucourt, undertook the perilous midday flight of over 200 miles into the German territory to destroy with bombs the far distant Krupp gun factories at Essen. Though this was a daylight raid, to better discern their target—over the enemy's guns the entire way through defensive aeroplane patrols subject to the imminent peril of engine failure, the courageous De Beauchamp undertook the mission with unfaltering spirit.

In order to first test his machine De Beauchamp flew over the trenches above the forest of Spincourt and practiced bomb-dropping on an enemy gun below. Returning satisfied with his preparations he discovered his comrade ruefully examining his

CAPTAIN DE BEAUCHAMP
The spectacular French bomber who made a daylight raid on the Krupp works. Killed in combat

machine gun, which was out of order and would not function. And the time of departure was at hand.

Without regard for his own defence, Captain de Beauchamp detached his own machine gun and threw it to the ground, directing his subordinate to do likewise. Motioning the mechanics to remove the blocks he sped his machine across the turf, closely followed by his companion, and as the clock in the hangar pointed to eleven, the watchers below saw the two bombing machines attaining the topmost ceiling as they straightened out their course for the distant objective.

So unexpected was their audacious attack the two Frenchmen encountered no opposition to their progress. Essen was finally in sight, the Krupp works were located, and descending low over the roofs, the incendiary explosives were released. Several bursts of mounting flames testified to the accuracy of their aim and the complete success of their exploit. Now for the return through an aroused country!

Relieved of their heavy burden the two aeroplanes swiftly climbed out of reach of the anti-aircraft shells. Several pursuing planes they shook off and lost by concealing themselves in the upper clouds. Their engines continued their healthy roaring, and at a few minutes past five o'clock in the afternoon they arrived in triumph over their home flying field, descending in several loop-the-loops to show that their energy was not yet exhausted. They had been flying for six hours over enemy territory and had covered 420 miles without a stop.

Captain de Beauchamp was adored by his pilots, notwithstanding the fact that the details of even his most remarkable exploits could not be wrung from him. Only by consulting the records did one ascertain that he possessed the Legion of Honour and the *Croix de Guerre* with six palms, each representing distinguished services. He never wore them on his breast and never exhibited them to his friends.

On November 17, 1916, De Beauchamp performed one of the most spectacular air exploits of the war. Crouched in his one-seater Sopwith, carrying six bombs and fuel for ten hours' flight, he left the aerodrome at Luxeuil, on the eastern edge of France, at eight o'clock in the morning. Straight east he flew, over the German lines in France, across the German border itself, over forests, rivers, and mountains until just at noon he found himself 320 miles away from home and over the busy streets of Munich. Secure in their remoteness, the people of the Bavarian capital had read with satisfaction of the panics caused in the cities of France by the daily visits of the bomb-droppers. Now it was their turn.

Flying low enough over the crowded streets to display the French circles on his wings, De Beauchamp watched the scurrying Boche citizens run for shelter. Round and round he circled, permitting them some fifteen minutes in which to realize their peril. Then he let go his explosives on the railroad station and freight depots, and climbing once more into the sky, set his course for Italy.

Rising to 12,000 feet he found himself just above the snow-crested Alps. Any engine failure here meant certain death. A hundred miles beyond he would find the Italian Allies, and safety.

The heroic De Beauchamp landed finally on an Italian flying field at four o'clock, after a continuous flight over enemy territory of 437 miles. The following day he and his aeroplane were on their way back to France. A little over a month later Captain de Beauchamp was killed in combat.

CHAPTER 13

The Belgian and Italian Aces

Adjutant Thieffry, The Belgian Ace

Before Lieutenant Thieffry entered aviation he belonged to the motorcyclist corps organized by General Leman as courier scouts and agents of liaison.

During a perilous patrol in 1915 Thieffry was captured, but he later succeeded in escaping and crossing over into Holland. There he was interned anew, but again he escaped and rejoined his corps. He then requested to be taken into aviation and was accepted.

He began his flying career as a bomber. He accomplished a number of night missions, and of long-distance reconnoitring by which he earned a reputation for bravery and skill. This existence, dangerous but rather monotonous, began to bore him, and he asked to be transferred into fighting aviation. After a long wait he obtained the desired permission and in December, 1916, began his training on a Nieuport.

Here he found exactly the work for which he was fitted. To the patience of the fisherman at the end of a line, so necessary to a chaser, he added a rare boldness and disdain of death. As soon as day dawned he took his aeroplane out of the hangar, and till twilight he sought out the enemy among the clouds. A few stops for his meals, and to fill up with oil and gasoline, were the only rests he permitted himself.

He spent his entire day in patrols and never hesitated to attack enemy aeroplanes as soon as they showed themselves, in however great numbers. With such principles one could not help bringing back victories. This Thieffry did, although he was in a sector where the Boches were few. Between times he accomplished extraordinarily brilliant missions.

It was he who on January 24, 1917, flew over Brussels at 100 feet altitude to terrorize the enemy and drop messages of hope to his countrymen.

On March 15th Thieffry succeeded in bringing down his first Boche. The 23rd he added a second victim to his score.

From that time on Thieffry became a furious hunter. His perseverance in stalking the Boche was crowned with success, since on May 12th he got his third victim and June 14th his fourth. And then on July 3, 1917, when attacked by a formidable enemy group, he brought down two of them in two minutes.

Thieffry was returning to Bruges on this occasion when he was suddenly attacked by fourteen Albatross who formed a network through which it seemed impossible to pass. The Ace did not hesitate. He dived into them, fired his machine gun right and left, bringing down first one Boche and then a second who opposed him, and so broke what had seemed the irresistible defence of the enemy. The twelve other astonished Albatross pilots ranged themselves in stupefaction along either side of his path homeward, none of them caring to dispute his passage further. Thieffry willingly accepted this Guard of Honour composed of enemy airmen, and waving a hand to the right and the left, at the same time keeping a wary eye to his rear, the intrepid Belgian passed through their formation and disappeared over his own lines.

On February 23, 1918, Lieutenant Thieffry, then the leading Ace of the Belgians with ten official victories on his score card, was seen to fall in combat within the enemy's lines. His aeroplane went down to earth a blazing mass which seemingly crashed to pieces at landing. Thieffry was reported killed in combat. But a few days later he was announced by the Germans as captured and imprisoned; having escaped death in an apparently miraculous manner.

Lieutenant de Meulemeester attained his tenth victory two months later and led the Belgian Aces with this score of enemies destroyed until the last of June, when Adjutant Coppens, a hitherto unknown pilot, suddenly leaped to the front with thirteen enemies downed, ten of which were observation balloons. By August 1st Coppens had totalled twenty-one aircraft destroyed in three months and had thus placed himself among the great airmen of the world. On September 1st he had 30 victims, and all but five were *drachens*.

Adjutant Coppens is a most remarkable specialist in this dangerous game against the *drachens*. In one week he destroyed in flames seven of these low-hanging balloons. No other airmen ever attained such a score of these victims in so short a period of time.

A Belgian Air Story

During the first months of the war, a Belgian biplane containing pilot and observer experienced motor trouble while some distance behind the German lines, and was compelled to come down. Pointing her nose towards home, the two officers hoped against hope that they might glide without power back to their own territory. But the wind was against them.

Leaning over the edges of their cockpits, the Belgians saw the earth rising nearer and nearer, while the speed of their craft continued distressingly slow. Everybody seemed firing at them!

The German trenches appeared, and they crossed them at less than one hundred feet above the enthusiastic riflemen. Their own trenches were two hundred yards distant. They could never make it.

The machine struck midway in No Man's Land and stopped. Ducking through the hail of bullets, both men succeeded in escaping to their trenches without a scratch, though they had no time to set fire to their machine.

Two days later, Captain Jaumotte, the pilot of the stranded aeroplane, learned to his amazement that his machine was still there. For two nights the Belgian trench men had so carefully

LIEUTENANT THIEFFRY
Belgium's foremost Ace, until taken prisoner
on February 23, 1918.

guarded it that the enemy had been unable to reach it. Jaumotte determined upon a rescue.

Securing an armoured motorcar, Jaumotte took along his two mechanics and two gunners and suddenly appeared in front of the abandoned aeroplane. While the gunners worked their machine guns, Jaumotte and the two mechanics busied themselves behind its protection with the disabled engine.

The German soldiers, stupefied with this incredible audacity, could only watch it through their periscopes. Every time a head appeared, the motorcar gunners raked the trench with their machine guns.

In fifteen minutes the work was completed. Climbing into his seat, Captain Jaumotte signalled the mechanic to turn the propeller. The engine roared, and with one wave of his hand, the audacious pilot swept away over his own cheering trenches, while the mechanics clambered back into the motorcar with their tools and returned home to their aerodrome.

For this feat, Jaumotte received a citation from the Belgian Army.

A Belgian Stratagem

One clear starlight night in the early winter of 1916, when the belligerent air forces facing each other across the flat lands of Flanders were bent upon bomb-dropping expeditions over enemy camps, two Belgian *escadrilles* took the air about ten-thirty to attack a German aeroplane factory near Ostend.

At one-minute intervals the sturdy Farmans rolled down the searchlight beam, cut into the still air, and began to climb. Circling at some five thousand feet above their aerodrome, they awaited their comrades, each machine displaying its wing-tip lights as warning signals against collision. Finally, sufficient time having elapsed to complete the formation, the Flight Commander flashed his signal, the squadron fell into line and disappeared northward into the night.

One slow climbing machine had experienced some difficulty in reaching the specified altitude. This tardy arrival was piloted by Adjutant Jenatzy and carried as bomber Lieutenant Rolin.

Rolin searched through the black sky with a night glass for his squadron, but the signal lights had been extinguished as the machines ceased their circling and straightened out their course for Ostend, and none of his comrades were in sight.

Suddenly Rolin observed below him a ghostly apparition swimming swiftly through the gloom north and eastward into the German lines. Another aeroplane followed closely behind it, and another and another.

Extinguishing his lights, he touched his pilot on the shoulder and pointed out to him the dim cruisers below.

"Boches—just returning home from a raid. Follow them!" he shouted in Jenatzy's ear. In another moment the Belgian aeroplane, with its heavy load of bombs swinging under it, was bringing up the rear of the Boche procession.

Evidently just returning from Dunkirk or its vicinity, the Fritzies passed over Furnes, then beginning to nose down, they approached a signal light ten miles beyond, which Rolin estimated must be near Ghistelles.

He was correct. Soon the whole circus was above the Ghistelles aerodrome, and one by one the German pilots flashed their signal from the air, the searchlights below flooded the landing field, hangars, and buildings, and the home-coming machines dropped down into the glare. The lights flashed out immediately the last machine landed.

A moment later came another signal from the air, and again the aerodrome was brightly illuminated. Rolin had imitated the same signal flashed by the German airmen, and in response to the magical *open Sesame*! his prize lay revealed below him. Now with motor cut off and her nose into the wind, the Belgian machine sailed overhead barely a hundred feet above the field.

With a shout of laughter at the success of his *impromptu* plot, Rolin let go the first heavy bomb into the centre of the group of aeroplanes and pilots. These latter were standing gazing up expectantly at the oncoming machine as the bomb struck them. A second later another bomb exploded in the centre of the largest hangar, and it burst suddenly into flames. Two more bombs were released on the return trip over other buildings.

Circling again and again over the demoralized enemy camp, the two Belgians laughed with schoolboy glee as they saw artillery shells intended for them burst many thousands of feet in the air above them. In the meantime they turned their machine guns on the fleeing Boches who were running in every direction with "noses to the ground."

Finally, shooting out the searchlight, they turned homewards, where they soon arrived and made their report. Next day's reconnaissance fully confirmed the extent of the damage their little surprise party had occasioned.

Major Baracca, the Italian Ace Of Aces

Major Baracca, the Italian Ace of Aces, was not only the most distinguished airman in Italy but his remarkable ability and industry in the air undoubtedly rank him among the greatest air fighters in the world.

Born in Italy, in 1883 Baracca was well above the age of the ordinary airman when war was declared. He was at that time an officer in the Italian cavalry. Another ace of his country, Colonel Piccio, who is credited with seventeen victories against enemy airmen, is now forty-one years of age—quite the oldest air fighter among all the Aces in the world.

Major Baracca has fought continuously and with great bravery against the Austrian and some German pilots who disputed the air along the line of the Italian front. He has led his Italian comrades in air successes as in industry and ability ever since the beginning of his career as a "birdman." Considerably over one thousand flights were made over enemy's lines by this great pilot, and some seventy bombing raids have been successfully carried out by him.

On June 21, 1918, after having accumulated thirty-six enemy aeroplanes to his credit, Major Baracca fell within the Austrian lines during a fierce combat. Five times on that day he had already made flights into the enemy sky, seeking enemy planes.

Major Baracca
Leading Italian Ace, who was killed June 21, 1918, with a record of 36 enemy planes.

He fought always with indomitable determination and persistence. On the occasion of his last fight he was engaged with an overwhelming number of enemy planes, when his machine was seen to fall in flames.

Subsequently the ground on which this great Ace fell was recovered by an advance of the army. Major Baracca's body was found near his machine, which latter was half consumed by fire. In Baracca's right temple was found a bullet hole which led to a report that the great airman had taken his own life in preference to falling prisoner into the enemy's hands.

He had frequently said that he would never permit himself to be captured so long as he had a bullet left. But from the circumstances of his flaming fall and the fact that he could probably have escaped before capture owing to the close proximity of his own lines, it is now believed that Major Baracca was killed by the bullet of an enemy.

Upon Baracca's death the title of Italian Ace of Aces passed to Lieutenant Flavio Barachini, a brilliant and daring rival of Baracca's for the past months. Barachini now has a total of thirty-one Huns and is considered a pilot without a peer in Italy.

Lieutenant Silvio Scaroni

Lieutenant Silvio Scaroni was the hero of a particularly brilliant exploit in the Italian air on the morning of December 26, 1917. He tells his own story of this great air-battle to the *Nel Cielo*, an aviation magazine published in Italy.

> This is the way it went. A little before nine o'clock in the morning word came to our aerodrome at X. that an enemy squadron of about twenty-five machines was headed in our direction from the front. I was in the captain's office at the time. I hurried out and climbed into my machine and then took my glass and searched the skies to the north of us. I made out a cloud of enemy aeroplanes, evidently on their way over to bomb and shoot up our flying camp. I counted twenty-three of them, then I dropped my glass, sped up my motor, and took off.

I had scarcely arrived at 4000 feet when the first group, composed of ten enemy machines, began to drop their bombs which fell some distance away from our hangars. Then they descended lower over our field, some of them getting down to 1000 feet and others down even to 600 feet. I had a moment of surprise at seeing them venture so low over our field, but that did not last long, for I hurled my machine suddenly into the midst of them and dived on one of them at the exact moment he was in the act of letting go some more of his bombs. I fired three or four bursts into him, some 150 bullets, at less than sixty yards. He had just time to fly half a mile from the camp before he hit the ground with a crash and burst into flames. .

This combat was hardly ended when I saw another big machine passing some 1500 feet over me. I opened my throttle and in less than a minute I was at his level. I placed myself fifty yards behind him and just under his tail and opened fire. I was in a spot where he could not possibly see me. He tried to swing to the right, then to the left in order to get out of my range, but I kept in his rear, imitating every manoeuvre he made and keeping myself out of the range of his machine guns. Finally he decided to volplane down to earth and get so low that I couldn't stay under him. Quickly I let him have a second, a third, and a fourth burst, and at the last he went down in a crash. With their guns they had fired, without exaggeration, over a thousand bullets at me without being able to get one hit. Hardly had the machine struck the ground when I distinctly saw the observer jump out of the fuselage and set fire to the wreckage. Everything burned up, including the unfortunate pilot, who was wounded and imprisoned beneath the *débris*. The observer was so excited that he had set his own clothes on fire, and I could see him running about rubbing himself and rolling in the grass to extinguish the flames. Finally he succeeded in putting them out, with the aid of some of our soldiers, and he was made a prisoner. He was a German major!

My comrades in my squadron had up to this moment brought down six other aeroplanes of the raiders.

Towards noon the German-Austrian aviators tried another raid, but this time they didn't even get to our aerodrome as the warning was quickly sent us and we had time to go up to meet them. I was in the vicinity of a sergeant of our group when we saw shell-bursts in the direction of Mt. Belluna. We put on the sauce and hurried there and found a group of enemy aeroplanes which immediately began a half-turn when they saw our machines coming to attack them. One of them, the one nearest me, was being pursued by one of ours. I flew in ahead of him and began to fire. In a few bursts he nosedived to the ground where he smashed. It was the biggest aeroplane I have ever seen, a twin-motor carrying three passengers. They were all killed. It was the third enemy machine brought down by our squadron in this combat.

That evening half a dozen of our trucks had the pleasure of going out to gather up the remains of eight aeroplanes fallen inside our lines and bring them to our aerodrome. We did not lose a single machine. I believe the enemy learned a sad lesson this day.

But in retaliation for this sad lesson the aeroplane fleet of the enemy that night returned and dropped bombs by the hundredweight into the open cities of Padua and Treviso.

The champion of this first great aerial battle in Italian skies, Lieutenant Silvio Scaroni, raised his total score of enemy aeroplanes brought down to nine, with his three victories on that day. And on January 12th he added another, two days later another, on the 28th still another, and on February 13, 1918, he won his thirteenth official victory.

Lieutenant Scaroni was born at Brescia and entered aviation at the beginning of the war. After two years' service in bombarding and regulating artillery fire, he applied for transfer to the fighting squadrons. He won his first combats on November

14, 1917, a double, and totalled his thirteen victories in less than three months, which I believe is a record unequalled so far by any other pilot in Italy.

Captain Ercole

Captain Ercole, a young pilot from Naples, Italy, is the hero of one of the most tragic stories recounted by the intrepid air pilots of the Italian Service. Early one morning in the spring of 1916, Ercole left his side of the Adriatic with a squadron of bomb-dropping Caproni machines to attack the enemy supply depots at Durazzo. He piloted one of the huge twin-engine machines, carrying over half a ton of explosives, besides two gunner passengers, Brigadier Mocellin and Captain Corbelli.

Arrived at the destination, the long line of Capronis dropped down one by one over each target, and let go their bombs. Enemy aeroplanes were about, and each pilot waited only to see the effect of his attack before heading back home at top speed.

Ercole's machine was the last in line as the Italian Squadron winged its way swiftly westward. Captain Corbelli, who sat guarding the rear with his machine gun, notified his companions of the approach of a Fokker from below. Brigadier Mocellin, inexperienced in shooting from aeroplanes, signalled Ercole to take the forward gun, and he himself took control of the machine while Ercole placed himself behind the gun.

They watched the darting little Fokker manoeuvre for its attack. Suddenly terminating his circles, he dived, and Ercole adjusted his piece upon him. Both fired simultaneously.

Ercole felt himself struck and fell in agony on to the floor. The next instant he felt another body fall upon him.

With great suffering, he extricated himself to discover Brigadier Mocellin lying dead beside him. Ercole's left arm was fractured, and streams of blood were flowing down his face. The aeroplane, self-guided, was plunging headlong down towards the sea.

Ercole looked about him. The Fokker had vanished. Perhaps it had been destroyed. At any rate, it was gone. His own squadron had likewise disappeared in the distance. But why did not Captain Corbelli jump to the controls? Ercole miserably dragged himself back to investigate.

There, to his horror, he found Corbelli lying crumpled up in his seat, a bullet through his heart. The machine was diving, unguided, to certain destruction.

Ercole crawled along forward and grasped the controls. Almost fainting with pain, he succeeded in straightening out the course of the aeroplane a few hundred feet above the sea. Ahead of him appeared land. It was the only chance. Without knowing where he was headed, he cut off his motor and with one supreme effort, negotiated the rough hillside successfully and came to a quiet stop.

Unable to move, Ercole sat patiently in his seat waiting for help. His two dead comrades lay where they had fallen. He could only gaze upon them and wait.

In the midst of this misery, when all his prayers were for human company, he suddenly heard shots and felt a succession of thuds through the body of his aeroplane. An Albanian soldier was standing fifty yards away, deliberately aiming at him with an automatic rule!

Spurred into activity, Ercole got to his aeroplane gun and turned it upon his newest enemy. The Albanian fell. In the distance other soldiers appeared, running towards him. Torn between duty and the horror of the sacrifice, and determined in spite of his physical suffering to prevent the enemy from seizing his aeroplane, Ercole prayed to his slaughtered comrades for forgiveness, set fire to the machine, and crawled away to the shelter of some bushes. The Albanians arrived and surrounded the blazing funeral pyre. They pointed out to each other the two dead men within. When the last flame died away, they shook their heads regretfully and retraced their steps. Ercole's escape was not suspected.

After a week's wandering, with wounds uncared for, and almost without having tasted food and drink, Captain Ercole appeared before an Italian sentry at the border. He was delirious with fever and in a critical condition, but after medical treatment, he was able to tell his remarkable story and describe to his comrades the mournful end of the two officers, Brigadier Mocellin and Captain Corbelli.

The records for long-distance flying and for height attained during the war go to Italian pilots.

When war broke, in 1914, Garros had flown across the Mediterranean; Bohn, the German, had flown without stopping for twenty-four hours in an Albatross biplane driven by a Mercedes motor; Oelerich, the Austrian, a scant two weeks before had climbed in his machine with a 100-horse-power motor to an altitude of 20,180 feet over the Lindenthal aerodrome; the swiftest aeroplane flew eighty miles an hour and carried a weight of five hundred pounds.

Since that day aeroplanes have flown one hundred and fifty miles per hour and have carried six tons, and have climbed to 30,000 feet.

In June, 1916, Lieutenant Antoine Marchal of France flew from Nancy, France, to Cholm, Poland, a distance of 807 miles-the world's record for long-distance flight without stop.

But on August 29, 1917, an Italian pilot, Captain Gulio Laureati, established a new world's record long-distance flight when he flew from Turin, Italy, to Naples and return—a distance of 920 miles without stop. This flight, however, was not over hostile territory.

Two Italian aviators flew from their lines on June 13, 1918, to Friedrichshaven, Germany, and back, a total distance of five hundred miles without stop. They took many valuable photographs of this aerial stronghold of the enemies and inflicted some damage before returning in safety to their own lines.

The world's height record for aeroplane carrying pilot and passenger was made by Lieutenant Papa of the Italian Army on December 14, 1917, at Turin, Italy, when he flew to 23,000 feet altitude on a Sia-Fiat two-seater biplane.

The time consumed in this record flight was one hour and three minutes.

3280 feet was reached in	2 minutes	
6561 " " "	5	"
9842 " " "	9	"
13123 " " "	15	"
16400 " " "	24	"
19685 " " "	37	"
21325 " " "	45	"
23000 " " "	63	"

In England Colonel William A. Bishop in July, 1918, climbed to 20,000 feet in nine minutes in a new single-seater machine which will appear at the front in due time. This same machine was subsequently driven by another pilot to the world's record height of 33,000 feet in an unofficial test.

CHAPTER 14

The American Aces

One thousand German aeroplanes were destroyed on the French and British front during May and June, 1918, according to an official announcement of the British Government. This report, to be exact, covered the two months from March 21, 1918, the date of the German Offensive against Amiens and the Channel ports, to May 21, 1918.

During the last half of that period American airmen accounted for thirty-two of this total, with a loss to our air fighters of but seven. Coincident with this news of the active engagements of our recently trained American pilots who may be said to have begun actual service at the front the middle of April, came the announcement that Lieutenant Douglas Campbell of California had brought down his fifth duly verified enemy aeroplane on May 31st, and had thus established himself the first American trained Ace in France.

It is true that Major William Thaw of Pittsburgh had likewise a total of five enemy machines shot down, but some of these were scored while Thaw was in the French service. Sergeant Baylies of New Bedford, Massachusetts, had eight victories, but Baylies too was fighting with a French *escadrille*, the celebrated Spad 3. Captain D. M. K. Peterson of the Escadrille Lafayette is another American boy with five hostile aeroplanes to his credit, but he too is wearing the French uniform. David Putnam of Brookline, Massachusetts, had brought down his fifth Boche in fact, but one of these was not credited to him as the necessary

Lieutenant Douglas Campbell
of California, the first American trained Ace in france

witnesses to the crash of the enemy were lacking.

Lieutenant Putnam then had four official victories, and Lieutenant Eddie Rickenbacher, the former automobile racer, had likewise four. His fifth, shot down on Decoration Day over the German lines, was not counted as official.

Lieutenant Campbell is twenty-two years of age, and is a son of the head of the Lick Observatory of Pasadena, California. The rapidity with which he mastered the science of aerial duelling marked him from the first as a fighter who would win a prominent place in the skies. He brought down his first enemy on April 14th, a few days after his first sortie over the German lines. For this victory he was awarded the *Croix de Guerre* by the French Army. His second victim fell May 18th, the third dropped on the following day, the fourth fell May 27th, a fifth, which was not credited, was shot down on May 28th, and his last official victory came on May 31st.

The French rule of recognizing a fighting pilot as an "Ace" after he has attained his fifth victory and thereafter giving him an official mention in the daily reports from the front is not followed by the other nations at war. The enemy has developed the suspicious habit of suddenly informing the world that a hitherto unknown pilot has achieved his twentieth official victory. As there are no possibilities of confirming this assertion, the Allied fliers may be pardoned the scepticism with which they receive these claims.

England, on the other hand, frowns upon the public's clamour for the names and victories of their successful airmen. With characteristic bluntness and scorn for display, and assuming that every Englishman must do his duty regardless of the limelight, Great Britain refuses to accord to the spectacular fighters in the air greater publicity than that accorded to the humblest trench fighter. It is therefore impossible to learn the full extent of the British flier's individual successes until his death reveals the facts or a well-merited decoration for valour and conspicuous brilliancy in combat tempts the officials to make public the number of his victories.

The American authorities apparently have followed the French method in this respect, and in this land of sportsmanlike rivalry among comrades much conscientious emulation should come of it. While our air fighters are doing no more than their duty and no more than their comrades in the trenches or on the sea, yet this duty requires from them far greater risks, more specialized training, and more particular fitness, both mental and physical, than is required of their brothers in the other arms of warfare.

America has furnished twelve expert air fighters who have proved their superiority over the Huns in no uncertain manner, ten of whom ran up their rapid successes in typical American fashion within a few months after they appeared at the front.

Lieutenant Baylies and Lieutenant Edwin C. Parsons of Springfield, Massachusetts, were members of the old Escadrille Lafayette and as they had received their training at the expense of the French Government, both of these Americans preferred to continue their services with the French fliers. Both were invited to join the Cigognes, the Spad 3, and under the tutelage of these famous masters both Parsons and Baylies rapidly acquired the skill that won for them many a combat in air.

Frank Baylies was born in New Bedford, Massachusetts, in 1896. He went to school at the Brown Preparatory School in Providence and after his graduation returned to New Bedford where he went into his father's business as an assistant.

As a boy Baylies was quiet and unassuming, fond of mechanics and somewhat noted for his love of sports and swimming. He drove a motor car about the streets of New Bedford and was thoroughly acquainted with every part of its mechanism.

A year before America entered the war Frank Baylies, then nineteen years of age, left for France to drive a car in the Ambulance Service. His devotion to duty brought him the following citation from the French Government:

> Frank L. Baylies served as a volunteer in the American Ambulance Field Service from February 26, 1916, to May 11, 1917. Faithful to the ancestral friendship of France and

the United States he devoted himself in the French Army to bring aid on the battle line to the wounded in the War for Right. Before entering the service of the United States he served in the Somme, at Verdun and in the Argonne as a driver in the American Sanitary Sections Nos. 1 and 3. He was cited in the orders of the 57th Division.

Transferred into aviation Baylies went through the training school at Avord with high honours. His conduct there attracted the attention of the fastidious Storks, and on October 1, 1917, he was invited to attach himself to that distinguished company.

Frank Baylies brilliantly justified his selection as a member of the Spad 3. His first victory was recorded on February 19, 1918, his second on March 15th. His third and fourth victims fell during the last half of April. In May Baylies shot down seven enemy aeroplanes, and on June 2nd he was officially credited with his twelfth victory. Eight more victories were actually won by the young American which were not credited—a total of twenty German aeroplanes destroyed by Lieutenant Baylies in less than six months.

One of his letters gives an account of the combats which brought him his fifth and sixth victories.

> I turned and started climbing. Number one passed directly over my head. The second was vertical. I pulled back on my stick, stood my Spad on its tail, and let Mr. Hun have the benefit of two perfectly well-regulated machine guns. He didn't have much to say went down out of control without a minute's hesitation. He hit the ground an awful blow and lay there a crumpled mass of *débris*.
> Poor devils! Their last ride. Still you have the consolation of knowing that they'd get you if they could.
> I turned around to attack the second but unfortunately both guns jammed (fortunately, I might add, for the Huns). Then I tried out again.
> Hadn't been over the lines five minutes before I spied five Hun double-seaters out for a few photographs. Dove on

the last at 1000 feet, shot at him as I passed by but missed. Came up again under his tail—ta-ta- ta-ta! Mr. Hun was no more!

Called it a day's work and came home for dinner just as the sun was setting. Doused my face with cold water, changed my shirt, and ate like a person famished. You know I have an appetite like a bear.

On June 17, 1918, Baylies left the aerodrome of the Cigognes about five p.m. in company with Lieutenant Parsons, his American comrade of the *escadrille*. Baylies had a very swift machine which soon carried him far ahead of his companion. At some twenty thousand feet over the lines Baylies discovered three German triplanes and with his usual ardour climbed up to invite them to a combat.

Suddenly Parsons saw a fourth enemy fighting plane dart out of the clouds and attack Baylies from the rear. With the first burst of fire the Spad fell over and started a long volplane into the enemy's lines. Smoke appeared from Baylies' machine, but no fire was visible. As his Spad continued under control, it was evident that Baylies was still master of his own movements. Parsons returned to camp unable to distinguish even the manner of Baylies' landing. For days his comrades awaited news of his fate.

On July 6th a German pilot swooped low over the French lines and dropped a weighted streamer. A *poilu* ran over and picked it up. It read:

Pilot Baylies killed in combat. Buried with military honours.

It was concluded that Baylies was badly wounded in the first attack of his enemy but that he lived long enough to bring his Spad down into the German lines for a perfect landing. His aeroplane was distinguishable from the front line trenches until darkness fell. The next morning it had been removed to the rear by the enemy.

Lieutenant Frank Baylies had the reputation among the French of a courageous and intrepid fighter. A Paris newspaper

LIEUTENANT FRANK L. BAYLIES
of New Bedford, Mass., killed June 20, 1918,
after 12 official victories in six months.

said of him some months before his death:

> About Baylies one may give this judgment. Either he will be shot down before long or else he will accumulate an unbelievable number of victories.

Both predictions were correct. No other American ever attained so many victories in so short a time nor vanquished his foes with more judgment and skill. If Baylies had but patterned his method on the cautious habits of his *escadrille* comrade, Fonck, this brilliant American hero would have taken first rank among the Aces of the world.

Baylies died possessing the War Cross, the Military Medal, the *Croix de Guerre* with eight palms for his eight citations, and the French Legion of Honour.

It was Parsons who avenged his late companion's death. He was flying alone when he saw a machine, which appeared to be French, approach him. It swooped down on him, firing incendiary bullets. The fight then began in earnest, Parsons gaining the position above the Hun, whose machine was camouflaged as a French plane, and firing a burst of not over ten shots. The enemy dropped like a stone from a high altitude.

Edwin C. Parsons was born in Holyoke, Massachusetts, September 24, 1892, but when he was a few months old his family moved to Springfield, Massachusetts. He was educated in the public schools and at Exeter Academy, Exeter, New Hampshire. He went over to France early in the war, enlisted as a second-class private in the Foreign Legion, and from December, 1915, to May, 1916, was in the ambulance at Neuilly-sur-Seine. He was made a corporal in the French Army, September, 1916, after having trained in the aviation schools, and in January, 1917, he went to the front as a member of the *Lafayette Escadrille*. Parsons, who is an accredited Ace, has won the *Croix de Guerre* and the *Médaille Militaire*.

Lieutenant David E. Putnam of Brookline, Massachusetts, the present American Ace of Aces[1] with a score of nine enemy

---
1. Lieutenant Putnam was killed on September 18, 1918.

aeroplanes officially accounted for up to June 10, 1918, has the brilliant record of five enemy aeroplanes destroyed in one combat on June 10th, but only three of these were verified by the French officials.

Lieutenant Putnam, a descendant of Israel Putnam of Revolutionary fame, was trained at the Avord Flying Field, entered the American Air Service in France upon obtaining his brevet late in 1917, and was attached to the *Lafayette Escadrille* under Major Thaw.

He at once attracted attention by the ardour of his scouting and the brilliancy of his tactics in his earliest duels in the air. On April 23rd Putnam, then a sergeant with three official victories, received the *Croix de Guerre* from the French government, and with his fifth official victory came his commission as lieutenant.

During the terrific air fighting along the French front early in June, 1918, Putnam distinguished himself by his repeated attacks on the German infantry, flying at low altitudes above the massed formations and spraying them with machine-gun bullets with bland indifference to the shots from the ground that riddled his wings with holes.

Winning his ninth official victory on June 9, 1918, Lieutenant Putnam the next day rolled up the greatest score of victories ever credited to an American flyer. Five certain successes were his in two combats which he fought behind the German lines, all duly witnessed by his comrades in the air, but unfortunately only three of which could be officially credited. But even this score of three is one which no American aviator had ever equalled in one day.

Lieutenant René Fonck of the French and Lieutenant Trollope of the British Flying Corps are two air duellists who have exceeded David Putnam's marvellous record. Both these airmen brought down six Hun aeroplanes in one day's fighting, thus sharing a record which Lieutenant Putnam will one day wrest from them. He has never been wounded, and the coolness and skill which have marked his combats in air promise a remarkable career for this youthful American Ace.

Lieutenant Paul Frank Baer of Fort Wayne, Indiana, terminated a spectacular career on May 22, 1918, when at the end of an unlucky combat behind the German lines he was forced down out of control and fell as a prize into the enemy's hands.

Baer was an American boy of twenty-two, trained at Avord for the *Escadrille Lafayette,* and assigned like Putnam to the squadron under command of Major Thaw. In six weeks' active fighting Baer shot down nine enemy airmen, a rapidity of successful action which established his reputation at once with his more experienced comrades. Eight further victories were claimed by this extraordinary pilot which were never made official.

Now a prisoner in an internment camp in East Prussia, Lieutenant Baer doubtless did not see the two citations from the French Army which appeared on June 4th and July 18th respectively. They read as follows:

> Lieutenant Paul F. Baer, a pilot of extraordinary audacity; made six flights in one day, bringing down two enemy aeroplanes.

The other read:

> Lieutenant Baer has shot down his eighth enemy machine and did not hesitate on the following day to attack an enemy patrol of overwhelming numbers with which he had a furious combat. From this combat he did not return.

The ninth official victory was later .credited him, and eight more unofficial successes are testified to by the members of his squadron, making a total of seventeen successes this remarkable pilot won in the course of his short career.

Another American Ace of remarkable talents is Lieutenant James A. Meissner of Brooklyn, New York, who left Cornell in his junior year to enter the Air Service of the United States, and who on April 9, 1918, under the tutelage of Raoul Lufbery, made his first flight over the enemy's lines.

On May 2nd Meissner had downed his fourth German aero-

LIEUTENANT DAVID E. PUTNAM
of Brookline, Mass., the American Ace, who brought down 5 huns in one day. Killed September 18, 1918.

plane and received in compensation the *Croix de Guerre* from the French. He had established an indisputable reputation for bravery on that day, for during the combat and after much unsuccessful manoeuvring on the part of both antagonists for a favourable opening, they at last ended their circling and came head on at each other, firing as they approached. It was a question as to which could hold his nerve the longest. A collision was inevitable unless one or the other swerved.

The Boche swerved, but not quite soon enough. The two aeroplanes collided. The Boche fell with his machine in fragments but also with several bullets through his body. Lieutenant Meissner was able to bring his own machine home to his flying field, where it was discovered that one of his wings was hanging by a single wire.

On July 7, 1918, Lieutenant Meissner brought down his fifth official enemy aeroplane and downed still another in the same combat which was not credited to him. And his antagonists in this fight were members of Germany's most celebrated fighting squadron the von Richthofen Tango Circus then commanded by Captain Reinhardt who has since been vanquished. Thus do our young American pilots prove their metal against the most celebrated air duellists of the enemy.

Captain James Norman Hall of Colfax, Iowa, author of "Kitchener's Mob" and "High Adventure", and one of the old members of the *Escadrille Lafayette* in the French service after his retirement from Kitchener's Mob, was shot down over Saint-Mihiel on May 7, 1918, during a hot combat with five Albatross machines of the Tango Circus. For days it was believed he had met his death, as his machine was seen to fall out of control some ten miles back in the enemy's lines.

On May 21st, however, word came from the German lines that Captain Hall was severely wounded and was under medical care in a German hospital.

Hall is a graduate of Grinnell College, class of 1910, and is now thirty years of age. He is a gifted writer and a much loved comrade, whose loss is mourned by public and soldiers alike.

Beyond the age when air fighting is easily learned, Captain Hall nevertheless did his share in the daily patrols with exemplary ardour. On March 2, 1918, he shot down two Boche aeroplanes during one combat, and on March 13th he destroyed a third. His fourth and last official victory was on May 2nd, when in company with Rickenbacher the two Americans downed two enemy aeroplanes which disputed their way.

Hall is said to be the first American pilot to have displayed the American insignia over the enemy's trenches. This insignia is a picture of the well-known plug hat of Uncle Sam tossed into the ring which Hall had painted on the side of his fuselage and which is now displayed by all the members of his squadron.

On March 13, 1918, Captain Hall received the Distinguished Service Cross of the United States Army.

Captain David M. Peterson of Honesdale, Pennsylvania, was informed on May 15, 1918, that he was to be decorated on that day by a French general with the *Croix de Guerre* for his distinguished conduct in having brought down two enemy machines in combats. To show his appreciation of this honour, the American captain went aloft with Lieutenant Edward Rickenbacher of his command, who likewise was to receive the same decoration, and before returning to ground Peterson destroyed two additional aeroplanes of the enemy.

Changing his flying clothes for a more suitable uniform, Captain Peterson attended the ceremony and received his decoration, together with the compliments of the general for his exploit of the morning.

A month later Captain Peterson brought down his fifth enemy and took his place among the fighting Aces of the United States. Lieutenant Rickenbacher likewise accounted for his fifth German machine on May 31, 1918, a marvellous record for this celebrated racing automobilist who did not enter aviation until the close of 1917.

Among the candidates for high honours in air fighting are the following airmen of the United States—their victories which are indicated being official and the record complete up to July,

1918.

Official American Victories in Air. to July 1, 1918

18 Major Raoul Lufbery, Wallingford, Connecticut, killed May 19, 1918.
13 Lieutenant David E. Putnam, Brookline, Massachusetts, three in one day.
12 Lieutenant Frank L. Baylies, New Bedford, Massachusetts, killed June 20, 1918.
9 Lieutenant Frank Baer, Fort Wayne, Indiana, captured May 22, 1918.
6 Major William Thaw, Pittsburgh, Pennsylvania.
6 Lieutenant Douglass Campbell, Pasadena, California.
5 Lieutenant Robert Magoun, Boston, Massachusetts, with Royal Flying Corps.
5 Adjutant Edwin C. Parsons, Springfield, Massachusetts.
5 Lieutenant H. Clay Ferguson, wounded March 12, 1918.
5 Captain David McK. Peterson, Honesdale, Pennsylvania.
5 Lieutenant Edward Rickenbacher, New York.
5 Lieutenant James A. Meissner, Brooklyn, New York.
4 Captain James Norman Hall, Colfax, Iowa, wounded and captured May 7, 1918.
4 Lieutenant Joseph C. Stehlin, Brooklyn, New York.
4 Lieutenant Norman Prince, Beverly Farms, Massachusetts, killed October 15, 1916.
4 Lieutenant Kiffin Yates Rockwell, Asheville, North Carolina, killed September 23, 1916.
3 Lieutenant Walter Rheno, Marthas Vineyard, Massachusetts.
3 Lieutenant Walter Lovell, Concord, Massachusetts.
3 Lieutenant Thomas Hitchcock, Jr., Roslyn, New York, captured March 10, 1918. He has since escaped.
3 Lieutenant Bert Hall, Bowling Green, Kentucky, retired December, 1916.

CAPTAIN JAMES NORMAN HALL(LEFT)
of Colfax, Iowa, Veteran American Aviator,
a wounded prisoner in Germany.
ADJUTANT EDWIN C. PARSONS (RIGHT)
of Springfield, Mass., an American Ace.

3 George Turnure, Lenox, Massachusetts, third on July 17, 1918.
2 Lieutenant Hugh Dugan, Chicago, Royal Flying Corps, captured April 6, 1918.
2 Lieutenant G. de Freest Lamer, Washington, D. C.
2 Captain Charles Biddle, Philadelphia, Pennsylvania.
2 Lieutenant Andrew C. Campbell, Chicago, missing.
2 Captain Phelps Collins, Detroit, killed March 18, 1918.
2 Lieutenant Didier Masson, New York.
2 Christopher Ford, New York, second on July 17, 1918.
2 Lieutenant W. A. Wellman, Cambridge, Massachusetts.
2 Sergeant James E. Connelly, Philadelphia, Pennsylvania.
1 Sergeant Victor Chapman, New York, killed June 23, 1916.
1 Sergeant Vernon Booth, Chicago.
1 Sergeant Austin B. Crehore, Westfield, New York.
1 Lieutenant Willis Haviland, Minneapolis, Minnesota.
1 Lieutenant Harry Sweet Jones, Harford, Pennsylvania.
1 Lieutenant Charles C. Johnson, St. Louis, Missouri.
1 Captain Robert L. Rockwell, Cincinnati, Ohio.
1 Lieutenant Stuart Walcott, Washington, killed December 14, 1917.
1 Lieutenant Alan F. Winslow, Rive Forest, Illinois
1 Lieutenant Edgar Tobin, San Antonio, on July 11, 1918.
1 Lieutenant Charles T. Merrick, Eldora, Iowa, on July 11, 1918.
1 Lieutenant Alexander O. Craig, New York, in Italy, on July 5, 1918.
1 Lieutenant Sumner Sewell, Bath, Maine, above Toul, on June 3, 1918.
1 Lieutenant William J. Hoover, Hartsville, South Carolina, on July 2, 1918.
1 Lieutenant Alfred A. Grant, Denton, Texas, on July 2, 1918.
1 Lieutenant John McArthur, Buffalo, New York, on July 2, 1918.

1 Lieutenant Tyler Cook Bronson, New York, on July 1, 1918.
1 Lieutenant Charles W. Chapman on May 8, 1918. Both he and victim fell in flames.
1 Captain Kenneth Marr on May 15, 1918.
1 Lieutenant Henry Grendelass.
1 Lieutenant Edward Buford, Jr., Nashville, Tennessee, on May 22, 1918.
1 Lieutenant William H. Taylor, New York, on May 21, 1918.
1 Ensign Stephen Potter, Boston, Massachusetts, killed April 25, 1918.
1 Lieutenant Walter Avery, Columbus, Ohio, captured and brought down Captain Menckhoff, the famous German Ace with 34 victories, in his first fight on July 25, 1918.

American Honour Roll in Aviation

Lieutenant Ernest A. Giroux, Somerville, Massachusetts, killed in action over German lines May 22, 1918.
Lieutenant Cyrus F. Chamberlain, Minneapolis, Minnesota, killed over French lines June 18, 1918.
Lieutenant Arthur Bluethenthal, Princeton, New Jersey, killed
June 7, 1918. Lieutenant Wilfred V. Casgrain, Detroit, Michigan, captured May 29, 1918.
Lieutenant Carter L. Ovington, Louisville, Kentucky, killed in action May 28, 1918.
Lieutenant William N. Hewitt, Enfield, Massachusetts, killed in accident May 31, 1918.
Captain James Norman Hall, Colfax, Iowa, captured, wounded, May 7, 1918.
Lieutenant Charles W. Chapman, Waterloo, Iowa, killed in flames May 8, 1918.
Lieutenant Thomas Ruff an, New York, killed in combat May 11, 1918.
Lieutenant Donald E. Stone, Mexico, New York, killed in

combat May 11, 1918.
Lieutenant Lloyd Skeddon, Brooklyn, New York, with Royal Flying Corps, killed in action May 11, 1918.
Lieutenant Richard Blodgett, Newton, Massachusetts, killed in combat May 20, 1918.
Lieutenant Alfred R. Metzer, Newark, New Jersey, killed in accident May 22, 1918.
Lieutenant Walter V. Barneby, Sumner, Washington, killed in accident May 22, 1918.
Sergeant Paul Kurtzson, Philadelphia, killed in combat May 24, 1918.
Lieutenant Roger Babiani, Cuba, killed in combat May 24, 1918.
Ensign Stephen Potter, Boston, Massachusetts, killed in combat April 25, 1918.
Lieutenant Paul Frank Baer, Fort Wayne, Indiana, captured May 22, 1918.
Lieutenant Frank L. Baylies, New Bedford, Massachusetts, killed in combat June 20, 1918.
Major Raoul Lufbery, Wallingford, Connecticut, killed in combat May 19, 1918.
Lieutenant Clarence Young, captured in Austrian lines June 22, 1918.
Lieutenant G. A. Phyler, captured July 7, 1918.
Lieutenant B. B. Battle, Columbus, Ohio, captured July 7, 1918.
Lieutenant J. Wilkenson, California, captured July 7, 1918.
Lieutenant Alan Ash, Chicago, killed in flames July 7, 1918.
Lieutenant Warren T. Hobbs, Worcester, Massachusetts, killed in combat July 7, 1918.
Sergeant James H. Baughan, Washington, D. C., captured July 1, 1918.
Quentin Roosevelt, killed in combat July 14, 1918.
Lieutenant Philip Davis, West Newton, Massachusetts,

killed in combat June 2, 1918.

Victor Chapman, New York, killed in combat June 22, 1916.

Kiffin Rockwell, Asheville, North Carolina, killed in combat September 23, 1916.

Norman Prince, Beverly Farms, Massachusetts, killed by accident October 15, 1916.

James McConnell, Carthage, North Carolina, killed in combat March 19, 1917.

Dennis Dowd, New York, killed in training August 11, 1916.

Edmond C. Genet, Ossining, New York, killed in combat April 16, 1917.

Erie A. Fowler, Long Island, killed, 1918.

Robert M. Hanford, Brooklyn, New York, killed, 1918.

Thomas Hitchcock, Jr., Long Island, captured May 10, 1918.

Ronald Hoskier, Orange, New Jersey, killed in combat April 23, 1917.

Charles Kerwood, Bryn Mawr, Pennsylvania, missing April 1, 1917.

Hugh Dugan, Chicago, captured April 6, 1918, with Royal Flying Corps.

Edward J. Loughran, New York, killed in combat, 1918.

L. Norman Barclay, New York, killed in combat, 1918.

James A. Bayne, Chicago, killed in combat June 19, 1918.

Leo Benoit, Attleboro, Massachusetts, killed in accident December 13, 1917.

Julian C. Biddle, Philadelphia, killed in combat August 18, 1917.

Everett F. Buckley, Kilbourne, Illinois, captured September 5, 1917, escaped June 6, 1918.

Thomas Buffun, New York, missing May 11, 1918.

Andrew Courtney Campbell, Chicago, missing 1918.

Captain Phelps Collins, Detroit, killed in combat March 18, 1918.

William H. Meeker, New York, killed in action, 1918.
Henry Palmer, New York, died pneumonia in France, 1917.
Paul Pavelka, killed in accident November 11, 1917.
Frank E. Starrett, Athol, Massachusetts, killed in combat 1918.
Wallace C. Winter, Chicago, killed in combat March 15, 1918.
William H. Tailer, Roslyn, New York, killed in combat February 5, 1918.
Charles Trinkard, Brooklyn, New York, killed in combat November 29, 1917.
Stuart Walcott, Washington, D. C., killed in accident December 14, 1917.
Harold Buckley Willis, Boston, captured August 18, 1917.
Herman Whitmore, Brunswick, Maine, missing April 6, 1918.
Houston Woodward, Philadelphia, missing April 1, 1917.

Appendix Aces of all Nations

Having examined their methods, peculiarities, and their characteristics, which account for their proved superiority both over their enemies and in comparison with their comrades, let us look at the complete score of the Aces of aviation of all the belligerent countries.

This score I have been tabulating since the war in the air began, and it is officially correct up to the date of August 1, 1918, with the exception of the list of British Aces, whose records are not made public until His Majesty is graciously pleased to confer upon them the Victoria Cross or the Distinguished Service Order for some extraordinary and brilliant performance of duty. Many British Aces must, therefore, be omitted from the following table.

56 FRENCH ACES LIVING TOTAL
616 SUCCESSES AUGUST 1, 1918

Lieutenant René Fonck	59
Lieutenant Charles Nungesser	38
Lieutenant Georges Madon	38
Lieutenant Maurice Boyau	29
Lieutenant Guérin	22
Captain Heurteaux	21
Lieutenant Deullin	20
Captain Pinsard	20
Lieutenant Coeffard	15
Lieutenant Jailler	12
Lieutenant Garaud	12

Lieutenant Marcel Hughes	12
Lieutenant Sardier	11
Lieutenant Tarascon	11
Lieutenant Ortoli	11
Sergeant Marinovitch	11
Adjutant Ehrlich	10
Lieutenant Nogues	10
Lieutenant Bourgade	10
Lieutenant de Sevin	10
Adjutant Herbelin	10
Lieutenant de Turrenne	10
Adjutant Chainat	9
Adjutant Casale	9
Adjutant Dauchy	9
Lieutenant Viallet	9
Captain Derode	7
Lieutenant de Slade	7
Lieutenant Lachmann	7
Lieutenant Flachaire	7
Adjutant Vitallis	7
Adjutant Sayare	7
Lieutenant L'Hoste	7
Sergeant Montrion	7
Lieutenant Raymond	6
Sergeant du Bois d'Aische	6
Lieutenant Covin	6
Lieutenant Bonnefoy	6
Lieutenant Gond	6
Lieutenant Soulier	6
Sergeant Boyau	6
Adjutant Dhome	6
Adjutant Peronneau	6
Sergeant Rousseau	6
Private Louis Martin	6
Lieutenant Leps	6
Lieutenant Borzecky	5

Lieutenant Paul Gastin	5
Adjutant Bloch	5
Lieutenant Regnier	5
Commander Marancourt	5
Adjutant Herrison	5
Adjutant Blanc	5
Lieutenant Marty	5
Sergeant Bouyer	5
Adjutant de Pralines	5

21 FRENCH ACES KILLED
TOTAL 231

Captain Georges Guynemer, missing September 11, 1917	53
Lieutenant René Dorme, missing May 25, 1917	23
Lieutenant Jean Chaput, killed May 5, 1918	16
Lieutenant de Meuldre, killed May 8, 1918	13
Lieutenant Navarre, retired wounded, April 10, 1917	12
Lieutenant de la Tour, killed December 21, 1917	11
Adjutant Maxime Lenoire, killed October 25, 1916	11
Sergeant Quette, missing May 16, 1918	10
Captain Georges Matton, killed September 10, 1916	9
Sergeant Sauvage, killed 1916	8
Lieutenant de Rochefort, killed 1916	7
Captain René Doumer, killed April 26, 1917	7
Captain Alfred Auger, killed July 28, 1917	7
Lieutenant Henri Languedoc, killed 1917	7
Lieutenant de Mortemart, killed March 20, 1918	6
Lieutenant Adolph Pégoud, killed August 31, 1915	6
Sergeant Marcel Hauss, killed 1916	5
Captain Lecour-Grandmaison, killed May 10, 1917	5
Lieutenant Georges Baillot, killed May 20, 1916	5
Adjutant Pierre Violet, killed December 27, 1916	5
Lieutenant Andre Delorme, killed 1916	5

91 BRITISH ACES
TOTAL 1231 HUNS

Major Raymond Collishaw	77
Colonel William A. Bishop	72
Major E. Mannock	71

Captain Philip F. Fullard	48
Captain Robert A. Little	47
Captain G. E. H. McElroy	46
Captain Henry W. Wollett	43
Captain J. I. T. Jones	40
Captain A. W. B. Proctor	39
Major Roderic S. Dallas	39
Captain F. R. McCall	34
Captain Frank G. Quigley	34
Major Albert D. Carter	31
Captain Cedric E. Howell	30
Captain A. E. McKeever	30
Major William G. Barker	25
Captain W. L. Jordan	25
Captain John Andrews	24
Captain M. B. Frew	23
Captain John Gilmour	23
Captain Burden	22
Captain A. H. Cobby	21
Lieutenant John J. Malone	20
Lieutenant Allen Wilkenson	19
Captain E. G. McClaughey	19
Captain P. C. Carpenter	15
Lieutenant Clive Warman	15
Lieutenant Fred Libby	14
Lieutenant R. T. C. Hoidge	14
Captain Murray Galbraith	13
Lieutenant Joseph S. Fall	13
Lieutenant A. J. Cowper	12
Lieutenant Alan Gerard	12
Captain Whitaker (in Italy)	12
Lieutenant, M. D. G. Scott	11
Captain Robert Dodds	11
Captain Gilbert Ware Green	9
Lieutenant K. R. Park	9
Lieutenant John H. T. Letts	8

Captain James A. Slater	8
Sergeant Dean I. Lamb	8
Lieutenant Boyd S. Breadner	8
Captain Wagour (in Italy)	7
Lieutenant Edward A. Clear	7
Captain C. A. Brewster-Joske	7
Lieutenant Lionel B. Jones	7
Lieutenant A. S. Sheppard	7
Lieutenant James Dennis Payne	7
Captain Lancelot L. Richardson	6
Lieutenant Cecil Roy Richards	6
Lieutenant Howard Saint	6
Lieutenant Fred John Gibbs	6
Lieutenant C. W. Cuddemore	6
Captain R. W. Chappell	5
Captain G. H. Boarman	5
Lieutenant F. T. S. Menendez	5
Captain Kennedy C. Patrick	5
Sergeant T. F. Stephenson	5
Lieutenant William Lewis Wells	5
Lieutenant E. D. Clarke	5
Captain Fred Hope Lawrence	5
Lieutenant Edward R. Grange	5
Lieutenant W. G. Miggett	5
Lieutenant Lawrence W. Allen	5
Lieutenant William D. Matheson	5
Lieutenant Stanley J. Coble	5
Captain S. T. Edwards	Many
Captain A. R. Brown	"
Captain A. T. Whealy	"
Captain T. F. Le Mesuries	"
Commander F. C. Armstrong	"
Commander E. L. N. Clarke	"
Commander R. B. Munday	"
Commander G. W. Price	"
Commander R. J. C. Compton	"

Lieutenant V. R. Stokes	Many
Lieutenant W. C. Canbray	"
Lieutenant H. T. Beamish	"
Lieutenant E. T. Hayne	"
Lieutenant G. W. Hemming	"
Lieutenant J. E. L. Hunter	"
Lieutenant W. A. Curtiss	"
Lieutenant G. R. Crole	"
Lieutenant Robert N. Hall	"
Lieutenant David S. Hall	"
Lieutenant M. J. G. Day	"
Lieutenant E. G. Johnson	"
Lieutenant M. H. Findlay	"
Lieutenant C. B. Ridley	"
Lieutenant S. B. Horn	"
Lieutenant K. K. Muspratt	"

20 BRITISH ACES, KILLED OR WOUNDED
TOTAL 398 SUCCESSES

Captain James McCudden, July 9, 1918	58
Captain Donald E. McLaren	48
Captain Albert Ball	43
Captain W. G. Claxton	37
Captain Brunwin-Hales	27
Captain Francis McCubbin	23
Captain G. E. Thomson, killed by accident	21
Captain J. L. Trollope, captured	18
Captain Stanley Rosevear	18
Lieutenant Leonard M. Barlow	17
Captain Walter A. Tyrrell, June 6, 1918	15
Captain H. G. Reeves, accident	13
Captain Noel W. W. Webb, August 16, 1917	12
Lieutenant Clive F. Collett, December 23, 1917	12
Lieutenant Rhys-David	9
Captain Henry G. Luchford	7
Captain H. T. Mellings, wounded	5

Commander R. F. Minifie, captured	5
Lieutenant Langley F. W. Smith	5
Lieutenant Ellis Vair Reed	5

14 ITALIAN ACES
TOTAL 193 HUNS

Lieutenant Flavio Barachini	31
Lieutenant Ancilotti	19
Colonel Piccio	17
Captain, Duke Calabria	16
Lieutenant Scaroni	13
Lieutenant Hanza	11
Sergeant Maisero	8
Lieutenant Parnis	7
Sergeant Poli	6
Lieutenant Luigi Olivi	6
Lieutenant Stophanni	6
Lieutenant Arrigoni	5
Major Baracca, killed June 21, 1918	36
Lieutenant Olivari, killed 1918	12

8 BELGIAN ACES
TOTAL 77 HUNS

Lieutenant Coppens	30
Lieutenant de Meulemeester	10
Lieutenant Jan Olieslagers	6
Adjutant Beulemest	6
Captain Jaquette	5
Lieutenant Robin	5
Lieutenant Medaets	5
Lieutenant Thieffry, killed February 23, 1918	10

14 UNITED STATES ACES
TOTAL 121 HUNS

Major Raoul Lufbery, killed May 19, 1918	18
Lieutenant David E. Putnam	13
Lieutenant Frank L. Baylies, killed June 20, 1918	12

Lieutenant Paul Frank Baer, captured May 22, 1918	9
Lieutenant Douglass Campbell, wounded	6
Major William Thaw	6
Lieutenant Robert Magoun, wounded April 8, 1918	5
Adjutant Edwin C. Parsons	5
Lieutenant H. Clay Ferguson, wounded March 12, 1918	5
Corporal David McK. Peterson	5
Lieutenant James A. Meissner	5
Lieutenant Edward Rickenbacher	5
Lieutenant Elliot Springs (with R. F. C.)	15
Lieutenant Reed Landis (with R. F. C.)	12

3 RUSSIAN ACES
TOTAL 28 HUNS

Captain Kosakoff	17
Captain Kroutenn, killed June 22, 1917	6
Lieutenant Pachtchenko	5

37 HUN ACES LIVING
CLAIM 748 SUCCESSES

Lieutenant Udet	60
Captain Berthold	39
Lieutenant Klein	33
Lieutenant Koenneke	32
Lieutenant Balle	31
Lieutenant Kroll	31
Corporal Rumey	30
Lieutenant Schleich	30
Lieutenant Laumen	28
Lieutenant Boerr	28
Lieutenant Huey	28
Lieutenant Blume	28
Lieutenant Arigi (Austrian)	26
Lieutenant Fiala (Austrian)	23
Captain Baumer	23
Lieutenant Jakobs	22

Lieutenant Cluffort	22
Lieutenant Adam	21
Lieutenant Goering	21
Lieutenant Grein	20
Lieutenant Buechner	20
Lieutenant Thuy	20
Lieutenant Kissenberth	17
Lieutenant Schmidt	15
Lieutenant Hess	13
Lieutenant Muller	13
Lieutenant Goettsch	13
Lieutenant Frickart	9
Lieutenant von Althaus	8
Lieutenant Esswein	6
Lieutenant Walz	6
Lieutenant Hehn	6
Lieutenant Koenig	6
Captain Zauder	5
Lieutenant Brauneck	5
Lieutenant Ullmer	5
Lieutenant Roth	5

64 HUN ACES, DEAD OR WOUNDED
CLAIM 1360

Captain von Richthofen, killed April 21, 1918	80
Lieutenant Lowenhardt, killed	53
Lieutenant Werner Voss Crefeld, killed September 24, 1917	49
Captain Boelke, killed October 21, 1917	40
Lieutenant Gontermann, killed November 3, 1917	39
Lieutenant Max Muller, killed January 15, 1918	38
Lieutenant Bongartz, wounded March 17, 1918	36
Captain Brunowsky (Austrian), wounded	34
Lieutenant Max Buckler, killed	34
Lieutenant Menckhoff, captured July 25, 1918	34
Lieutenant Loerzer, wounded June 15, 1918	33
Lieutenant Cort Wolff, killed September 15, 1917	33
Lieutenant Schaeffer, killed June 7, 1917	30
Lieutenant Almenroder, killed June 27, 1917	30

Lieutenant von Richthofen, wounded May 18, 1918	29
Lieutenant Prince von Bulow, killed May 19, 1918	28
Lieutenant Wuesthoff, killed	28
Lieutenant Kirstein, killed July 20, 1918	27
Captain von Tutscheck, killed March 17, 1918	27
Lieutenant Barnett, killed October 13, 1917	27
Lieutenant Dosler, killed January 1, 1918	26
Lieutenant Peutter, killed	25
Lieutenant Link Crawford (Austrian), killed	25
Lieutenant Veltgens, killed	24
Lieutenant Erwin Boehm, killed December 1, 1917	24
Lieutenant Friedrichs, killed July 20, 1918	21
Lieutenant Billik, killed	21
Lieutenant Wimdische, killed	21
Lieutenant von Tschwibon, killed November 22, 1917	20
Captain Reinhardt, killed by accident June 10, 1918	20
Lieutenant von Eschwege, killed 1917	20
Lieutenant Bethge, killed March 17, 1918	20
Captain Behr	19
Lieutenant Thulzer	19
Lieutenant Baldamus	18
Lieutenant Wintgens, killed September 25, 1916	18
Lieutenant Frankel, killed April 8, 1917	17
Lieutenant Geigel, killed May 13, 1918	15
Lieutenant Schneider	15
Lieutenant Immelmann	15
Lieutenant Nathanall	14
Lieutenant Dassenback	14
Lieutenant Festner	12
Lieutenant Pfeiffer	12
Lieutenant Manschatt, killed March 12, 1917	12
Lieutenant Hohndorf, killed September 12, 1917	12
Lieutenant Muttschaat	12
Lieutenant Buddecke, killed December 16, 1916	12
Lieutenant von Kendall, killed April 6, 1917	11
Lieutenant Kirmaier	11
Lieutenant Theiller	11
Lieutenant Serfert	11
Lieutenant Mulzer	10
Lieutenant Banfield (Austrian), wounded June 7, 1918	9

Lieutenant Leffers, killed December 27, 1916	9
Lieutenant Schulte	9
Lieutenant Parschau, killed July 26, 1916	8
Lieutenant Schilling	8
Lieutenant Immelmann, killed June 18, 1916	6
Lieutenant Fahlbusch	5
Lieutenant von Siedlitz	5
Lieutenant Rosenkranz	5
Lieutenant Habor	5
Lieutenant Reimann	5

Manford von Richthofen, favourite of the Kaiser, and the pride of the German army, was the celebrated commander of the enemy air squadron officially known as Judgstaffel No. 11, but familiar to all airmen as the Tango Circus. Of aristocratic birth, he was a lieutenant of *Uhlans* before the outbreak of the war. The former air champion, Captain Boelke, induced him to enter the Air Service in 1915, and his first victory was won in September, 1916. In seven months the flying squadron which he led shot down 200 aeroplane antagonists.

In less than fifteen months' active flying, von Richthofen personally brought down 70 aeroplanes and 10 observation balloons, mostly British. He flew the swiftest type of aeroplanes that German constructors could build, and he mounted upon them two Spandau machine guns that fired straight ahead between the blades of the propeller. His machine he painted a bright red, and for the past eight months his menacing presence thus courted identification from his enemies with a self-confidence and audacity truly admirable.

He was shot down April 21, 1918, over the Somme River, at the Amiens front, and his new Fokker triplane, a personal gift to him from Fokker himself, fell into the British lines.

This machine flew 140 miles per hour and climbed 15,000 feet in 17 minutes. Orders found in his pockets indicated that the enemy army commanders desired this sector cleared of British aeroplanes on the morning of April 21 at all costs. But it is doubtful whether the fall of Amiens itself would have compensated Germany for the cost she paid in the loss of her great Ace.

www.ingramcontent.com/pod-product-compliance
Lightning Source LLC
Chambersburg PA
CBHW031622160426
43196CB00006B/239